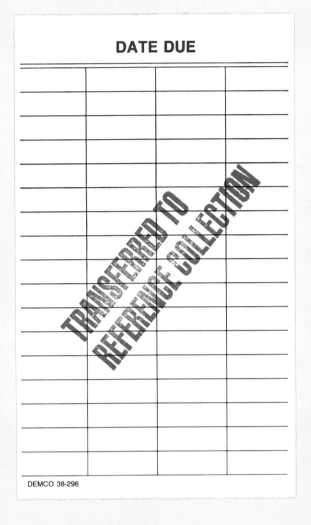

DATE DUE

DEMCO 38-296

THE ENCYCLOPEDIA OF
BUTTERFLIES

Idea leuconoe (Tree nymph)

THE ENCYCLOPEDIA OF
BUTTERFLIES

John Feltwell

Prentice Hall General Reference

New York • London • Toronto • Sydney • Tokyo • Singapore

A QUARTO BOOK

Copyright © 1993 by Quarto Publishing plc

First published in Great Britain in 1993 by Quarto Publishing plc

Prentice Hall General Reference
15 Columbus Circle
New York, New York 10023

Library of Congress Cataloging-in-Publication data

Feltwell, John.
    The encyclopedia of butterflies/John Feltwell.
    p.   cm.
    Includes bibliographical references (p. 288) and index.
    ISBN 0-671-86828-4
    1. Butterflies – Encyclopedias. I. Title.
QL541.5.F44 1993
595.78'9'03 – dc20   93-12184

This book was designed and produced by
Quarto Publishing plc
The Old Brewery, 6 Blundell Street,
London N7 9BH

Senior Editor: Kate Kirby
Editors: Barbara Haynes, Maggi McCormick
Senior Art Editor: Amanda Bakhtiar
Designers: Penny Dawes, Terry Jeavons
Photographer: Stephen R. Steinhauser
Maps and Symbols: David Kemp
Illustrator: Brian Hargreaves
Picture Manager: Rebecca Horsewood
Art Director: Moira Clinch
Publishing Director: Janet Slingsby

Typeset by The Brightside Partnership, London
Manufactured in Singapore by Colour Trend
Printed in Hong Kong by Leefung Asco

**All the specimen butterflies were photographed at
the Allyn Museum of Entomology/Florida Museum of
Natural History. We would like to thank the curators of
the Museum, Dr. Jacqueline Y. Miller and
Dr. Lee D. Miller for all their help in
the production of this book.**

With thanks to Sally Butler.

10 9 8 7 6 5 4 3 2 1

First Prentice Hall Edition

Contents

Introduction

For some of us the first exposure to the world of natural history began with our early observations on butterflies, nature's most elegant yet scientifically spectacular organisms. Through these early encounters, we quickly learned the interdependence of nature and that butterflies play a variety of roles in the ecosystem. However, similar to other organisms, butterflies are subject to uncertainty with respect to adequate food supply, predators, changes in climate, and available habitat among other factors.

With more than 753 species currently recorded, the study of butterflies in the U.S. has sometimes taken a circuitous route. The introduction of a binomial sys-

Pachliopta aristolochiae
(*Rose swallowtails*)

tem of nomenclature by Linnaeus (1758) provided a framework for future identification and enabled researchers to properly document species, but the detailed studies of Abbot and Smith (1798), Scudder (1889), Edwards (1862–1897), and Holland (1898) began the lengthy inventory of butterfly species. With the introduction of Klots (1955) and other popular volumes, the study of North American butterflies was brought within the grasp of every inquisitive naturalist and professional entomologist. Our knowledge and appreciation of these insects continues to grow at an accelerated rate, but every question answered results in another series of questions proposed. Many of these queries have been resolved through the combined interest and study by both professional researchers and enthusiastic naturalists of all ages. Despite these efforts, our knowledge is still limited, especially with respect to docu-

mented life history and authoritative identification of their preferred larval hostplants and adult nectar sources. In addition, the behavior of butterflies in the field, where and how they perch, diurnal flight patterns and periods, and interaction with other species is often absent from published records.

With this present volume, Dr. John Feltwell takes a refreshingly distinctive approach to the study of worldwide butterflies. It is written for those naturalists and entomologists – amateur and professional – whose curiosity about things observed in nature extends beyond a passing fancy. Three aspects of the book are particularly noteworthy. With more than 1000 butterfly species illustrated in color, the reader is introduced to the broad biological diversity and breathtaking beauty which exists among this extraordinary group of insects from every part of the globe. Dr.

Feltwell has included an extensive list of opportunist or generalist species such as Danaus plexippus *and* Vanessa atalanta, *that are widely recorded throughout North America in addition to unusual species infrequently encountered, such as* Dryas iulia, Siproeta stelenes, *and* Chlorostrymon maesites. *With the balanced geographic representation, other efforts have been directed toward the illustration of species previously excluded from more popular volumes; such intriguing butterflies as* Parantica schenki (Solomon), Oreixenica kershawi (Australia), Mycalesis messena (Bachan), *and* Deudorix antalus (Africa) *are featured. Each butterfly is defined further with a brief diagnosis, range distribution, larval hostplant and its current conservation status.*

Today there is a growing awareness of how human activities can disrupt and destroy the delicate balances of nature. Butterflies are excellent biological indicators, and the greatest threat to their survival is the loss of habitat. With an ever increasing human population, agricultural practices have adjusted and now include the farming of marginal areas, formerly hedges, woods, areas along streambeds and rural roads once reserved for nesting birds, butterflies, and other wildlife. Such practices have reduced the available habitats for breeding populations and in the cases of extremely limited ranges, for example, the Xerces blue (Glaucopsyche xerces), *these species are now extinct. Often native plant species have been replaced with introduced plants, further diminishing the available habitat and associated larval hostplants. As one of the better recognized European conservationists, Dr. Feltwell is keenly aware of these problems and has focused on those species of some conservation concern, especially those butterflies listed in the* Red Data Book of Threatened Swallowtails of the World. *It is hoped that this information will make both casual and professional naturalists aware of the voids in our current scientific database, especially in regard to the ecological requirements of butterflies, and prompt further study before additional species slip into extinction.*

Papilio
machaon
(Swallowtail)

JACQUELINE Y. MILLER
Associate Curator
Allyn Museum of Entomology,
Florida Museum of Natural History

How to Use this Book

In addition to the color plates, information is given about the butterfly species in two ways: in the text and in the symbols. The examples below will help to clarify the system used and explain the symbols which appear in each entry.

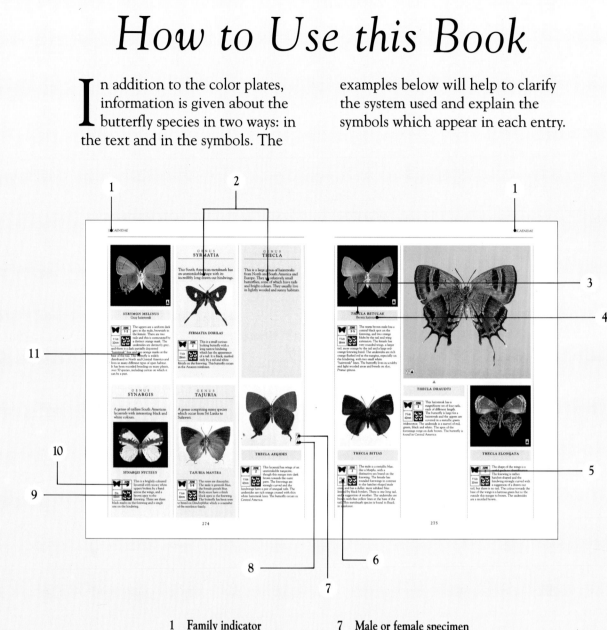

1 Family indicator
2 Introductions to genera
3 Scientific name
4 Common name
5 Family indicator
6 Size
7 Male or female specimen
8 Ventral or dorsal view
9 Conservation status
10 Zone of origin
11 Text entry

1 and 5 Family indicator

Each of the four butterfly families is included, but leaving out the skippers which many experts do not now regard as true butterflies.

(1) The heading at the top of each page indicates to which of the four families the specimens on the page belong.

(5) In addition, each entry has a stylized shape symbol, denoting family membership:

Papilionidae (swallowtails)

Pieridae (whites and sulphurs)

Nymphalidae (brush-footed butterflies)

Lycaenidae (hairstreaks, coppers and blues)

Note: the author has chosen to follow current trends and has amalgamated four traditional families of butterflies – the brush-footed butterflies (*Nymphalidae*), the browns (*Satyridae*), the monarchs (*Danaidae*) and the snouts (*Libytheidae*) to make a single family, the *Nymphalidae*. This makes much better sense, from a "lumpers" point of view (rather than a "splitters" point of view), since on structural grounds, at least, all these butterflies have two pairs of functional legs. The brush-footed nature of all the butterflies is embodied in the forward-projecting "brushes" which are the redundant front pair of legs.

Butterfly families are subdivided by taxonomists, people who study classification, into separate genera. The number of butterfly species in a genus varies from one to several hundred. In some cases the precise number is known; in others, particularly those of tropical habitats, it is not always known. Then, with hindsight, taxonomists move some species from one genus to another because of the recent discovery of useful diagnostic features, and the number changes again.

Within each family the butterflies are arranged alphabetically by scientific name.

2 Introductions to genera
Each genus has an introduction which looks at some of the typical characteristics of the species within the genus.

Species within the same genus are unified by a matching tint panel behind the butterfly's name, so you can see at a glance which butterflies belong to the same genus.

3 Scientific name
Scientific Latin names are always in a state of flux. The author has used the most up-to-date classification. In this he has drawn on the expertise of Dr. Jacqueline Y. Miller and Dr. Lee D. Miller, curators of the Allyn Museum in Florida, who are at the forefront of butterfly taxonomy.

The genus name is given followed by the species name and, where appropriate, the subspecies.

A butterfly's scientific name reflects something about its morphology, structure, behavior, coloration, or food plants – as in the case of *Aglais urticae* (the small tortoiseshell) which breeds on nettles (*Urtica*).

4 Common name
Where a common name is known, the European common name is given first, followed by the US common name.

Common names are a source of confusion because different species can have the same common names.

5 Family indicator
See above under 1.

6 Size
The sizes given in this book are for the wingspan. The wingspan is the distance between the tips of the outstretched forewings. This is a little larger than twice the forewing length since it includes the width of the thorax which may be $1/4$in (6mm) in some species. The figure given is for the maximum size of the female, since the female is usually larger than the male.

Convention dictates that the forewing length is taken as a measure of wingspan, but there are numerous tropical butterflies where the hindwing is much longer than the forewing. In *Papilio androcles* from Southeast Asia, the forewing length is $2^3/8$in (60mm) compared to the hindwing length of $3^3/4$in (95mm), 2in (50mm) of which is made up of the tail itself. The various Mistletoe hairstreaks, *Iolaus* species from tropical Africa, have significantly longer hindwings than forewings, too.

Another point to note about size is that the butterflies in the color plates are not to scale. For this reason the size of the image does not reflect the actual size of the butterfly. To show the butterflies in proportion to each other would mean that the smallest specimens would be so small as to be unidentifiable, as the example below demonstrates.

Vacciniina optilete
(22mm/$^7/8$in)

Ornithoptera
goliath samson
(210mm/$8^1/4$in)

7 Male or female specimen

Most of the specimens shown are male. However, in cases where a female specimen is shown, then a female symbol appears in the frame with the specimen. If the specimen is male no symbol appears.

8 Ventral or dorsal view

Most of the specimens have been photographed to show their dorsal (upperside) surface. However, in some cases the ventral (underside) surface is more colorful and is more useful for identification purposes. In cases when the ventral surface is shown, the symbol, above, will appear in the frame with the specimen.

9 Conservation status

It is noted whether a butterfly is in any way conserved or protected (in the widest sense), and a special section on conservation follows in this introduction. All butterflies which are protected by individual countries, or by conservation groups, have been given a conservation symbol; so too have butterflies which are in decline or have become locally extinct. Although some of these species are not being actively conserved, they are mentioned simply to direct attention to them. The fact that their numbers and populations are at risk or declining is often the first stage in the conservation awareness of a species. The symbol indicating an unprotected species

represents the status of the butterfly as it is known at the present time. However, conservation research is not well funded enough to allow all species that require protection status to be known or awarded it.

Status conserved or protected in some way.

Status neither conserved nor protected at the present time.

10 Zone of origin

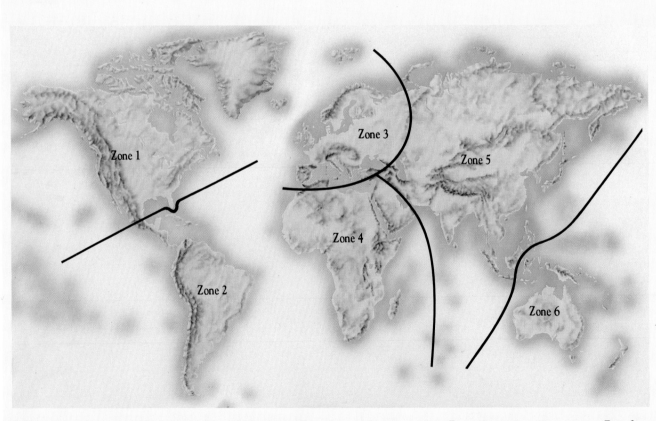

For the purposes of this book, the world has been divided into six regions; North America, South America, Europe, Africa, Asia, and the Australian region (see map).

The key to these regions is as follows:

North American region..................Zone 1
South American region..................Zone 2
European region.............................Zone 3
African region.................................Zone 4
Asian region.....................................Zone 5
Australian region............................Zone 6

THE NORTH AMERICAN REGION: this is all that area north of a line drawn roughly east-to-west through Mexico, and includes the United States (including Alaska), Canada, and Greenland. Of the 700 or so species that could be counted as North American, many are interesting butterflies of the tundra and arctic region, particularly the *Erebia*. There are also perhaps 200 species out of the total which are directly influenced by population reinforcement from Central America or the Antilles which are relatively close by.

THE SOUTH AMERICAN REGION: this covers an area south of a line drawn roughly east-to-west through Mexico, and includes Central and Southern America and the West Indies. This latter region includes the Greater and Lesser Antilles. Within the general South American region, there are two very rich butterfly areas: the Amazon basin and Central America, both of which are likely to yield new butterfly species. Costa Rica is particularly rich in butterflies.

THE EUROPEAN REGION: this includes a small part of the African continent and species found as far west as the Atlantic islands of Azores, and as far east as the Black Sea. Within the area there are about 400 butterfly species, of which 30 percent are endemic (found nowhere else in the world). Despite there being probably more butterfly enthusiasts in Europe than anywhere else, the caterpillar food plants of about 60 species of European butterfly are still unknown.

THE AFRICAN REGION: this comprises the whole of Africa, except the small part of European influence along the north coast, and includes the butterfly-rich island of Madagascar. There are 3,207 species of butterfly in Africa, of which 15 percent are hesperids. Butterflies do not always fit neatly into this region. For instance, there are butterflies found in northern and eastern Africa which are found also in Arabia, and there are species which are found in Madagascar which have affinities with the Indian subcontinent.

THE ASIAN REGION: the largest region, it includes the areas from Arabia east via the Indian subcontinent, via Burma, Thailand, Philippines, the Indonesian islands lying west of Wallace's Line (see box, below), and the greater part of the CIS, as well as Japan and China.

THE AUSTRALIAN REGION: this comprises all of the mainlands of Australia and New Zealand, but also includes a highly significant number of tropical islands north of the Australian continent, east of Wallace's Line. These include New Hebrides, New Caledonia, Papua New Guinea and its gaggle of islands to the west, the Moluccas, Timor, Lombok, and Sulawesi. This whole area is very rich in butterflies and accounts for many of the butterflies of the Australian region. Some of the butterflies of the rainforests of this chain of islands are also found in the tropical rainforests of northern Australia.

11 Text entry

Each entry in the directory section follows the same format:

DESCRIPTION: there is variation in every living creature, and there can be no such thing as a finite definition of a particular species. In the general description, the author therefore attempts to cover all possibilities of identification.

NUMBER OF GENERATIONS EACH YEAR: the information is given if it is known.

MIGRATION: if a species is not described as a migrant, it is likely that it is a resident and one which stays very much in the same habitat in which it emerged. However, there is no clear line of division between resident and migratory butterflies. There are butterflies which are strongly resident, ones which are strongly migratory, and others which show local movements, but the borderline between the groups is very imprecise.

It is, though, very clear that certain genera of butterflies have more migratory species than others. For instance, there are various important migratory butterflies belonging to the following genera: *Appias, Colias, Colotis, Danaus, Delias, Inachis, Papilio, Pieris,* and *Vanessa.* The vagaries of butterfly migration are discussed in more detail on pages 22 to 23.

FOOD PLANTS: the food plants of caterpillars is an area where an enormous amount of information is still required. There still exist in Europe about 60 species of butterfly for which the larval food plants are unknown, and in North America the food plants for about 100 butterfly species remain unknown. The situation becomes more acute in tropical Central and South America and tropical Southeast Asia, where the food plants of whole groups of butterflies are unknown.

The larval food plants are mentioned in the introduction to the genus if they are similar for all the species. Where the food plants of individual species are known, these are mentioned in the text entry concerned. Where butterflies use numerous food plants, these are often referred to by the name of the plant family or families to which they belong.

THE WALLACE LINE

There is a highly significant, but imaginary, line drawn from north to south through the Indonesian islands. This is called the Wallace Line after Alfred Russel Wallace (1823–1913), a contemporary of the naturalist Charles Darwin, who carried out a great deal of field work in this region of the world.

His attention was drawn to the way that different characteristics of the Asian, Malaysian, Philippine, and Australian biogeographical areas seemed to come together on the island of Sulawesi. This observation has caused considerable debate, which continues to this day, as to the origins and evolution of the widely differing groups of plants and animals, including many butterflies, found within the region and more significantly either east or west of the line.

Superlatives

This book contains many superlatives. In terms of the largest butterflies in the world, it has to be Queen Alexandra's birdwing, *Ornithoptera alexandrae*, which has a wingspan up to 11^1/$_8$in (280mm) and occurs in New Guinea. It was first collected when it was shot down from the rainforest canopy; perhaps the marksman thought it was a large bird. Queen Victoria's birdwing, *Ornithoptera victoriae*, whose wingspan is a mere 6^7/$_8$in (175mm), was also shot. The largest butterfly in the Asian region is *Trogonoptera trojanus* with a wingspan up to 8in (200mm).

In North America, the largest butterfly, a swallowtail, is the Homerus swallowtail, *Papilio homerus*, with a wingspan up to 6in (150mm), but it occurs more in Central America than in its occasional presence in North America.

Also included in this book are the largest white in North America, *Ganyra josephina* (2^3/$_4$in/73mm), and the largest white in Asia, the Great orange tip, *Hebomoia glaucippe* (4in/100mm). The largest butterfly in Africa, the African giant swallowtail, *Papilio antimachus* (9^1/$_8$in/230mm), is included; so too is the largest white in South Africa, the Large vagrant, *Nepheronia argia* (3^1/$_8$in/83mm).

Members of the blues figure among the smallest butterflies in the world and the North American Pygmy blue, *Brephidium exilis*, is probably the smallest butterfly in the world, with a wingspan of ^{1}/$_2$–^{3}/$_4$in (15–19mm). A relatively common butterfly, the Small blue, *Cupido minimus*, is the smallest butterfly in Britain and common throughout much of Europe. However, the smallest in Europe, the Grass jewel, *Freyeria trochylus*, with a wingspan of ^{3}/$_4$in (19mm), is not described here.

Abundant and widespread butterflies

Many abundant and widespread butterflies are described in this book. They include the most common butterfly in Japan and China (in July), *Papilio xuthus*; the most successful butterfly in Africa, *Catopsila florella*; and the most common butterfly in Costa Rica, *Phoebis sennae*. One of California's most abundant butterflies is the Chalcedon checkerspot, *Euphydryas chalcedona*.

THE MOST BEAUTIFUL BUTTERFLY

Beauty is always subjective, but there is often general agreement about some of the world's most beautiful butterflies, such as Australia's most spectacular butterfly, the Blue Mountain swallowtail, *Papilio ulysses*. The Victorian collector, Alfred Russel Wallace, collected the first specimens of the superlative *Ornithoptera croesus*. There can be no doubt that the most beautiful fritillary in North America is the Diana, *Speyeria diana*.

The Red-spotted purple, Basilarchia arthemis astyanax, drinks nectar from a rose. This is a Batesian mimic of the Pipevine swallowtail, Battus philenor, which it resembles on both the upper and lower surfaces; and it is not too dissimilar from the blue female of the Diana whose range it overlaps.

Euploea core is among the most common butterflies in Australia and in India. In Europe, the Small tortoiseshell, *Aglais urticae*, is among the most common, perhaps vying with the Meadow brown, *Maniola jurtina*, or the Large and Small whites, *Pieris brassicae* and *P. rapae* respectively. A major contributory factor to the success of these butterflies is that they are migrants, or they have common larval food plants, or both. The Monarch or Milkweed, *Danaus plexippus*, of North America is

This is the Common eggfly, Hypolimnas bolina, *one of the most widespread and frequently encountered butterflies in the* tropics. *It often visits garden flowers for nectar and is seen here on a zinnia.*

very common and is perhaps the world's most researched migrant butterfly. One of the world's most widespread browns is *Melanitis leda*, which occurs in Africa, Asia, and Australia.

On a worldwide basis, the most widespread butterfly is the Danaid eggfly, *Hypolimnas misippus*, which occurs on six continents. Not far behind is the Painted lady, *Cynthia cardui*, which is, perhaps, both the most widespread and common butterfly in the world, although another strong contender is the Long-tailed blue, *Lampides boeticus*.

Butterfly families

The butterflies described in the book have been arranged according to four butterfly families, starting with the most colorful of butterflies, the swallowtails (*Papilionidae*). The remaining three families follow taxonomic convention with the whites and sulfurs (*Pieridae*) grouped together, the brush-footed butterflies (*Nymphalidae*), and, finally, the hairstreaks, coppers, and blues (*Lycaenidae*).

EXCLUDING THE SKIPPERS

This is the first encyclopedia of butterflies to exclude the skippers (*Hesperiidae*). Although formerly classified as butterflies, the skippers show more similarities to moths, and there is a growing awareness that skippers should be separated from the true butterflies. The moth-like features that skippers possess include small size; thick, hairy bodies which are large in relation to the small wings; uniform drab colors; and, probably as important as anything, hooked antennae which are not neatly clubbed as in true butterflies. Some skippers even rest with their wings laid flat, not vertically like most butterflies. Of course, there are exceptions to most of these criteria used to disqualify skippers as butterflies, and this simply serves to demonstrate that the separations between butterflies and moths are subjective and somewhat arbitrary.

In the field, butterflies can be readily sorted into the four major families. Inspection of their wing shape, venation, and number of legs give some vital clues. For example, swallowtails are large and colorful, with six large legs, and wings with or without tails.

Papilionidae

The swallowtails are usually recognized by the presence of tails, but these are absent in many species including festoons and apollos. They are also large butterflies and count among their number some of the largest in the world. They are a worldwide group, and species such as the swallowtail enjoy wide distribution over different continents. The colors of swallowtails are usually bright, including yellows, oranges, and red.

The most overriding characteristic of the swallowtails is the long tail, as in this Tiger swallowtail, Papilio glaucus, *but there are many exceptions. The bold black "tiger" stripes present on both surfaces are widely found in swallowtails.*

Pieridae

The whites and sulfurs are easy to identify from their bright colors, from which they derive their name. The whites are a large and widespread group which have white and cream colors, and they tend to exploit larval food plants belonging to the cabbage family, *Cruciferae*. The sulfurs include many of the clouded yellows, some of which are noted migrants.

Nymphalidae

Brush-footed butterflies include groups such as the browns, milkweeds, aristocrats, and snouts, all of which have previously been classified as separate butterfly families (*Satyridae, Danaidae, Nymphalidae,* and *Libytheidae* respectively). They are all combined here as one family, *Nymphalidae*, since they have one overriding characteristic: four functional legs. Their first pair of legs are redundant: they do not function for locomotion. They are so reduced as to be not recognizable as legs and are often overlooked. They exist as simple appendages tucked under the head. Nymphalids are generally fairly powerful butterflies and include some noted migrants.

Lycaenidae

This family includes three main groups of butterflies, the hairstreaks, coppers, and blues, each identified by various external characteristics. Butterflies belonging to this family are relatively small, and the biggest they become is up to about 2¹/₂in (65mm) in some of the Asian tropical *Arhopala* species. Many lycaenids have one or two pairs of tails, often short, though in the case of the Congo long-tailed blue, *Iolaus timon*, one of the tails is about as long as the forewing. The total hindwing length including the long tail is 1³/₈in (35mm) compared to the forewing length of ⁷/₈in (22mm). Like some swallowtails, some lycaenids exhibit back-to-front mimicry, where the tail and an eye-spot mimic the real head, compound eye, and antennae. This confuses predators so they don't know where to strike effectively. The butterfly, therefore, has a 50:50 chance of surviving an attack with only its tails knocked out.

The hairstreaks are named after a fine line which runs across the underside, usually across most of the hindwing. The line may be partial, or a series of dots, or absent. The coppers are named after the fiery copper colors of the upper surfaces, which are most pronounced in the males. The flashy color is also seen in the males of the blues. Males are usually bright blue, while female blues are usually brown, sometimes with a dusting of blue.

ABOVE *The hairstreaks, blues, and coppers are among the smallest and most colorful butterflies in the world. This Dusky large blue,* Maculinea nausithous, *typical of lycaenids, has a spotted underside combined with beautiful iridescent uppers. Not all lycaenids have "tails."*

LEFT *The Plain tiger,* Danaus chrysippus, *has typical markings of many danaids, though there is great variation, from yellowish to gray hues. The Browns or satyrids and the Snouts or libytheids are also placed in Nymphalidae, since they all have four functional legs.*

ABOVE *The pierids may be white, cream, pale green, lemon, yellow, or orange, like this Clouded yellow,* Colias croceus, *or even maroon. Many species are white with black spots. Sexes can look completely different and unrelated.*

Morphology

The butterfly body is made of three parts: head, thorax, and abdomen. The head has a pair of antennae or feelers which are usually long and knobbed at the ends. The antennae are sensitive to touch and smell, and have a specific number of segments, sometimes of use in identification. There is a pair of compound eyes, one on each side of the head. The eyes are beveled so that a wide angle of vision is possible. The sight of butterflies, like many other insects, is good for detecting movement, but not details. Each compound eye is made up of thousands of tiny eye modules, called ommatidia, each of which has a small lens connected to the optic nerve. The other main feature on the head is the tongue, or proboscis, used for sucking up liquids. Its structure resembles two straws fused together and zipped up.

The thorax

The thorax is a muscle box with three segments. The three pairs of jointed legs arise from the thorax, one from each of the three segments. In some butterflies the front pair of legs are nonfunctional and much reduced in length. The thorax contains the flight muscles, which are attached to the base of the wings. There are always two pairs of wings, and these arise from the second and third segments.

The abdomen

The abdomen contains the bulk of the digestive system, and the excretory system. At the tip of the abdomen are the sexual apparatus, called the genitalia, whose internal characteristics are useful in identifying different species.

The outer body

The outer body of the butterfly is covered with small sensory hairs. A newly emerged insect is obviously downy in appearance, but as it gets older, its body becomes balder, and the tiny scales which cover the wing membranes gradually fall out of their slots.

Butterflies also have specialized scales on their wings which contain highly volatile insect hormones, called pheromones. These hormones are released into the air during mating and affect the behavior of the opposite sex.

Wing mechanism

Rapid flapping of wings is achieved by alternating the contraction and relaxation of the muscles inside the thorax. Upstroke occurs when the *inside muscles contract and the outer ones relax, and downstroke by the outside muscles contracting and the inside ones relaxing.* *A slight change in the shape of the thorax occurs during flight, which helps to move hemolymph (blood) around the body.*

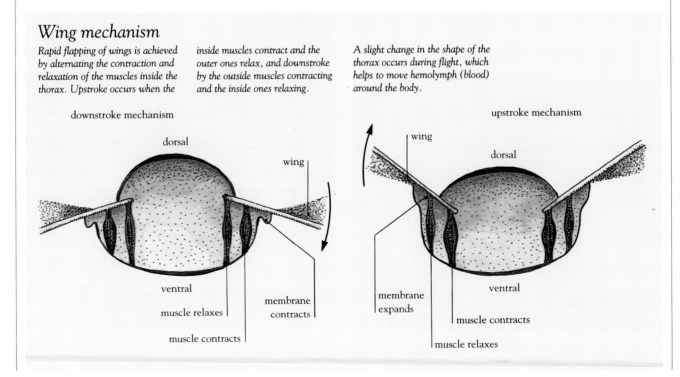

downstroke mechanism

dorsal

wing

ventral

muscle relaxes

membrane contracts

muscle contracts

upstroke mechanism

wing

dorsal

membrane expands

ventral

muscle contracts

muscle relaxes

Head and body

This is a typical butterfly in the style of a Swallowtail. Tails, when present, are on the hindwing. The wings show the veins which support the wing structure. The body is hairy, which is typical of a freshly-emerged insect. Three legs are shown, one pair to each segment. In some butterflies there are just two pairs of functional legs. Notice the backward-facing defensive spines on the legs and claws on the tips. The proboscis or tongue is shown partially extended. It is normally curled up like a watch spring under the head and may be difficult to spot. The antennae are always clubbed in a butterfly, but they may be long or short.

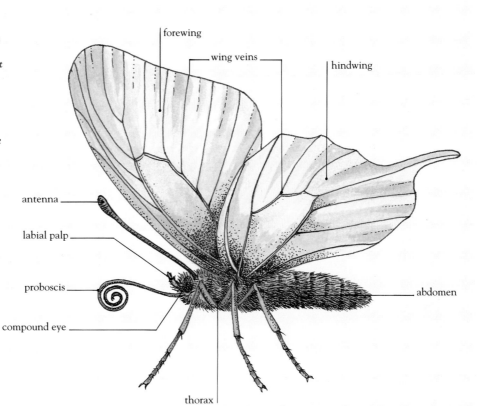

forewing

wing veins

hindwing

antenna

labial palp

proboscis

compound eye

abdomen

thorax

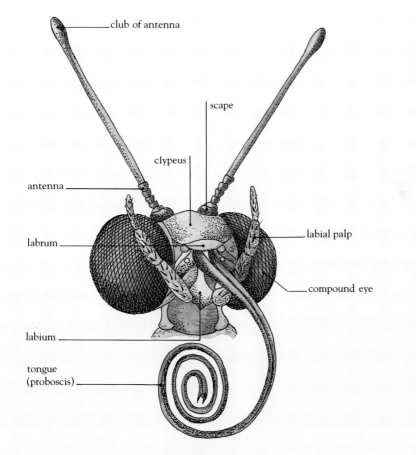

club of antenna

scape

clypeus

antenna

labrum

labial palp

compound eye

labium

tongue (proboscis)

The head carries a great deal of sensory apparatus for the butterfly. The largest features are the pair of compound eyes which are made of an array of thousands of individual eyes, each with a tiny lens and a tiny fraction of view. The beveled nature of the compound eye means that the butterfly is aware of its immediate environment through a very large angle. The pair of antennae, or feelers, arise from the head, and the paired proboscis, which is fused and normally kept rolled up, is a major feature. The proboscis is used for sucking up nectar from flowers. The head is covered with minute bristles and hairs which are sensitive to touch, as are the labial palps and the labrum.

Butterfly life cycles

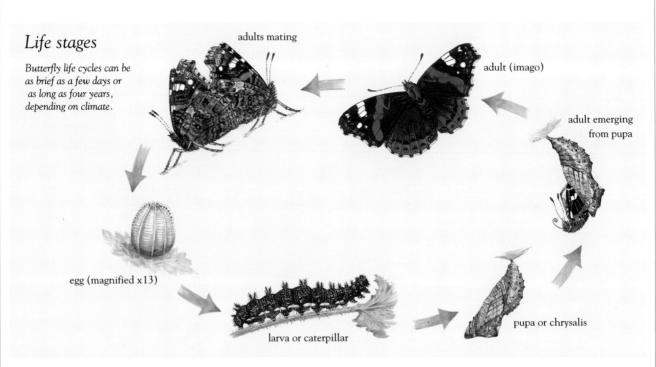

Life stages

Butterfly life cycles can be as brief as a few days or as long as four years, depending on climate.

adults mating

adult (imago)

adult emerging from pupa

egg (magnified x13)

larva or caterpillar

pupa or chrysalis

All butterflies (and moths) go through four stages in their life cycle: egg or ovum, caterpillar or larva, pupa or chrysalis, and adult or imago (imagines). The fact that the life cycle has a pupal stage marks butterflies out from other insects which simply have early stages which look like miniature adults. Butterflies therefore have a type of metamorphosis which is termed complete, in contrast to other insects which have an incomplete metamorphosis.

In temperate climates the typical life cycle from egg to adult is often accomplished during a year, in which case the butterfly is said to have a single generation. Two generations a year is quite common among many butterflies, but up to five or six annually is unusual.

Cold winter weather slows up life cycle development in butterflies, so they have evolved many means of overcoming it. Some butterflies hibernate as adults, others as eggs, young larvae, or as pupae.

During hibernation insects, at whatever stage they are in, have adaptations for overcoming intense cold. During hibernation the insects simply "turn over." This means they do not burn up a lot of energy and do not feed. It is known that glycerol and sorbitol are found in the blood of some butterflies which act as a natural antifreeze to help them overcome infrequent bursts of cold weather, such as snow and hail during short summers.

Hot weather can sometimes be a problem to butterfly development, though usually it is not. Butterflies in tropical habitats do not demonstrate winter hibernation, but they may have periods of seasonal inactivity which coincide with the dry season. This may involve estivation, which is a sort of summer hibernation when the butterfly rests during the hottest (and driest) period. Estivation is not exclusive to butterflies of tropical

When the Peacock, Inachis io, emerges from hibernation in the spring, it is often a little sluggish.

If it is disturbed, it displays these large "eyes"

areas, since some temperate species do this, too. The Meadow brown, *Maniola jurtina*, in central Italy estivates during the hot summer months.

However, the butterflies of the rainforest are really in synchronization with the natural vegetation, which does not show any pronounced seasonal change. Their life cycle continues from one generation to another, so during a year there may be several generations, but no period of marked inactivity. Much work on population biology needs to be done. It may be that the butterflies of the *Taygetis* genus in South and Central America have periods of inactivity and live for a few months. Early-stage larvae of the Western seep fritillary *Speyeria nokomis*, in Mexico may estivate during periods of droughts.

Adult life span

For butterflies which hibernate or estivate, the life span may be up to ten months. Butterflies which emerge from a pupa during the summer in a species which has a few generations a year may live from one to four weeks.

The purpose of a butterfly is to reproduce. Males and females have to find each other, court, mate, then the female lays her eggs. It is usual for the

THE HIGH LIFE

Parnassian swallowtails have been found up to 13,500ft (4,115m) on Mt. Everest. These are probably the world's highest-living butterflies, but are rivaled by *Ancyluris formosissima* from Peru and Ecuador, which is found up to 10,000ft (3,000m).

male to seek the female, and in this endeavor he is helped by powerful scents and colors of the female. Sexes are often different colors, males usually being the brighter, females usually drab. The larger female often has slightly rounded forewings. The larger wing surface makes a larger aerofoil for flight. She has a large abdomen which becomes swollen with eggs. The bright colors of males are due to three forces, sexual selection by the female, competition from other males, and antipredatory devices.

Egg-laying

When mating is completed, which may take an hour or so, the female then lays eggs. She has to find the correct food plant for the caterpillars, and she will diligently search vegetation using her pow-

The Large tortoiseshell, Nymphalis polychloros, is widespread across Europe. It often feeds on spring blossoms when it emerges from hibernation.

ers of scent and sight. In most cases, the female carefully lays her eggs on the right food plant, showing perhaps the only form of parental control in butterflies. However, in just a few species, the female lays her eggs broadcast over the food plant — usually coarse grasses. The Silver-washed fritillary, *Argynnis adippe*, lays its eggs on a tree trunk near some violets, the food plant, thus forcing the caterpillars to walk to the food.

Eggs are different shapes and sizes according to the species, and are sometimes useful identification clues. They may be tall ($^3/_{16}$in/4mm), round, pitted, ribbed, yellow, white, blue, but they darken with age as the caterpillar develops inside. The female may have 200–500 eggs to lay. These are often

After mating, the female Giant swallowtail, Papilio cresphontes, visits citrus groves and gardens where it lays its eggs individually on young citrus leaves.

THE MATING GAME

Males can be very territorial and pugnacious in their endeavors to find females. *Phoebis philea* is known to knock a female to the ground and mate with her within 15 to 30 seconds of her flying overhead. This species and others have small serrations on the forewings which may be involved with courtship — making them very formidable warriors of the butterfly world.

Butterflies mate soon after emergence. These are Common blues, Polyommatus icarus.

Males have other strategies for finding females, they engage in hill-topping; females do this as well. The top of a hill or mountain is a logical topographical meeting place for butterflies. If they all fly uphill by using upcurrents, they are likely to find a mate.

Another way of finding mates is lekking, that is, gathering in suitable places. This is what many of the South American ithominid butterflies do in forest clearings, sunny places, and tracks. They form groups or leks comprising individuals of a number of species in which courtship and mating takes place. New members recruited to the group stand a better chance of finding a mate.

deposited on the underside of the leaf, or on stems, singly or in groups, but are always glued to the surface so that they do not fall off. They may be chemically protected by pigments or physically protected by scales from the female's abdomen. It is useful for the species if the female can fly abroad to lay her eggs, or deposit them over a wide area; then there is less competition for available food plants.

The caterpillar stage

The first stage caterpillar, or instar, hatches from the egg. It may or may not eat its eggshell, depending on the species. Eggshells generally have useful nutrients in them which are recycled by the caterpillar. They may also have useful substances in them which the caterpillar may need to deter would-be predators.

Each time the caterpillar grows bigger, it sheds its old skin in a process of molting. This it usually does five times, though it can vary in a few species of the South American tropical *Nymphalidae* between four and seven. The outer skin of the caterpillar is very tough, but when the old skin is sloughed off, the replacement skin underneath is soft for just a short while. The caterpillar is able to swell up a little at first until the skin dries and then spends the rest of its time consolidating the available body space until it is almost bursting for

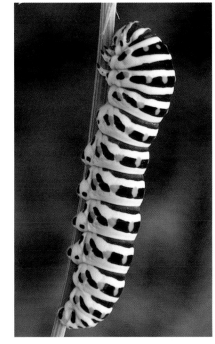

The fully grown caterpillar of the swallowtail, Papilio machaon, *is of striking appearance, banded black and white with orange dots. It has an orange osmeterium which it everts from behind the head if disturbed.*

The small but beautifully marked Silver-studded blue, Plebejus argus, *feeds on the flowers of wild clematis. The color on the inside of the wings is blue in the male. It breeds on gorse, broom, and rock rose.*

another skin change. Each stage of the caterpillar's development is called an instar, so in most caterpillars there are five instars.

The time taken for a caterpillar to pass from its first to its final instar varies from three to six weeks in most species. For those arctic and tundra species which take two summers to complete their larval stages during the short summers, the caterpillar may live for up to 18 months. Caterpillars which hibernate in temperate zones may live for nine months.

When the fifth instar caterpillar is fully grown, it suddenly stops eating and goes into a wandering stage. It wanders, sometimes relentlessly, around the locality until it has found a suitable place to pupate. During this period of wandering, the caterpillar usually loses any bright color it had and changes into somber hues. This helps the caterpillar become less noticeable as it moves over different surfaces. It is during the wandering stage that many caterpillars are easily spotted by naturalists, especially when the caterpillars are crossing roads and tracks or walking up walls.

The pupa

The criteria for good pupation sites vary between species, but include a sheltered site, not necessarily in full sunshine, in grass and litter on the soil surface, or on a tree trunk. Generally speaking, butterflies do not spin silk cocoons to protect the pupa, but all caterpillars have silk glands. One extraordinary pierid in South America, *Eucheira socialis*, spins a large cocoon in which many larvae pupate. Many lycaenids spin very weak nets of silk around their pupae. But many butterflies use their silk for spinning either a firm base on which to fasten the pupa, or a silken girdle around the middle of the pupa to support it to a stem or twig. The pupa of many butterflies is attached to a stem in full sunshine and is not in a protected position, although they do have the protection of being camouflaged in color, shape, and pattern.

Emergence of the butterfly

After about ten days, or in the following spring for those species which hibernate as a pupa, the adult emerges. In the few hours before emergence, the color of the pupa changes to reflect the fast-developing butterfly inside. Where the body will be, the color is often black, and the wing cases hint at the color and patterns of the adult wings in miniature. Then two weak lines along the head and legs rupture, and the insect scrambles out.

The fresh butterfly pulls itself free of the pupal case and hangs upside down, with its wings wet and limp. Immediately, the butterfly inflates its wings to their full size, using its blood pressure to aid inflation. During this period the butterfly must expand its wings to their full extent; otherwise, the wings will dry hard and crippled. Emergence is usually timed for a quiet period, for instance in the morning, when disturbance will be at a minimum. The butterfly is very vulnerable and defenseless until its wings have dried, which may take an hour or so, and it can then take its first flight.

Migration

In general terms, some of the most common and widely seen butterflies of the world are regular migrants. They may be seen migrating in most climatic regions, for instance in the tropics, subtropics, and in temperate regions, sometimes in extraordinarily large numbers.

The advantages of migration

In temperate climates where there are distinct seasons, the reason butterflies migrate is clear. They have to migrate in order to exploit new resources as the seasons progress. As the northern hemisphere warms up in spring due to the ever increasing elevation of the sun, so the snow melts, the plants grow, and the butterflies and other insects move northward to exploit the new flush of flowers. Birds then move in to feed on the insects and butterflies.

In the tropics, where there are no clear-cut seasons, some butterflies demonstrate another reason to migrate away from the immediate area in which they grew up as caterpillars, and to establish new colonies. If all butterflies stayed where they emerged, mated, and laid eggs, the caterpillars would have too much competition and starve to death. So it is in the interest of the species to move abroad and find new territories. This is the reason for most migration; getting away from the parental area is good for the species.

There is a hard core of regular migrants in this book. These often migrate in large numbers and are generally large and powerful butterflies of their genus. Two of the characteristics of a migrant are that they often enjoy a much larger distribution than a non-migrant species, and that they are usually fairly constant in their color and pattern. Their conformity of appearance is due to the large mix of genetic material effected by crossbreeding over a large area. This is always better for a species, than if it did not rely entirely on crossbreeding.

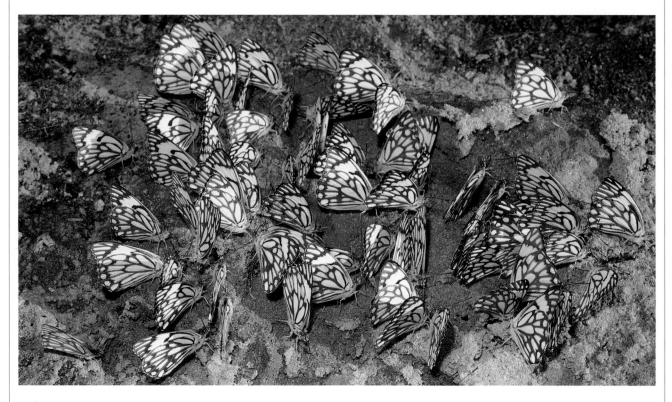

These South African Brown-veined whites, Belenois aurota, alight on damp ground to drink water and recharge their energy reserves on their potentially dangerous migration across desert.

GREAT MIGRANTS

The major migrant in North America is the Monarch or Milkweed, *Danaus plexippus*, which makes a return migration to its winter roosts from the Canadian border to the southwest of the United States. Here it remains through the winter, clinging by the million to conifers high in the mountains and often covered with winter snow. In the spring the butterflies leave these protected sanctuaries and return to points north and northeast.

Map 1

Key

—— indicates migratory routes

- - - assumed, but unconfirmed, routes

Painted lady, *Cynthia cardui* (Map 2).

Another great migrant is the Painted lady, *Cynthia cardui*. It regularly moves from North Africa, north and north-westward to Britain and Europe beyond. This journey of about 800 miles (1,290km) is considerable for a butterfly with such simple wings. It is well known that when a migratory stream of butterflies is in motion, other butterflies join in the flow, and this includes both regular and irregular migrants, as well as a few other nonmigratory butterflies caught up in the general flow. A companion of the Painted lady is the Red admiral, *Vanessa atalanta*, which meets up with hibernating individuals that now increasingly survive the winters in northwestern Europe.

Map 2

Monarch, *Danaus plexippus* (Map 1).

Resident butterflies

The opposite of a migrant is a resident species which remains in the immediate area around which it developed as a caterpillar. Such a butterfly's powers of dispersal are often poor, and it may stay the rest of its life in the same meadow, field, or woodland clearing in which it emerged as an adult. The majority of butterflies, and certainly those mentioned in this book, are resident. No attention is specifically drawn to them, and the assumption can be made that, in the absence of any comments about the species being migratory, it is resident.

The extent of migration

Being a migrant or a resident is too neat a designation, and there are variations between these two extremes. There are strong regular migrants, weak irregular or occasional migrants, and species which undergo what is called local movement. Local movement differs from migration in that it is limited. These local movements may be regular or irregular, but they are not long-distance migrations over hundreds of miles. Vagrant is another term which is used. This implies that the butterfly is a migrant, but that it turns up only irregularly from a long way away. It is represented on local fauna lists as an occasional vagrant.

Technically, migration is the movement from one place to another, and back again. Butterflies never actually do this, though there are examples of weak return migration, especially over the Pyrenees. A strong powerful movement of butterflies, for instance, down or up the foothills of the Himalayas may be called a migration, but often it is witnessed as a one-way movement. Birds engage in repeated migration year after year, but butterflies do not live so long and cannot engage in long-term migration. Fragile butterflies, at least in the northern temperate climate, are severely hampered in any return migration by the inclement weather which terminates this possibility.

Immigration refers to butterflies (or other animals) coming into a particular place or country, and emigration refers to butterflies leaving a certain place or country, it all depends on the point of reference. Lepidopterists of particular countries refer to butterflies as immigrants. For instance, "immigrants from the continent," are referred to in England. They may also be vagrants. Vagrants help to "top up" populations of butterflies.

In any butterfly population, even a migratory one, there will be individuals which are resident, and others which are migratory. The migrants will eventually meet up with resident members of the same species, but at great distances from where the migrant emerged.

The beautiful Orange long wing or Julia, Dryas iulia, is very variable throughout its range in South and Central America and Southern US. Some specimens have no dark marks on the uppers; others have pronounced dark marks. This strong flier often stops to visit flowers and breeds on passion-flower vine

Conservation

Conservation is a major theme in this book. As we race to save the rainforest (just one of several important butterfly habitats), we also race to identify the butterflies found there. Just like plants of potential medicinal importance which are disappearing before they are discovered, butterflies are also inevitably disappearing before they are discovered. Our loss is the biological diversity, the great gene pool of butterfly genetics at risk to degradation and loss. Butterflies are just as important for their genetic diversity as some plants are important for their medicinal properties.

Butterfly houses are useful in stimulating butterfly awareness and increasing butterfly *populations. These are owl butterflies,* Caligo, *feeding on fruit juices.*

The Large blue, Maculinea arion, *is seen here in southern France feeding on pitch trefoil,* Psoralea bituminos. *It became extinct in* *Britain in 1979, due to loss of food plants. It survives elsewhere in Europe, but its habitats are often under threat.*

The value of a richer, more complete world with its full quota of insects, especially butterflies, is almost immeasurable. Esthetics are difficult to quantify, but we can be sure that it is a great loss when any butterfly species becomes extinct.

Butterflies are indicators of a healthy environment. So much emphasis is now given to butterflies in the western world that numerous, relatively small nature reserves have been set up to protect particular species or butterfly-rich habitats. These allow the butterflies to prosper in areas threatened by people who would otherwise urbanize greenfield sites, build leisure centers and shopping malls, or simply destroy primary or secondary vegetation. In the tropics, huge national parks have been established, but these range from being completely unmanaged, and therefore a disaster for butterflies, to others which are regulated.

Exploitation of swallowtails

Of the four major butterfly families, the swallowtails have attracted the most conservation attention. The most collectable swallowtails live in the most evocative of all habitats, the rainforest, and of these some are very rare, hardly seen, and very difficult to capture, thus putting an extra price on their heads. The lure of the chase has always motivated collectors; rare and exciting examples of swallowtails were traded for a great deal of money, and, sadly, some still are. The passion to collect and kill runs very deep in lepidopterists — a curious phenomenon and justified by some, even in high places — but the vast majority of ordinary lepidopterists abhor all such collecting.

Various museums around the world bear witness to expeditions where, decades on, the pinned specimens are still being identified, their genitalia dis-

TOP *The Zebra swallowtail,* Eurytides marcellus, *is named after its conspicuous black-and-white markings. It is common along the eastern side of North America, from Canada to Florida.*

ABOVE *This handsome swallowtail,* Papilio demetrius, *is common in Japan and China. However, in Korea, it is thought to be endangered or possibly extinct.*

sected, and their names haggled over. This work, known as taxonomy (the study of plant and animal classification), will undoubtedly continue for many decades to come. Not much information about the biology and ecology of butterflies will be gained from continued taxonomic research, and the vagaries in the naming of butterflies will not help to conserve butterflies or their habitats. But taxonomic research is essential for a fundamental understanding of butterfly nomenclature.

Butterflies under threat

It is because the swallowtails have attracted the collector that this family of butterflies has been singled out for critical attention by IUCN – The World Conservation Union. IUCN has published a number of IUCN *Red Data Books* covering major groups of plants and animals, which catalogue those species which are most threatened. Butterflies figure in two of their books, *The IUCN Invertebrate Red Data Book* and *Threatened Swallowtail Butterflies of the World: The IUCN Red Data Book*. Another publication, *Swallowtail Butterflies, an Action Plan for their Conservation* aims to provide an operational way forward and proposes priority field projects. It is an attempt to redress the situation by proposing conservation work that will allow threatened species to recover; recovery plans and projects are all-important.

In the IUCN invertebrate book, 23 butterfly species are listed, including some skippers. *The Threatened Swallowtails Butterflies of the World: The IUCN Red Data Book* includes details on 78 swallowtail species under threat. Most of these threatened species are mentioned in this encyclopedia. Data for each swallowtail species was collated from 1983 until publication of the *Red Data Book* in 1985. It has been ascertained from the senior author of the book, Dr. Mark Collins, that current data on the threats to swallowtails do not indicate any major shifts in the conservation status, so that the comments made about each species — whether it is Endangered, Vulnerable, Rare, Indeterminate, or Insufficiently Known — have not changed. There also exists the *British Red Data Books: 2. Insects* which deals with British fauna, and only seven species of butterfly are mentioned. All seven, except the Chequered skipper, are included in this book.

Other butterflies have been included which are of conservation interest. These include butterflies

Rainforest edges and clearings are often populated by fluttering danaid butterflies, showing off their markings, which are used in mimicry associations. This danaid is Euploea mulciber, *seen resting on* Lantana camara.

which are successfully bred in captivity, although in some cases the early stages have not yet been described in the wild. The fact that a species is being bred in captivity means that it is being conserved and that its genetic compliment is being safeguarded. There can be no doubt that butterfly centers serve a respectable conservation role in maintaining populations of butterflies, some of which may be endangered in their country of origin. It may be that some of the common species found in butterfly centers will become extinct in the wild before it is realized, so inefficient is the monitoring of tropical butterfly habitats.

Rainforests

The tropical rainforest is a major habitat which seems to be more important for butterfly conservation than other habitats elsewhere. This is not necessarily so, since in the temperate northern hemisphere, and in Western Europe in particular, which is overpopulated, over-explored, and has experienced gross habitat loss, the ecology and biology of some relatively common butterflies still remain overlooked. What focuses the attention on tropical rainforests is that they have not been over-explored, and that butterflies (and other insects) are in urgent need of identification and investigation. The fruits of these forests are richer than those of temperate climes and therefore the demise of habitats and their attendant species (both flora and fauna) are much more acute. There is a great deal of conservation of wildlife to do in the tropical rainforest.

RAINFOREST OR JUNGLE?

What is tropical rainforest exactly? The term is a non-specific way of describing a group of completely different habitats. In common parlance rainforests and jungles are often confused. In fact, they are completely different habitats exploited by different sorts of butterflies.

A rainforest, as the name suggests, is a wet or damp habitat where it rains frequently, often every day. In contrast, a jungle is mostly a dry habitat made up of thickets of thorny vegetation (those in India and Africa are typical), separated by grassy areas often called savanna. The only things which jungles and rainforests share are that they are both found in tropical areas, and they both have thorny vegetation. The jungle has more dry thorny vegetation than rainforests, but rainforests have their own share of thorny rattan climbers as an understory. The butterflies of jungles enjoy flitting between groups of trees and thickets in bright sunshine; rainforest butterflies, on the other hand, are found in the half-light of the rainforest understory or in full sunshine in the rainforest canopy.

Heliconid butterflies, such as Heliconius charitonius, *live in the rainforests of South America. They all have long wings and bright colors. Heliconids are usually abundant and roost communally.*

Different types of rainforest

Some rainforests can be more humid than others because of the local topography and altitude, and this may be called cloud forest. Some cloud forest is perpetually shrouded in a fine cloudy mist. There are certain butterflies which live specifically in cloud forest and have adaptations to this relatively dark and damp environment. In rainforests generally, the rain comes frequently, very locally, very suddenly, and with a vengeance. Butterflies only have seconds to find refuge under leaves or deep in the thick forest where the torrential rain on the canopy is reduced to a fine drizzle.

In very broad terms, the rainforest can be described as lowland and upland. Lowland rainforest tends to be a thick, impenetrable tangle of vegetation that needs to be cut with a machete to make any progress, although there are plenty of ways through for skillful butterflies. The higher the altitude, the more the understory of vines, bamboos, and other plants thins out to create a park-like effect where it is possible to look between the cathedral-like columns of branchless trees for some considerable distance, something which is impossible in the thick, lowland forest.

There are different types of rainforest depending on the kind of soil, just as there are different types of temperate forest. However, the diversity of species is relatively rich and quite unlike temperate forests, which tend to be dominated by a single species, such as oak or beech. In West African rainforests, there may be over 250 tree species per acre, which represents great choice for butterflies and other insects.

Male Graphium *swallowtails congregate beside a rainforest river to sip up salts in solution from the damp sand. The* butterflies often congregate in groups of their own species and become very flighty; they imbibe soluble salts to make scents.

Habitats in the rainforest

There are three places in virgin rainforests where butterflies live: in the rainforest canopy, along rivers, and in the half-light of the rainforest itself. This is in virgin rainforest, but in areas where rainforest has been felled, it is customary for secondary vegetation to spring up within weeks and form a tangle of mixed tropical vegetation. The species which form the secondary vegetation are not necessarily related to the original forest felled.

This secondary vegetation is a potent and very viable habitat for butterflies and is well worked by butterfly enthusiasts. In effect the edge of the rainforest, where the new settlements tend to be, is where prodigious growths of vegetation occur, and where butterfly studies are often undertaken. It is infinitely more practicable, and often more productive, than deep in the rainforest. And the tendency for forest people to cultivate crops and colorful flowers, such as the widespread bougainvillea, oleander, and cannas, attract passing butterflies, too. Lantana, *Lantana camara*, and sensitive plant, *Mimosa pudica*, often grow wild as an understory to palm plantations, and these are of great interest to nectar-feeding butterflies.

The rainforest canopy is the most unworked of the rainforest butterfly stations. It is a difficult environment to study, 150ft (46m) above the ground. A canopy walkway is essential, strung up among the branches by shooting ropes across to secure a passage. Few people have spent much time in this prestigious habitat inhabited by scores of butterflies which rarely, or never, descend to the

Appias nero *is a very fast flier with curved forewings. It is usually only the male which is found as it descends from the rainforest canopy to river* corridors and clearings. The female spends most of its time in the rainforest canopy and has rarely been found.

ground. Many canopy butterflies are known mostly from males which feed at ground level, but leave their mates high in the canopy. However, by comparison, few people have spent much time in the canopy of woods in temperate climates, so there could be some ecological surprises there, too.

Fogging

Taxonomists in rainforests have employed one method of studying canopy butterflies without clambering to the dizzy heights, and that has been by fogging. Pioneered both in South American and Asian rainforests, the technique involves fogging a

BUTTERFLY JEWELS

Just consider *Morpho aega*, one of the most collected and well-known butterflies through the use of its blue metallic wings in "butterfly jewelry." The males jink about over the rainforest canopy in such numbers that pilots have often recorded the phenomenal flashing of blue light over the forest. Incidentally, it is thought that this common butterfly can sustain the six million males removed from the population each year without detriment!

Birdwings, such as this Golden birdwing, Troides haliphron, from the rainforest canopy in Southeast Asia, are greatly prized by collectors. All species are listed in Appendix II of the Convention of International Trade in Endangered Species of Wild Fauna and Flora (CITES), which restricts their trade. Birdwings are among the largest and most collectable swallowtail butterflies in the world, and the easiest way of seeing them is to visit a butterfly house.

reflecting the local downpours in the surrounding upland rainforest, thus exposing fresh mineral deposits in the sand. Following the course of a tropical river will make any lepidopterist's heart race with the super-abundance of butterflies.

On the river banks, butterflies will be living in a twilight world of sunshine and shade, sometimes flitting deep inside the dark forest. Many tropical butterflies of the sunny edge are speckled white and black to make themselves more inconspicuous. The intensity of the light is so strong that the difference between light and dark is like white and black, so the speckling is very appropriate. However, some butterflies which live in the twilight world of the rainforest are dark, such as *Euthalia evelina*. Others appear to fly only at dusk, which is unusual for butterflies, for instance *Eryphanis aesacus*, *Opsiphanes* in South America, the Jungle glory butterfly, *Thaumantis diores* of India, and the Bamboo tree brown, *Lethe europa*, in Asia, which is even attracted to lighted windows.

Commercial demand

The demand for spectacular butterflies of the rainforest shows no sign of diminishing, though there are some cases of sustainability. There are butterflies which are wantonly collected as trophies from the forest since they command high prices, especially in Asia. Such species include the Birdwing, *Ornithoptera meridionalis* (at $1,000 a specimen); and *Graphium wallacei*, *Papilio albinus*, *P. bridgei*, and *P. euchenor* are also high on the list. Bernard D'Abrera recounts how specimens of *Papilio chikae* are traded by Japanese collectors for 35mm cameras. There are collectable butterflies in South America, too; the *Agrias* butterflies are regarded by some as the most sought-after butterflies in the world, and their larval food plant is kept secret by suppliers.

Quite a number of rainforest butterflies are farmed or ranched to meet the demands of the trade. The distinction between the two is that farming requires that the insects are captive bred, while ranching means that suitable food plants are planted in the locality to attract the adults to breed. In either case, the butterfly populations are artificially enhanced, and adults are cropped from the system. Among the species farmed are *Papilio woodfordi* and *Graphium codrus* in New Guinea, while species ranched in Brazil include *Papilio thoas*, *P. cleotas*, and *P. hectorides*.

small area of canopy with a mixture of diesel and insecticide. This is done using a special gun which is hauled into the canopy on ropes and, in the early morning, when there is little or no wind. The dead insects, of all orders, and other arthropods fall into large canvas funnels which direct them to containers of pickling alcohol.

This knock-down technique upsets lots of butterfly enthusiasts. However, taxonomists argue it is essential to know what is there in the first place. It is impossible to conserve anything without knowing first of all about a species' biology and ecology. Some results in South America show that up to 80 million arthropod species may live in the rainforests, of which only a relative few are butterflies. Recent research indicates the total number of arthropods is much less.

Riverbanks and forest edges

Perhaps the most worked parts of a virgin rainforest are the rivers and rainforest edges. Progress through a rainforest is often best accomplished along a river, and it is here that butterflies congregate. They use the river as a corridor for moving through the forest, often in the direction of the flow. It is often males which are on the move, and they gather at good mud-puddling sites on the exposed banks of the river. The river level goes up and down several times a day, accommodating and

This is the Chinese yellow swallowtail, Papilio xuthus, which is often kept in butterfly houses. Here a group of butterflies feed on an ice plant, Sedum. This butterfly is found in Asia and is not thought to be threatened in the wild.

31

Butterfly watching

Butterflies are partial to flowers and sunshine, so wherever these two go hand-in-hand, butterflies are likely to be found. The flowers imply damp conditions sufficient for the seeds to germinate and plants to grow. Plants provide leaves and buds to sustain the larvae, and flowers to sustain the energy requirements of the butterfly. Suitable damp habitats for butterflies include along streams and rivers, along ditches, beside hedges and roadsides, damp patches in alpine habitats which ooze moisture and attract masses of butterflies, as well as gulches and washes in North America. Sun is critical for many butterflies; but there are many species which only like dappled light or shun sunlight completely, like some of the rainforest butterflies.

Watching a butterfly emerge is always an absorbing occupation. Here, in a bog locality in western Ireland, a Marsh fritillary, Euphydryas aurinia, *comes to adulthood.*

Likely habitats

Many good habitats for butterflies are the result of human activity, such as roadsides and woodland trails, woodland glades and hedges, and especially gardens. Forestry rides and clearings provide sheltered sunny areas for butterflies. Trails are much better for butterflies when they inter-connect and provide a corridor for movement from one place to another. The ithominids of South America are by their very nature so much on the move that they are not characterized by any one habitat, since they occur in any natural, semi-natural, and disturbed habitat.

The bright colors of the lycaenids are easy to spot along roadsides; especially the male coppers, such as Heodes virgaureae. *Although scarce, this butterfly is widely distributed in central Europe.*

SEX SCENTS

Male butterflies of many tropical species can only manufacture the right pheromone, or sex scent, when they have imbibed the appropriate chemical from external sources, usually various plants. These plants tend to be different from the larval food plants, or those from which the butterflies obtain nectar. The important plants have volatile chemicals, such as pyrrolizidine alkaloids, which are exuded from the stem and bark. Mud-puddling males also drink mineral-rich liquids from moist sandy banks by rivers and streams, and even from dung and places where animals drink and urinate, in order to manufacture their pheromones and attract a mate.

In the tropical rainforest, the canopy is one of the best, least researched habitats for butterflies. Apart from that, the river corridors, tracks, and clearings are also very rich habitats. Male butterflies gather for mud-puddling by rivers and streams, where they can be seen in great abundance.

Where the rainforest has been cut down, secondary vegetation often grows, providing butterflies with an enormous diversity of food plants which scramble for survival in the open cleared areas. Many a lepidopterist has met with more success in secondary vegetation which exists along roads, around villages and edges of the forest, than in the deep recesses of the virgin rainforest.

Another place for butterflies is at the tops of hills, ridges, and mountains. Males and females congregate to court and mate. Butterflies have an ability to endure great heat, as well as great cold. Species which inhabit tops of mountains fly over alpine meadows in the heat of the day when it is almost too hot for people to be outside. Butterflies delight in sunshine, basking on hot rocks with their wings open, cruising up and down, sailing and floating in the gentlest breeze on a summer's day, and gliding forever on the thinnest air.

ABOVE *It is uncanny how some butterflies, such as this Moroccan orange tip have evolved colors to blend in with their nectar sources.*

TOP *There is much to learn by simply observing butterflies, like this swallowtail,* Graphium sarpedon, *and trying to gain knowledge of their food plants. The function of the color and pattern of butterflies is interesting, too.*

There are those butterflies which are resident and found only in specific localities where their caterpillar food plant grows. Other, more mobile butterflies which are wanderers and adventurers can turn up unexpectedly in many different types of habitat. They are among the most successful butterflies, which exist in widely differing habitats and exploit common plants for breeding purposes.

ATTRACTING BUTTERFLIES

Butterflies will often be tempted out of their foliar refuges by the smell of rotting fruit, juicy carrion, dung, or, in some cases, by certain plants. A piece of plant belonging to the borage family, *Boraginaceae*, will attract ithominids in South America. Other butterflies, for example, *Morpho* species, respond to lures of bright flashy colors.

Planting a wildflower garden is an ideal way to attract butterflies. Even small patches of nectar-rich Verbena patagonica *are sufficient to lure visitors.*

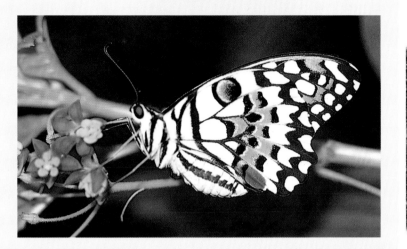

PAPILIONIDAE

These are the swallowtails, a family of large and generally colorful butterflies, mostly, but not exclusively, with long swallow-like tails. They include the widespread swallowtail, and the birdwings of Southeast Asia, which are the largest butterflies in the world. The "tails" are used for gliding and also in mimicry, especially the back-to-front imitation of head and antennae. Among the swallowtails are the tailless festoon butterflies.

Swallowtails have attracted a lot of attention from collectors, and many now have legislative protection. Many species are protected in various countries, and attempts are in hand to farm and ranch them. They may be seen in butterfly centers where they have become a popular attraction. Swallowtails are represented widely throughout the world, although more species are found in the equatorial regions.

(The butterfly above is *Papilio demodocus*.)

GENUS
ALLANCASTRIA

A small genus which is closely related to the parnassians.

ALLANCASTRIA CERISYI CYPRIA
Eastern Festoon

ZONE 3

2³⁄₈in 62mm

The small tails on the scalloped hindwing help to distinguish this butterfly from the *Zerynthia* festoons. It has a pale yellow ground with black markings. There is a single generation each year. The butterfly flies over alpine meadows in search of *Aristolochia* species, its caterpillar food plants.

GENUS
ARCHON

This genus has a single species and is related to the parnassian butterflies.

ARCHON APOLLINUS
False Apollo

ZONE 3·5

2³⁄₈in 60mm

The female is larger than the male, with orange and a stronger shade of red on the hindwing uppers. The forewings are mottled gray with bold black marks on the leading edge. It breeds on poisonous *Aristolochia* species and has a single generation each year. It is protected in Greece.

GENUS
ATROPHANEURA

Members of this genus are closely related to the *Troides* swallowtails, but are smaller with shorter wings. Many are models for mimics. Males may be tailed, or tailless, and they have an interesting dorsal fold from which its scents arise. Species occur from India to China, via Sulawesi.

♀

ATROPHANEURA JOPHON
Ceylon Rose

ZONE 5

5in 130mm

The rose color from which this butterfly takes its name is found as a series of sub-marginal spots on the hind-wing. The ground color is black, but on the forewing there are a number of light-colored markings. It is classified as Vulnerable in the *Red Data Book of Threatened Swallowtail Butterflies of the World*. It is endemic in Sri Lanka.

ATROPHANEURA HAGENI

ZONE 5

6¼in 160mm

The ground color of this butterfly is black. The hindwing is dusted with silvery blue interspersed with black spots. The underside of the abdomen is red. The underside of the forewing is flushed with light scales. This species is a model for the female *Papilio forbesi*. The butterfly is found only in Sumatra, Indonesia, and occurs on high plateaus. It is not threatened.

ATROPHANEURA LIRIS

ZONE 6

5in 130mm

This is a tailed swallowtail with long drawn-out forewings. There is a lighter area which suffuses most of the forewing, especially in the larger female, and the suffusion carries onto the hindwing. Five red spots occur on the underside of the hindwing, and these are more pronounced in the female than the male. At least six subspecies are known. It is found on several Indonesian islands and is not threatened. There is an old and dubious record of a siting in northwestern Australia.

ATROPHANEURA LUCHTI

The hindwings have a bright flash of lemon yellow on this otherwise dark butterfly, making it very attractive. It is typically a rainforest species, but its caterpillar food plants and complete life cycle are as yet unknown. It is classified as Rare in the *Red Data Book of Threatened Swallowtail Butterflies of the World.* It is endemic to eastern Java.

ATROPHANEURA NEPTUNUS
Yellow-bodied Club-tail, Yellow Club-tail

ZONE 5

5in 130mm

The most notable feature is the "club-tail" after which a lot of similar butterflies are named. The female has rounded wings; otherwise the sexes are similar. The black ground color is interrupted by a small flash of bright red on the hindwing. The tip of the abdomen is yellow, but this is also seen in other species. This is a very variable butterfly with eight known subspecies. It flies in open woods in the lowlands and is not threatened.

ATROPHANEURA SEMPERI SUPERNOTATUS

ZONE 5

5½in 140mm

This glamorous swallowtail is marked with varying amounts of red and pink depending on the subspecies and the sex. The male can have all-black wings with a touch of red on the anal part of the hindwings, and is distinguished by his red body. The female is larger and lighter in color, with pale brown forewings and a generous amount of red on the hindwings. There are seven subspecies which occur on various Indonesian islands. The butterfly inhabits rainforest and is not known to be threatened.

G E N U S
BARONIA

A genus of a single species, it exhibits primitive butterfly features.

BARONIA BREVICORNIS

ZONE 2

2⅜in 60mm

A "living fossil", this butterfly with short antennae is a dirty brown-orange with lighter patches toward the base of the hindwing. It is classified as Rare in the *Red Data Book of Threatened Swallowtail Butterflies of the World* and occurs only in a small area of Mexico.

GENUS
BATTUS

There are 17 species belonging to this exclusively New World genus. They are related to the *Troides* swallowtails and breed on the same range of food plants, the birthworts, *Aristolochia* species. Birthworts are poisonous, and the caterpillars are able to store the plant poisons in their own tissues and pass them to the adult butterflies, via the chrysalis.

BATTUS POLYDAMAS LUCIANUS
Gold rim swallowtail, Polydamas swallowtail

ZONE
1·2

4in
102mm

A large dark brown migrant butterfly with a row of orange marks forming a gold rim around the margins of the wings. On the underside of the hindwing, a row of red spots is also present. The hindwings are strongly scalloped. The butterfly flies along waysides and scrubby areas where its caterpillar food plants, the *Aristolochia* species, occur. In the tropics it is continuously brooded. Butterflies live for about a week.

GENUS
BHUTANITIS

A small genus of butterflies which are listed in the *Red Data Book*, two of them are designated as Rare. Further details on the ecology and biology of this genus is required.

BATTUS PHILENOR
Pipevine Swallowtail

ZONE
1

3¹/₃in
86mm

This is a large migrant butterfly with iridescent blue over its black wings, especially pronounced toward the margin of the hindwing which has a row of orange spots. Males are usually more showy than females. The butterfly is named after its *Aristolochia* food plants, variously called Dutchman's pipe and snakeroot. Gardeners have helped to encourage this butterfly, since it takes nectar from many plants under cultivation such as azalea, buddleia, lilac and milkweed. Because this butterfly is poisonous, it is mimicked by other butterflies.

BATTUS ZETIDES
Zetides Swallowtail

ZONE
2

1⁵/₈in
41mm

The butterfly is quite distinctive with a tapering row of rich yellow ocher marks crossing the wings, against a ground color of reddish brown. A key feature is the series of long and pointed white marks on the inside of the underside of the hindwing, and the four pointed triangles toward the margin. Little is known about this scarce butterfly. It is classified as Vulnerable in the *Red Data Book of Threatened Swallowtail Butterflies of the World*.

BHUTANITIS MANSFIELDI

ZONE
5

3¹/₈in
80mm

The butterfly has long forewings crossed by about eight broad white lines. The shape of the wings is a key feature, with a deeply scalloped hindwing and a lobed tail. This species is only known from a few specimens taken in Bhutan in 1933-4, and more information about it is urgently required. It inhabits mountainous areas and probably breeds on *Aristolochia*. It is classified as Insufficiently Known in the *Red Data Book of Threatened Swallowtail Butterflies of the World*.

BHUTANITIS THAIDINA

ZONE 5

3³/₄in 96mm

The peculiar shape of the wings is a good guide to identification, especially the elongated hindwing and the spatula-shaped tail. The bright red and blue marks on the hindwing link in with web-like yellow marks which cover the forewing in an orderly manner. The life cycle is yet to be elucidated. The species occurs in China and Tibet. It is classified as Rare in the *Red Data Book of Threatened Swallowtail Butterflies of the World*.

GENUS
CRESSIDA

This genus has one species. Males lack claspers, and females develop a sphragis.

CRESSIDA CRESSIDA

ZONE 6

4in 100mm

The sexes are dissimilar. The male has dark bases to its wings and a series of red spots around the margin of the hindwing and two prominent black spots on the forewing. The female is much paler with wider forewings which are partially transparent.

GENUS
ELEPPONE

An Australian genus which breeds on citrus. The males are territorial.

ELEPPONE ANACTUS
Dingy Swallowtail

ZONE 6

2³/₈in 60mm

This species has a black ground with large cells of white toward the base of the hindwing, and off-white cells all over the forewing. There is a row of subdued red spots around this butterfly's hindwing. Males defend sunny spots and are powerful fliers.

GENUS
EURYTIDES

A genus of 50 species confined to the New World. The butterflies have short antennae which are curved upward, and a short body. Some of them mimic *Parides* and *Heliconius* butterflies, while others have long tails and are called "kite swallow-tails." They are fast fliers and engage in mud-puddling. Many breed on members of the custard apple family, *Annonaceae*.

EURYTIDES BELLEROPHON

ZONE 2

4in 100mm

The sexes are similar, but the female is larger than the male. The pattern and color is similar to the Old World *Iphiclides podalirius* with its overall white ground color, long impressive tails and black tiger stripes. This species aggregates at mud-puddling stations and visits plenty of flowers for nectar. It is not threatened.

EURYTIDES CELADON
Cuban Kite Swallowtail

ZONE 1·2

3¹/₈in 80mm

Fairly similar to *E. marcellus*, but the red line on the underside lacks a white inner part. The pattern on the uppersides of the wings is repeated on the undersides, and there is one large area of white which is continuous over both the fore- and hindwings. This is a resident of Cuba and a possible rare stray into Florida.

EURYTIDES DUPONCHELII

ZONE 2
4¹/₈in 104mm

A sexually dimorphic species, the male is brighter than the female with a pale yellow band crossing the wings and a row of bead-like red spots running around the hindwing. The all-brown and undistinguished female has an extremely small tail. Woodland habitats are exploited by this species. Although it is currently not under threat, it is collected and offered by dealers at high prices.

EURYTIDES LYSITHOUS PLATYDESMA
Harris' Mimic Swallowtail

ZONE 2
3¹/₈in 80mm

The dark forewings have a pale patch toward the trailing edge and the hindwings have a central pale area, but the most interesting feature is the series of pink marks around the hindwings. The dark tails are unmarked, and the edges of the hindwings are scalloped. The butterfly has suffered total habitat loss in the area of Rio de Janeiro in Brazil, and is currently listed in that country as threatened with extinction. It is classified as Endangered in the *Red Data Book of Threatened Swallowtail Butterflies of the World*.

EURYTIDES MARCELLUS
Jamaican Kite Swallowtail, Zebra Swallowtail

ZONE 1·2
3¹/₂in 89mm

A most spectacular butterfly with its dark zebra bands which cross both wings and terminate in the long and elegant tails. There is a bright red spot on the inside edge of each hindwing, and the light ground color is palest green in fresh specimens. The butterfly is a regular nectar-feeder, and the male exhibits patrolling behavior. The species is endemic to Jamaica. It is classified as Vulnerable in the *Red Data Book of Threatened Swallowtail Butterflies of the World*.

EURYTIDES IPHITAS
Yellow Kite

ZONE 2
3³/₄in 95mm

The key feature is the dark border which runs around the wings and is continuous with the dark forewing apex. There are three yellow flashes in the dark apex, and the ground color of the rest of this tailed butterfly is deep orange. Not much is known about this species, which has not been seen recently in Brazil and is thought to be in decline. It is classified as Vulnerable in the *Red Data Book of Threatened Swallowtail Butterflies of the World*.

EURYTIDES MARCHANDI

ZONE 2

4in
100mm

A splendid-looking butterfly, similar in both sexes with long, slightly curved tails and yellow markings over a dark brown ground. There is some variation in ground color and paler yellow forms exist, including two sub-species. The butterfly inhabits highland rainforest up to 3,500 ft (1,000 m) but its caterpillar food plants are unknown.

EURYTIDES PAUSANIAS

ZONE 2

3½in
90mm

Mimicry of the heliconid butterflies, possibly *Heliconius clytia* and *H. wallacei*, has been perfected by this swallowtail, which shares the same rainforest glades and open areas. The forewings are long in typical heliconid shape, and there are simple splashes of dull red on the tip and yellow in the center of the wing. The butterfly is possibly under threat since it is not a common species, and more information on its life cycle is urgently required.

GENUS
GRAPHIUM

This is a large genus of about 150 species from Africa, Europe and Asia. Many, but not all, have tails, some very long. Many engage in mud-puddling behavior. Separate species groups of graphiums can be seen mud-puddling together – *they* can recognize their own kind very easily! Most graphiums have a speckled pattern, and they are fast fliers. Caterpillars have three pairs of spines behind their heads.

EURYTIDES MOLOPS
HAETERIUS

ZONE 2

3½in
90mm

A superb butterfly with distinctive black marks and bands on the forewing, and black markings around the scalloped white hindwing. The tail is exceptionally long and gracefully curved, and if the wingspan of the insect is measured from the hindwings (instead of the forewings), it would be 4¾in (120mm). The butterfly is found typically in rainforest clearings and along rivers. It is not under threat.

EURYTIDES PHILOLAUS
Dark Zebra Swallowtail

ZONE 1·2

3½in
89mm

As its name suggests this is a dark swallowtail, and the white to pale cream marks on the wings join up to make a pronounced wedge shape. The leading edge of the forewing has a few thin white lines, and the margins of all wings have a series of lunules and chevrons. This common butterfly aggregates for mud-puddling along tracks, in wooded areas and clearings.

GRAPHIUM AGAMEDES
Glassy Graphium

ZONE 4

2½in
65mm

The ground color is black-brown with a broad white band across the wings. This band is broken by black veins and some of the white area on the forewing is transparent. The sexes are similar. This butterfly frequents tropical rainforest and, although uncommon, is not threatened.

GRAPHIUM AGAMEMNON
Tailed Jay, Green-spotted Triangle Butterfly

The collection of jazzy green spots on the wings help the butterfly to merge into the background as it flies through the dappled sunlight of the rainforest in which it lives. There is a very small and modest tail, and the sides of the body are covered in green bars.

GRAPHIUM ANGOLANUS
Angola White Lady Swallowtail,
White Lady Swallowtail

A tailless swallowtail whose black and white colors are in strong contrast to the orange-yellow on the side of the abdomen and orange spot on the inside of the hindwing. The black areas are mostly around the margins of the wings, which are also speckled white. There are three subspecies known. Caterpillars feed on plants of the *Annonaceae* family. The butterfly is common and widespread.

GRAPHIUM ANTIPHATES
Fivebar Swordtail

This butterfly takes its name from the five long black bars which occur on the forewing and lead toward the dark apex. The apex is marked by a series of five small spots in a straight line. The hindwing is scalloped with a long tail emphasized by a central black line. The base of the hindwing is very pale, reflecting the underside pattern. It is a widespread butterfly, and at least 12 subspecies are known. It is threatened only in Sri Lanka though it occurs through to Malaysia.

GRAPHIUM ANDROCLES

Overall the butterflies appear very white in strong sunlight; and this is enhanced by their long tails; in fact, the apex of the forewings is black. The females are larger than the males, but otherwise the same. Two subspecies are known. Groups of males mud-puddle on the banks of rainforest rivers; although very nervous, they make a splendid sight. The butterfly is entirely confined to the Indonesian island of Sulawesi (between New Guinea and Borneo) where it is a resident. G. *androcles* is not a threatened species

GRAPHIUM ANTHEUS
Large Striped Swordtail

This butterfly has long curved tails and large wings. It is a powerful flier. The sexes are similarly patterned, although the female is slightly larger than the male. Males exhibit mud-puddling behavior. Females lay eggs on members of *Annonaceae* including custard apples. This is a common butterfly and not under threat.

GRAPHIUM ARISTEUS
Fivebar Swordtail

The five bars on this swordtail are comparatively thick and black and contrast with the white basal parts of the forewing. The butterfly has a beautiful pair of curved tails, and there is a white lunular line around the margin of the hindwing. It shares its common name with a variety of other butterflies which have similar coloration and patterning. This species is a little smaller than G. *antiphates*.

42

GRAPHIUM DELESSERTI
Zebra, Malayan Zebra

ZONE 5	
3½in 90mm	

This species mimics some of the danaid butterflies which are poisonous, and thus its appearance confers some protection from birds. Not only are the color and pattern mimicked, but the slow flight of the model is also perfected. In both sexes the ground color is whitish with black veins, though the male has larger and darker markings than the female. Mud-puddling behavior is exhibited by the males.

GRAPHIUM CODRUS

ZONE 5·6	
3¾in 95mm	

Probably the most distinctive features of this species are the pale base of the hindwing and the trailing edge of the forewing. The tail on the elongated hindwing is relatively blunt. There is a variable yellow-green band across the forewing in both sexes. So far 14 subspecies have been recorded. The butterfly is a resident of the rainforest canopy, but little is known of its life history. It is collected and farmed in its rainforest habitat.

GRAPHIUM COLONNA
Mamba, Black Swordtail

ZONE 4	
3⅛in 80mm	

This is a very black butterfly with thin pale green stripes crossing the wings, and two red spots on the hindwing. The sexes are similar in appearance. It is a powerful flier, and the males mud-puddle regularly in groups along roads and on river banks. This butterfly lives in wooded areas and breeds on *Artabotrys*, a genus of plants belonging to the *Annonaceae* family.

GRAPHIUM EPAMINONDAS

ZONE 5	
3⅓in 86mm	

The butterfly has long tails typical of a swordtail and is black, white and orange. The orange is particularly well marked on the underside of the hindwing. It is a species of the lowland rainforest, which, unfortunately, is the sort of habitat constantly under threat of clearance. The butterfly is classified as Insufficiently Known in the *Red Data Book of Threatened Swallowtail Butterflies of the World*. It occurs as one of three endemics on the Andaman Islands in the Indian Ocean, where there are 13 swallowtail species known.

GRAPHIUM EUPHRATES

ZONE 5

2⁵⁄₈in
70mm

This is similar to G. *androcles*, but smaller and with much more black on the hindwing and tail. The forewings are heavily marked with four bold black discontinuous stripes. The hindwing is scalloped. At least three subspecies are known. The butterfly is not threatened and is common in places.

GRAPHIUM IDAEOIDES

ZONE 5

5in
130mm

This is a large butterfly with a large expanse of wing. It has a gray-white ground speckled all over with black. The sexes are similar. The butterfly lives in rainforest clearings and along rivers where it is a perfect mimic of *Idea leuconoe*. The butterfly is classified as Rare in the *Red Data Book of Threatened Swallowtail Butterflies of the World*.

GRAPHIUM LEONIDAS
Common Graphium, Veined Swallowtail

ZONE 4

3¹⁄₂in
89mm

The sexes of this pale green-yellow speckled butterfly are similar. The base of the hindwing has the largest pale green area. It is commonly found in woodlands, waysides and gardens, where it sucks nectar. Caterpillars feed on members of the *Annonaceae* (custard apple) family.

GRAPHIUM GELON

ZONE 6

2³⁄₈in
60mm

The pattern and color are close to that of G. *sarpedon*, but the turquoise blue area is much reduced on both surfaces and the uppers are mostly rich brown-black. There are three white marks on the forewing. The hindwing is significantly scalloped. This butterfly is only found on New Caledonia and Loyalty Island, in the Pacific Ocean, where its current status is not thought to be threatened.

GRAPHIUM KIRBYI
Kirby's Swordtail

ZONE 4

3¹⁄₈in
80mm

This species has a well-defined and regular white band which crosses the dark uppers. The hindwing has a faint dusting of white scales. The tips of the majestic long "swordtails" are white. The undersides reflect the pattern of the uppers, and there are several distinctive red marks. It flies in coastal forests.

GRAPHIUM MACFARLANEI

ZONE 6

3¹⁄₂in
90mm

Typical of many rainforest butterflies of this genus, the wings are speckled with mustard-green marks. Running across the wings and getting larger toward the base is a series of green marks which form a distinct band. This is a tailless swallowtail found in Australia and New Guinea. Caterpillars feed on various members of the *Annonaceae*.

GRAPHIUM MENDANA

ZONE 6

4¹/₈in
104mm

This is a magnificent butterfly with indented forewings and a heavily scalloped hindwing drawn out as a long blunt tail. There is a series of uniform yellow spots which run across the forewing and contrast well against the rich brown ground. The anal part of the hindwing is white in males. The species only occurs in the Solomon Islands. It is classified as Rare in the *Red Data Book of Threatened Swallowtail Butterflies of the World*.

GRAPHIUM MORANIA
White Lady Swallowtail

ZONE 4

2⁵/₈in
70mm

This tailless swallowtail, similar in both sexes, has black and white markings. The key features are the kidney-shaped white marks on the forewing. There is much white on the hindwing, which has only a dark speckled margin, and a lot of white on the leading edge of the forewing. The butterflies occur in open country, savanna and forest edges. Caterpillars feed on species of *Annona*.

GRAPHIUM PHILONOE
Eastern Graphium,
White-dappled Swallowtail

ZONE 4

3¹/₈in
80mm

The wing margins are dark speckled with light marks, while the inside of the wings has large blocks of light marks. The base of the hindwings is distinctly white-cream. The butterfly lives in light woods and forests as well as coastal sites, where it breeds on *Annona* species.

GRAPHIUM POLICENES
Common swordtail, Small striped swordtail

ZONE 4

3¹/₈in
80mm

This beautiful butterfly is speckled yellow-green, with larger blocks of color toward the base of the wings. It has a long sweeping tail and a single red mark on the inside edge of the hindwing. There is a red stripe on the underside of the hindwing. It lives in forests and woods, and breeds on *Uraria caffra* and *Artabotrys* species.

GRAPHIUM PROCLES

	ZONE 5
3¼in 85mm	

The forewings are indented on the outer margin, and the hindwings are scalloped and tailless. The black ground color has a weak green band crossing the wings and light spots near the margin. The species is endemic to Sabah and Malaysia, and is classified as Indeterminate in the *Red Data Book of Threatened Swallowtail Butterflies of the World*.

▲

GRAPHIUM STRESEMANNI

	ZONE 6
3⅛in 80mm	

This is a brown butterfly with yellow spots toward the apex of the forewing and a series of small white spots by the margin. Pale blue markings occur on the forewing with pale green near the base of the hindwing. The butterfly is found in rainforest, but its caterpillar food plants are not known. It is related to *G. sarpedon* and, in keeping with members of this close alliance, they probably feed on members of the *Hernandiaceae*, *Lauraceae*, *Monimiaceae* and *Winteraceae*. The butterfly is classified as Rare in the *Red Data Book of Threatened Swallowtail Butterflies of the World*.

GRAPHIUM SANDAWANUM

	ZONE 5
2⅝in 70mm	

Seen on the wing, this may be confused with *G. sarpedon*, but it has a much larger expanse of yellowish green over its wings, and the hindwing is more scalloped with a more pronounced stubby tail. The butterfly was only discovered in 1977, even though it is sometimes quite common. Although it occurs in Mt. Apo National Park, Mindanao, Philippines, this does not safeguard its habitats in the humid mountain rainforest. It is classified as Vulnerable.

GRAPHIUM SARPEDON
Common Bluebottle, Blue Triangle

	ZONE 5·6
3½in 90mm	

A series of broad blue-green transparent windows cross the wings. These windows are very effective in the strong sunlight, helping to enforce the colors for use in defense and courtship. The butterfly is swift in flight and engages in mud-puddling. It frequents forest clearings, edges and waysides. Caterpillars have exploited at least five plant families including *Lauraceae*, *Myrtaceae* and *Sapotaceae*, a factor which has contributed to this species great success.

GRAPHIUM THULE

ZONE 6

2³/₄in 72mm

The overall appearance of this butterly is black with horizontal slats of white on the forewing and uniform white spots. The hindwing has a large patch of white in the center. This pattern may be mimicking some of the dark-speckled danaids of the rainforest. Subspecies and forms are known to occur. This butterfly only lives in Irian Jaya (Indonesia) and on New Guinea. It is typically a rainforest species, but it has been little collected to date.

GRAPHIUM TYNDERAEUS SORRELOANTHUS
Green-spotted Swallowtail

ZONE 4

3¹/₃in 86mm

A tailless swallowtail well-marked in yellowy green. There is a broad broken band of yellowy green which crosses the wings and is prominent at the base of the hindwing and on the trailing edge of the forewing. The edge of the hindwing is distinctly scalloped, and the forewing edge is noticeably curved. It lives in forest and probably breeds on members of the *Annonaceae*.

GRAPHIUM WEISKEI
Purple Spotted Swallowtail

ZONE 6

3¹/₈in 80mm

A tailed swallowtail of which the male is spectacularly colored with a mixture of pink and green at the base of the wings, and green toward the tip of the forewing. The hindwing margin is scalloped and the forewing curved and indented. The female is brown. The butterfly frequents the rainforest canopy in New Guinea and is most frequently found in highland rainforest areas. Its life cycle has still to be described.

GENUS
IPHICLIDES

Two species belong to this Old World genus; both have very long tails.

IPHICLIDES PODALIRIUS
Scarce Swallowtail

ZONE 3

3¹/₂in 90mm

The wings are white crossed with dark bands. This butterfly may be described as "flying backward" when it glides for the back-to-front-mimicry with long tails and false-eyes is so convincing. It frequents flowery hamlets and waysides where it breeds on *Prunus* species and other fruit trees.

GENUS
LUEHDORFIA

This is a genus of Asian butterflies whose taxonomy is still to be clarified. Three species are listed in the *Red Data Book*.

LUEHDORFIA CHINENSIS

ZONE 5

2³/₈in 60mm

This is a relatively small butterfly with black bars over a cream ground color. The hindwing margin has a pattern of red, blue, black and yellow around the inside. Very little is known about the biology and ecology of this species. It is classified as Insufficiently Known in the *Red Data Book of Threatened Swallowtails of the World*.

LUEHDORFIA JAPONICA

The patterning is typical of a swallowtail, with black bars crossing the wing over a pale yellow ground, and this species is closely related to the parnassian swallowtails. There is a modest tail. The scalloped hindwing has a distinctive blue eye-spot surrounded by a curved band of yellow. The butterfly occurs in open woodland in Japan, as its specific name suggests. Like *Polygonia c-album*, this butterfly has staggered generations: in this case the pupae have different diapause modes. It is classified as Vulnerable in the *Red Data Book of Threatened Swallowtail Butterflies of the World*.

GENUS
MEANDRUSA

An Asian genus of three species which have bifid claws and lack androconial folds.

MEANDRUSA PAYENI EVAN
Yellow Gorgon, Outlet Sword, Sickle

This has extremely curved and pointed forewings. The hindwing is curved to a point in its long tail, more pointed in the female than the male. It is dark brown, lighter toward the base of the wings. The life cycle of this rainforest butterfly is unknown. It is Vulnerable in Malaya.

GENUS
ORNITHOPTERA

There are 13 species in this genus of birdwing butterflies, which are restricted to the Australian region. They fall into two groups: ones where the males have a scent patch (*priamus* group) and those without (*paradisea* group). In most species the caterpillars feed on members of the *Aristolochiaceae*. Highly prized and collected, all are listed by CITES, and trade in these butterflies is restricted.

ORNITHOPTERA AESACUS

The male has iridescent turquoise green over all its wings and a thick black bar across the forewings. The female is brown with white spots and yellow-gray hindwings. Very little is known about this butterfly, and its only location is on Obi Island in the Moluccas, Indonesia. It is classified as Indeterminate in the *Red Data Book of Threatened Swallowtail Butterflies of the World*.

ORNITHOPTERA ALEXANDRAE
Queen Alexandra's Birdwing

This is the largest butterfly in the world, with an incredible 11¹⁄₈in (280mm) wingspan. The male is green and black with uniquely shaped wings, the female is distinctively brown and white. The yellow abdomen is distinctive. This butterfly lives in the canopy of lowland rainforests and also exploits areas of secondary growth rich in vines. The first-ever specimen collected was shot. It is classified as Endangered in the *Red Data Book of Threatened Swallowtail Butterflies of the World*.

ORNITHOPTERA CHIMAERA
Chimaera Birdwing

The male has iridescent green and gold on the forewings with black markings; the female has a brown ground. It is a butterfly of the highland rainforests found on New Guinea and Irian Jaya. There is considerable potential in farming this species for the butterfly trade. It is classified as Indeterminate in the *Red Data Book of Threatened Swallowtail Butterflies of the World*.

ORNITHOPTERA CROESUS
LYDIUS

	ZONE 6
7½in 190mm	

This butterfly has splashes of orange-brown color, from which it takes its name, along the leading edge of the forewing against a black ground color. The hindwing is mottled over orange with yellow. It is found on various islands of the Moluccas where it is endemic. Its preferred habitats include lowland swamps. The butterfly is classified as Vulnerable in the *Red Data Book of Threatened Swallowtail Butterflies of the World*.

▲

ORNITHOPTERA
MERIDIONALIS

	ZONE 6
6in 150mm	

A thinner streak of green or yellow on the leading edge of the forewing distinguishes this species from the fairly similar *O. paradisea*. Its habitat in the lowland rainforest is threatened. The butterfly is legally protected in Papua New Guinea and is classified as Vulnerable in the *Red Data Book of Threatened Swallowtail Butterflies of the World*. Unfortunately it is a collectable species, and a pair has been offered recently for over $1,000.

ORNITHOPTERA GOLIATH
SAMSON
Goliath Birdwing

	ZONE 6
8³⁄₈in 210mm	

Although the goliath bird-wing is not the largest birdwing species, it is, nevertheless, impressive seen flying in its green iridescent livery among the vegetation of lowland rainforests. The hindwing is yellow with a black margin and 3 yellow-black spots. The female, like those of so many other birdwings, is a much subdued brown color with contrasting black areas surrounding the wings. This butterfly is classified as Vulnerable in the *Red Data Book of Threatened Swallowtail Butterflies of the World*.

ORNITHOPTERA PARADISEA
ARFAKENSIS
Paradise Birdwing, Tailed Birdwing

	ZONE 6
6¼in 160mm	

The hindwing is a unique shape and a useful identification guide, together with the modest curved tail. The male butterfly has a yellow abdomen, which is a feature shared by many birdwings. The yellow hindwing is edged in black, and a large black band crosses the green iridescent forewings. Females look completely different with their gray-brown forewings. The butterfly spends a lot of time on the canopy of upland rainforest. It is classified as Indeterminate.

ORNITHOPTERA PRIAMUS
Priam's Birdwing

ZONE 6

5in
130mm

The yellow abdomen contrasts with the green and black wing markings of the male. The female is black, white and yellow, and much larger. This is a very variable butterfly, and 14 subspecies have so far been identified. The butterfly frequents rainforest canopies and breeds, like so many of the birdwings, on *Aristolochia* vines. It is one of few birdwings which occur in the rainforest of Northern Australia.

ORNITHOPTERA ROTHSCHILDI
Rothschild's Birdwing

ZONE 6

6in
150mm

The forewings of the male are mostly dark with smudges of green along the leading edge and toward the apex, and a larger area of green by the trailing edge. The hindwing is the reverse, with more yellow over the wing, a black margin and some black spots to the inside. The female is altogether much duller, light brown with gray-white spotting, particularly on the hindwing. The butterfly prefers highland rainforest. It is classified as Indeterminate in the *Red Data Book of Threatened Swallowtail Butterflies of the World*.

ORNITHOPTERA TITHONUS

ZONE 6

4³/₈in
110mm

This has iridescent forewings with a black bar and margins, and the male has four black spots on the hindwing; otherwise it is fairly similar to *O. goliath*. There are four known subspecies. This butterfly is found in highland rainforest. It is classified as Insufficiently Known in the *Red Data Book of Threatened Swallowtails of the World* and is also listed by CITES.

ORNITHOPTERA URVILLIANUS
D'Urville's Birdwing

ZONE 6

7¹/₄in
185mm

The central part of the forewings are a rich velvet brown-black, and around the forewings and all over the hindwings is a suffusion of velvet blue. The abdomen is yellow. This birdwing is farmed in the Bismarck Archipelago (New Ireland) and on Bougainville, as well as being found in the Solomon Islands.

ORNITHOPTERA VICTORIAE
Queen Victoria's Birdwing

ZONE 6

6⁷/₈in
175mm

Unique-shaped wings like stubby spatulas, and hindwings almost wrinkled or deformed, characterize this species. The green base of the wings and the yellow spot on the black forewing of the male are also distinguishing marks. It is named after Queen Victoria, as specimens were shot down from the rainforest canopy by members of the British navy when they visited the Solomon Islands.

GENUS
PACHLIOPTA

There are over a dozen species in this genus from the Indian and Australian regions of the world. The genus is sometimes merged with *Atrophaneura*. Individual species often have red marks on the body which warn predators of their unpleasant taste. Most species breed on poisonous members of the genus *Aristolochia* and store the poisons in their bodies for their own defense.

PACHLIOPTA POLYDORUS UTUANENSIS
Red-bodied Swallowtail

ZONE 5·6

3¹/₈in
80mm

Females are generally larger than males, but both sexes have dark uppers with some highlighted areas brushed over the surface, and occasionally a series of red spots on the hindwing and on the underside and tip of the body. A very variable butterfly, since 31 subspecies have been described so far. The one found in Queensland, Australia, is one of the smallest. The species is generally secure and not threatened.

PACHLIOPTA POLYPHONTES

ZONE 6

3¹/₈in
80mm

The butterfly has elongated forewings which are black with a touch of gray scales. The hindwing is also elongated with a white window in the center and a series of dull red spots around the margin of the tailed hindwing. Another variable swallowtail found on several Indonesian islands, it exists in at least five subspecies. One of the subspecies, *P. polyphontes rosea*, has a rose-colored suffusion on the hindwing.

GENUS
PAPILIO

This is one of the most widespread of genera, and there are over 200 species. Most are tropical, and most have been favored by collectors. The majority of the butterflies have tails. Many are migratory. Caterpillars exploit species belonging to the *Rutaceae*, *Lauraceae* and *Umbelliferae*. *Citrus* (a lauraceous genus) is widely used as a food plant.

PAPILIO ALEXANOR
Southern Swallowtail

	ZONE 3
2½in 66mm	

The southern swallowtail lacks quite a few of the black marks found on the wings of *P. machoan* or *P. hospiton*. However it does have the typical tail and red and blue spot. This butterfly frequents alpine meadows, where it breeds on various members of the *Umbelliferae*. It is quite rare and confined to various localities. It has a single generation each year and may be found up to 4,300ft (1,300m). The butterfly is classified as Vulnerable in the *Red Data Book of Threatened Swallowtail Butterflies of the World*.

PAPILIO ANCHISIADES
Red-spotted Swallowtail

	ZONE 1·2
3¾in 95mm	

This is a mimic of various *Parides* species and is mostly brown-black with red and white marks in the center of the hindwing of the female, and a blur of white in the center of the forewing. Found mostly in Central and South America, this migrant species has successfully exploited part of the southern United States. Adults are frequently found ovipositing on citrus plants in the orchards. The caterpillars, like those of some other swallowtails, are called orange dog because they have an orange-colored osmeterium as a deterrent against predators.

PAPILIO AEGEUS ORMENUS
Orchard Swallowtail

	ZONE 6
3½in 90mm	

A large black butterfly with enormous patches of white on the hindwing and two or three very small white marks on the forewing. The wings are fairly rounded and the hindwing scalloped. Caterpillar, pupa and female butterfly have different color forms which are adaptations to avoid detection by predators. This butterfly occurs in Australia and New Guinea and, as its name implies, frequents gardens and orchards to breed on citrus. The early stages of the caterpillar look like bird droppings, typical of so many swallowtails

PAPILIO AMYNTHOR

	ZONE 6
4½in 115mm	

This is a dark brown butterfly with a large white flash on the hindwing and a white bar on the forewing. The tailed hindwing is scalloped. It is found on the islands of New Caledonia and Norfolk Island, where it breeds on citrus. It is common, and its populations are not threatened.

PAPILIO ANDROGEUS
Queen Page

	ZONE 1·2
4⅛in 105mm	

The sexes are completely different. The male is the brighter with a large yellow bar across its wings, while the female is very dark and tailless with subtle blue suffusions over the hindwing. The sexes differ in their behavior, too. The female is reclusive and not often seen, while her mate spends a lot of time on the forest canopy, occasionally coming down to engage in mud-puddling. Caterpillars feed on citrus.

PAPILIO ANTIMACHUS
African Giant Swallowtail, Giant Papilio

ZONE 4

9 ¹⁄₈ in
230mm

This, the largest butterfly in Africa, has long curved forewings with prominent dark brown tips. A thick bar of orange radiates from the base of the forewing, and orange chevrons are also present. The hindwing is mostly orange marked with round black spots and a black border. Females, which can be 4in (100mm) smaller than males, are rarely seen. Males engage in mud-puddling and may be found along forest edges and by pools. It is continuously brooded in some places.

PAPILIO ARISTOR
The Scarce Haitian Swallowtail

ZONE 2

4 in
100mm

The warm brown ground is crossed on the forewing by a row of bead-like white spots which splits into two. There are yellow chevrons on the hindwing and a single eye-spot. The rarely seen female is slightly larger and paler than the male, with larger yellow spots. The butterfly is endemic to Hispaniola. Habitats include dry scrub and it probably breeds on citrus. It is classified as Indeterminate in the *Red Data Book of Threatened Swallowtail Butterflies of the World*.

PAPILIO ASCOLIUS

ZONE 2

4 ³⁄₈ in
110mm

This swallowtail has an almost typical heliconid shape with elongated forewings, and a color pattern similar to some rainforest-dwelling heliconids. The female has more orange around the base of the wings than the male. It has a wide distribution in South America. The caterpillar food plants of this species remain unknown.

PAPILIO ARISTODEMUS PONCEANUS
Schaus' Swallowtail, Dusky Swallowtail

ZONE 1

3 ³⁄₄ in
95mm

On the upperside the wings have a thick yellow bar with yellow marks inside the margin, and a black tail. The yellow-orange undersides have red and a band of silvery blue on the hindwing. One of five subspecies, it occurs in tropical Florida. It is protected and classified as Threatened.

PAPILIO ASTYALUS
Astyalus Swallowtail

ZONE 2

4³/₈in
110mm

The ground color of this migrant is dark brown to black, and in the male there is a very wide yellow band which crosses the wings. The base of the hindwing is totally yellow. A series of six yellow chevrons is placed submarginally on the hindwing. The female is very dark all over, and may or may not have a tail. Like many other *Papilio*, the caterpillars breed on citrus. The butterfly is found in areas forested with tropical hardwoods. Its distribution reaches from Central America into the southern United States.

PAPILIO BJORNDALAE
Bahamas Swallowtail,
Andraemon Swallowtail

ZONE 2

3¹/₂in
92mm

A large yellow and brown swallowtail which bears a reddish wedge-shaped mark on the underside of the hindwing. This subspecies, one of three, occurs only on the Bahamas. The species, *P. andraemon*, is found on Cuba, the Bahamas and the Cayman Islands. It was introduced to Jamaica where it has become a pest on citrus. The butterfly may occasionally reach Florida. It lives in open flowery areas and breeds on members of the citrus family.

PAPILIO BLUMEI

ZONE 6

4³/₄in
120mm

This is a magnificent butterfly found only on the island of Sulawesi (Indonesia), mostly the north of the island. Sexes are fairly similar, and striking. The ground color is black dusted in green scales, and there is a prominent iridescent green band crossing both wings. Green chevrons ring the hindwing, and the tail is a stunning blue color, sometimes greenish. There are at least two subspecies recorded. The butterfly occurs in the rainforest and is much sought by collectors.

▼

PAPILIO BENGUETANUS

ZONE 5

4in
100mm

Heavily netted veins at the base of the wings characterize this species, but toward the margins the wings are heavily darkened in black. A series of flat yellow lunules is present submarginally on the hindwing, and there is a small eye-spot on the anal region of the hindwing. The tails are long and fine. The butterfly is only found in one part of the Philippines and is classified as Vulnerable in the *Red Data Book of Threatened Swallowtail Butterflies of the World*.

PAPILIO BREVICAUDA BRETANENSIS
Short-tailed Swallowtail, Maritime Swallowtail

This is a dark-colored swallowtail, with a reasonable-length tail, but it is shorter than that of *P. machaon*, for example. There are two rows of orangey-red marks on the underside of the wings. The butterfly may be found in coastal areas and on hilltops where males find females. It is uncommon, but not under threat at present. It breeds on various members of the *Umbelliferae*.

PAPILIO BROMIUS
Broad Blue-banded Swallowtail

This is a tailless swallowtail with a single broad blue-green band crossing the black wings. Toward the margin of the hindwing there are also a few dots. The sexes are similar, the female just a shade duller. The butterfly lives in rainforests and breeds on *Teclea* and other members of the *Rutaceae*. A common species, it is not threatened at present.

PAPILIO CANOPUS
Canopus Butterfly

Simple in design, the male is brown with a cream-white band divided by dark veins. The female is larger with a dark brown ground color and a discontinuous cream band. There are 12 subspecies recognized. It breeds on members of *Rutaceae*, including citrus. The butterfly ranges from Indonesia to the tropical rainforests of Northern Territory and Queensland, Australia. It is relatively common and not currently under threat.

PAPILIO BRIDGEI

This is most impressive on the underside with a medley of light and dark, especially on the hindwing. The underside of the forewing is brown with large irregular smudges of white and a white checkering of the edges, while the underside of the hindwing has a line of black scalloped marks which contrast with the white lunules and spots. This is a common butterfly of the Solomon Islands and Bougainville. Its numbers are being increased, since it is bred captive on butterfly farms especially for the trade.

PAPILIO CAIGUANABUS
Poey's Black Swallowtail

This is a pretty butterfly distinguished by the bright yellow band which runs around the hindwings, wider on the hindwing than on the forewing, where it is white. There is a bold reddish area on the anal part of the hindwing. The sexes are similar. The butterfly is endemic to Cuba and is classified as Indeterminate in the *Red Data Book of Threatened Swallowtail Butterflies of the World*.

PAPILIO CHIKAE

Discovered as recently as 1965, this butterfly has the most amazing iridescent green and blue marks around the margins of the hindwing and a large lobed tail. The forewings are black dusted in green. Habitats include open mountainous regions, but the food plants have yet to be found. This is a butterfly with a price on its head – it is collected and offered for sale on the world market. The butterfly is endemic to the island of Luzon in the Philippines and is classified as Endangered in the *Red Data Book of Threatened Swallowtail Butterflies of the World*.

PAPILIO CLYTIA
Common Mime

ZONE 5
4³/₄in
120mm

Its name suggests that it mimics other butterflies. In fact it exists in a large number of forms and subspecies, and seven subspecies have been described. Judging by its colors, which range from smoky brown to yellow-brown with speckled black markings, to yellowy green, it is not surprising that this group is in dire need of revision. The distribution of this species is large, ranging from India to China. It is a common species which is not currently threatened, although one subspecies in India is protected by law.

PAPILIO CRESPHONTES
Giant swallowtail, Orange dog

ZONE 1·2
5¹/₂in
140mm

This large brown migrant butterfly has a band of yellow crossing the wings and a series of yellow spots around the margins. There is a red mark at the anal position on the hindwing. The tail is long containing a yellow blob on the tip. The butterfly is regularly found in gardens where it breeds on citrus, and, because of its size, is easy to recognize. It is widespread and common.

PAPILIO DARDANUS
Mockler Swallowtail

ZONE 4
4³/₈in
110mm

An exceedingly variable butterfly with two completely different color forms. The cream-yellow male has a tail. The female is much smaller, darker and tailless, and with three color forms which vary between their combinations of black, white, orange and yellow. A black and white female form mimics *Amauris niavius*. This is a common and widespread species. The males are most usually seen, the female being rather reclusive. It breeds on *Citrus* among many other genera.

PAPILIO CONSTANTINUS
Constantine's Swallowtail

ZONE 4
4³/₈in
110mm

The key feature of this swallowtail is the yellow spot by itself in the cell area of the forewing; otherwise there is an extensive band of yellow spots, somewhat divided on the forewing, which crosses the wings. The tail has a pair of yellow marks on each side. Females are usually slightly larger with bolder markings, but are fairly reclusive. Males visit nectar sources in forest edges and scrubby areas.

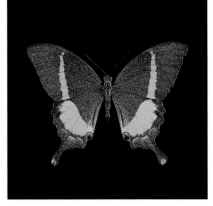

PAPILIO CRINO
Common Banded Peacock

ZONE 5
4in
102mm

The magnificence of this species centers on the broad band of green-blue iridescence which pervades the wings. The tail is bold, lobed, and with a touch of green. Butterflies are regular visitors to garden flowers, such as *Lantana*, where they imbibe nectar. The butterfly is found only in southern and western India and Sri Lanka, in dry lowland country. It is not threatened.

PAPILIO DEMOLEUS
Lime or Lemon Butterfly,
Checkered Swallowtail

ZONE 5·6
3¹/₂in
90mm

This widespread butterfly is speckled yellow over a brown ground color. It is tailless and has a red false-eye at the anal area of the hindwing. Six subspecies are known. It is a common butterfly which enjoys a very wide distribution from the Middle East through to China and Japan, as well as Australia. It is probably a migrant.

PAPILIO DEMODOCUS
Citrus Butterfly, African Lime Butterfly,
Christmas Butterfly, Orange Dog

ZONE 4

4½in
115mm

This is a common butterfly which has a pale yellow speckled pattern over a dark brown ground. It has no tail, but there are two red false-eyes on the hindwing. This species occurs in Africa and in Arabia, and it is replaced in Asia and Australia by *P. demoleus*, which looks similar. The butterfly enjoys open forested areas and gardens. It breeds on citrus and cosmos in gardens and is sometimes a pest of citrus crops. It has been introduced to Madagascar.

PAPILIO DEMOLION
Burmese Banded Swallowtail,
Banded Swallowtail

ZONE 5

4⅛in
104mm

This species is very uniform in its symmetry with the dark forewings curved and indented, and the hindwing rounded with a long lobed tail. Apart from the distinct chevrons around the hindwing, there is a large cream band which dominates the wings. Three subspecies exist of this common and widespread butterfly which occurs from Indonesia, via the Philippines to Burma and Thailand. This species is not threatened.

PAPILIO ESPERANZA

ZONE 2

4⅜in
110mm

This is a very rare butterfly which is only found in one part of Mexico. For its conservation, all details of the locality are being kept secret. Caterpillar food plants are so far unrecorded, but the butterfly favors mountain cloud forest at about 5,500ft (1,700m). Two broods are produced each year. This butterfly is classified as Vulnerable in the *Red Data Book of Threatened Swallowtail Butterflies of the World*.

PAPILIO EUCHENOR

ZONE 5·6

2¾in
72mm

Strongly contrasting colors are typical of this species, which has an irregular band of cream crossing the wings emphasized on each side by velvety black. The margins of the hindwing are scalloped, and there are three small cream marks near the forewing tip. The butterfly exists in at least 13 subspecies. The butterfly occurs in the eastern part of Indonesia and on New Guinea, where it is collected for the butterfly trade. The species is not regarded as threatened.

PAPILIO GAMBRISIUS BURUANUS

ZONE 5

6¼in 160mm

This swallowtail is identified from the underside, which is a patchwork of white bars highlighting the dark ground color to give an impression of scalloping on the margin. The hindwing underside has a dominant area of white and to the outside of this is a row of blue scales, a row of white marks, and a false eye in the anal position. Two subspecies are known from Indonesia.

PAPILIO EURYMEDON
Pallid Tiger Swallowtail

ZONE 1

3⅛in 80mm

The black tiger stripes run across the wings and link up with the dark tail. The ground color is white, but the margins have dark markings and, overall, the contrast of white and dark markings is striking. It exhibits back-to-front mimicry like so many tailed swallowtails. This migrant occurs across the southern United States with some distribution into Central America. It is a common species of open flowery meadows where it breeds mostly on members of the *Rosaceae*. It is not threatened.

PAPILIO FUSCUS
Yellow Helen, Black and White Helen, Banded Helen

ZONE 5·6

5½in 140mm

This is a large butterfly with dark curved forewings, and there is a flash of yellow on the upperside of the hindwings. This pattern is repeated on the undersides, but in white with a scattering of red marks. There are 22 subspecies known. The butterfly enjoys widespread distribution through much of Asia and into Northern Australia. It is relatively common and is not threatened. It breeds on citrus.

PAPILIO GARLEPPI

ZONE 2

4in 100mm

This resident butterfly has a widely separated distribution in Peru, Brazil, Bolivia and Guyana. The butterfly is very rare and is in need of much research. The food plants are unknown, but likely to be members of the *Rutaceae*. Specimens have reputedly come from high altitude (up to 16,500ft/5,000m) as well as lowland valleys; most butterflies do not show such a large range. It is classified as Insufficiently Known in the *Red Data Book of Threatened Swallowtail Butterflies of the World*.

PAPILIO GLAUCUS
Tiger Swallowtail

ZONE 1

4¹⁄₈in
105mm

This is a bright yellow butterfly with a long tail. A series of black tiger marks run across the wings, which have a distinct black border. In the dark margin of the hindwing are some yellow marks and a red blotch at each end. The Washington State Department of Game list this as a Special Species, though it is a relatively widespread with a number of subspecies. It seems to move locally rather than to migrate.

PAPILIO HELENUS
Red Helen

ZONE 5

5¹⁄₂in
140mm

This is a large dark-colored butterfly with a greenish tinge. The conspicuous feature is the pale yellow-cream flash near the leading edge of the hindwing, covered up at rest, and used to surprise predators. Thirteen subspecies are known. One of the largest is *P. helenus mooreana*, whose female can have a wingspan up to 5¹⁄₂in (140mm). The butterfly frequents open forested areas and visits nectar sources in yards. It breeds on citrus and is not threatened.

PAPILIO HORNIMANI
Horniman's Swallowtail

ZONE 4

4in
100mm

This is a large black-tailed swallowtail which has a brilliant metallic blue band crossing the wings, and a series of blue spots inside the hindwing margin. The butterfly lives in highland rainforest. It is continuously brooded, but is most common immediately after rains. Males exhibit mud-puddling behavior; females are seen less frequently. The butterfly is not threatened.

PAPILIO HECTORIDES

ZONE 2

3³⁄₈in
88mm

The sexes are completely different. The male has a dominant white-cream band which crosses the dark wing and a series of fine chevrons around the hindwing. There are some red spots on the hindwing. The female has many more red spots on the hind-wing to the outside of a white area which is continuous with a small white band which crosses the forewing. The butterfly is found widely in Argentina, Brazil, Paraguay and Uruguay and is not under threat. It is ranched in Brazil.

PAPILIO HOMERUS
Homerus Swallowtail

ZONE 2

6in
150mm

This is a resident butterfly with contrasting light and dark markings, similar in both sexes. A white-cream band crosses both dark wings, and the hindwing has a row of submarginal spots. It frequents rainforests in both lowland and highland areas. It is greatly threatened by habitat destruction. An attractive butterfly, it has been much collected. It is only found in Jamaica and is classified as Endangered in the *Red Data Book of Threatened Swallowtails of the World*.

PAPILIO HOSPITON
Corsican Swallowtail

ZONE 3

3in
76mm

The very short, almost blunt tails distinguish this resident butterfly from the other large swallowtails seen in Europe. The dark base of the wings, and the dark margin infused on the hindwing with blue marks, are also characteristic. The butterfly is only found on Corsica and Sardinia in mountainous areas, where it breeds on *Ferula communis*, giant fennel. There is a single generation each year. This species is classified as Endangered in the *Red Data Book of Threatened Swallowtail Butterflies of the World*.

PAPILIO INDRA
Indra Swallowtail,
Short-tailed Swallowtail

ZONE 1

3¼in
93mm

This is a dark swallowtail with a short tail. The key feature is the black abdomen, which often has a dash of yellow toward the back. There are a number of subspecies among which the length of the short tail varies. The butterfly lives in rocky and forested areas in mountainous sites where males engage in hill-topping to find females. The females lay their eggs on a variety of umbelliferous plants. The butterfly is listed for protection by the Washington State Department of Game. It is not threatened.

PAPILIO ISWARA
Great Helen, Large Helen

ZONE 5

6¼in
160mm

This large and magnificent butterfly has brown wings lightly dusted with lighter scales, especially along the veins. However the magical parts of its color scheme are the large patches of cream-yellow on the leading edge of the hindwing. There are also two brown-centered spots on the inside edge of the hindwing. There are two subspecies. The butterfly lives in hilly areas. It is not threatened.

PAPILIO JORDANI

ZONE 6

6⅔in
170mm

The sexes are completely different. The male is black with a band of merged blue-white spots large on the hindwing and tapering-off on the forewing. The female is larger and dressed in dowdy dirty white with light brown emphasizing the brown veins. There are wavy dark marks around the trailing edge of the hindwing. The female mimics *Idea* species. The butterfly is endemic on the island of Sulawesi, Indonesia, and very little is known about its life cycle. It is classified as Rare in the *Red Data Book of Threatened Swallowtail Buttterflies of the World*.

PAPILIO INOPINATUS

ZONE 5

5in
130mm

The key features on the underside are a white band toward the apex of the forewing and an irregular red spot in the anal region of the hindwing. The overall color is dark brown to black, and the butterfly has no tail, though the hindwing margin is scalloped. Two subspecies are recognized in Indonesia. The butterfly lives along forest margins, but is not threatened.

PAPILIO JACKSONI
Jackson's Swallowtail

ZONE 4

3½in
90mm

The sexes are different. The male is brown with a white band across the hindwing linking up with a broken band on the forewing. The female is slightly larger and in place of the hindwing band has a yellow patch. There is a beading of white marks around the inside of the hindwing. Five subspecies are recorded. The butterfly lives in lowland and upland forest. It breeds on *Teclea* and *Fagara* species and is continuously brooded throughout the year.

PAPILIO LAGLAIZEI

ZONE 5·6

3⅞in
98mm

Mimicry of a moth, *Alcides agathyrsus*, is perfected in this species with black margins and a black apex to the forewing. The undersides are much lighter, especially the hindwing. A curved broad greenish band takes up most of the uppers inside the dark margins, and there is a short white tail. The butterfly lives on the canopy of the rainforest where it mingles with its model, the moth. The butterfly is found in various parts of Indonesia and New Guinea. It is not threatened.

PAPILIO LORMIERI
Western Emperor Swallowtail,
Emperor Swallowtail

ZONE 4

5in 130mm

This is a familiar-looking butterfly, since it has the colors and patterns of *Papilio demodocus*, but with the addition of a tail. Yellow marks pepper the wings, and there are two distinctive orange and blue eye spots on the hindwing. The butterfly is continuously brooded in rainforests through the year and breeds on citrus. It is not a threatened species.

PAPILIO LORQUINIANUS

ZONE 5

4¾in 120mm

This tailed butterfly has magnificent turquoise blue over its wings, particularly on the basal half of all the wings. There are smudges of green scales on the apex of the forewing and muted turquoise chevrons around the hindwing. Five subspecies are recorded of this scarce butterfly. It is found on various islands of Indonesia, but it is not threatened.

PAPILIO MACHAON
Artemisia Swallowtail, Swallowtail

ZONE 1·3·5

3in 76mm

A most attractive migrant butterfly and easily recognized in flight. There are an enormous number of subspecies of all sorts of colors ranging from very dark black to very orange. There is always a pair of tails on the hindwing. The American name of the butterfly reflects its food plant, artemesia, but in Europe the food may be wild carrot, fennel or milk parsley. The full-grown caterpillars have the same colors as the adult, and they evert an orange osmeterium from behind the head to scare away predators.

PAPILIO MARAHO

ZONE 5

4¾in 120mm

The key feature is the shape of the hindwing, which is generously edged in pink and is grossly indented which emphasizes the broad tail. The forewings are dark, and the hindwings are edged in huge pink chevrons while toward the base is a large flash of cream. The color scheme seems to mimic some of the *Atrophaneura* species. The butterfly is endemic to Taiwan, where it lives in mountainous rainforest. It is classified as Vulnerable in the *Red Data Book of Threatened Swallowtail Butterflies of the World*.

PAPILIO MEMNON
Great Mormon

6in
150mm

ZONE
5·6

This is a widely distributed and variable butterfly with at least 13 subspecies recorded. Forewings are generally pale brown between the heavier marked veins, and the base of all the wings is very dark. Female forms may or may not have tails. Males are usually black and never have tails. The butterfly breeds on citrus and is common visiting flowers along lowland rainforest paths.

PAPILIO MULTICAUDATA
Two-tailed Tiger Swallowtail,
Three-tailed Tiger Swallowtail

5in
130mm

ZONE
1·2

There is a maximum of three tails on each hindwing, hence the alternative common names. Like the other tiger swallowtails, it has typical black tiger stripes crossing the wing. It breeds on *Fraxinus* (ash), *Prunus* (sloe) and *Quercus* (oak), and may be found in mountainous regions and foothills where the adults are avid nectar feeders.

PAPILIO NIREUS
Green-banded Swallowtail,
Narrow-blue-banded Swallowtail

4in
100mm

ZONE
4

The green or blue band which crosses the wings is variable according to the four subspecies, which occur over much of Africa. This is a common butterfly which breeds on citrus and may be found sipping nectar from wayside flowers in woods, forests and savanna. It is not threatened.

PAPILIO MONTROUZIERI

2³/₄in
72mm

ZONE
6

The brilliant metallic sky blue which covers most of the wings is impressive. The outer part of the wings is dark, especially the apex of the forewings. The dark margins of the hindwings are scalloped. The tails are lobed at the end. The butterfly is only found in New Caledonia, where it is not threatened.

PAPILIO NEUMOEGENI

3¹/₈in
84mm

ZONE
5

A delightful metallic green covers much of the tailed hindwing, more so in the male than the female, and a green dusting covers the forewings. The female is slightly larger and duller, and more reclusive. Males are likely to be found in rainforest glades. Caterpillar food plants are unknown. It is classified as Vulnerable in the *Red Data Book of Threatened Swallowtail Butterflies of the World*.

PAPILIO NOBILIS
Noble Swallowtail

4³/₈in
110mm

ZONE
4

The bright orange-yellow is distinctive for a swallowtail. The female is slightly larger than the male with darker markings around the margins. The female also has a darker smudge in the region of the forewing cell leading toward the base, and a series of dark spots on the hindwing. Three subspecies are known. The butterfly is found in highland rainforest, where it breeds on *Wahlenbergia*, a member of the *Campanulaceae* (bellflower) family.

PAPILIO OENOMAUS

ZONE 5

6in
150mm

This is a large black butterfly, which has gracefully curved forewings containing a white band, and a scalloped and tailed hindwing. There are two subspecies recorded. This is a common species of the Lesser Sunda Islands of eastern Indonesia, and it is currently not threatened.

PAPILIO PALINURUS
Banded Peacock, Burmese Peacock, Moss Peacock

ZONE 5

3¹⁄₈in
84mm

Of the several Asian butterflies which are predominantly green, this species is recognizable by its finer shape and curves of the wings, together with a white or red spot on the leading edge of the hindwing. It is a widespread butterfly of forests and generally common. There may be up to five subspecies of which one subspecies in Malaysia may be vulnerable.

PAPILIO ORNYTHION
Ornythion Swallowtail

ZONE 1·2

4³⁄₈in
110mm

The sexes look alike, but the female is the larger. The shorter tails differentiate this species from *P. thoas* and *P. cresphontes*. The brown ground color is broken by the large band of yellow which crosses the wings, and a series of yellow chevrons run inside the margin of the hindwing. The butterfly may be found in open wooded areas and gardens where it breeds on citrus. Some of its flights reach into the southern USA. It is not threatened.

PAPILIO PALAMEDES
Laurel Swallowtail

ZONE 1

3¹⁄₂in
90mm

The undersides of this butterfly are useful for identification since there are two rows of red-orange marks crossing the wings. Yellow chevrons cross the upper forewing. It is a migrant species which has made adaptations to living in the swampy areas of the eastern and southeastern part of the USA. It breeds on various native trees including *Persea* and *Sassafras* species. The butterfly is widespread, common and not threatened.

PAPILIO PELAUS ATKINSI
Pelaus Swallowtail,
Prickly Ash Swallowtail

ZONE 2

2in
50mm

The brown ground color is crossed on the forewing by a curved yellow band and on the tailed hindwing by a series of red spots. There is a small eye-spot at the anal region of the hindwing. There are three subspecies. The butterfly occurs only in Jamaica, where it is widely distributed, flying in shady wooded areas. It is not threatened.

PAPILIO PELODORUS
Eastern Black and Yellow Swallowtail

ZONE 4

4³/₄in
120mm

The key feature of this tailed swallowtail is the series of irregular-sized pale yellow spots on the submargin of the hindwing. There is also a large band of yellow which crosses the wings. The strongly curved forewings give this butterfly of the mountain forests the ability for strong flight. It may be found throughout much of the year and engages in mud-puddling.

PAPILIO PERICLES

ZONE 5

3¹/₈in
82mm

The hindwings are much longer than the forewings, since the hindwing is drawn out with an elongated tail, lobed at the tip. The base of the wings has a pleasing blue suffusion in contrast with the brown ground color. The margin of the hindwing is also scalloped. The butterfly is found in the Lesser Sunda Islands of Indonesia where, although it is uncommon, it is not threatened.

PAPILIO PHESTUS

ZONE 6

3¹/₈in
80mm

The forewings are drawn out with very rounded features and are almost completely black with only a little light dusting. The hindwing has the strong contrast of white and black with a touch of red by the anal part of the wing. The butterfly is found in Papua New Guinea and the Solomon Islands. It is not threatened.

PAPILIO PHORBANTA EPIPHORBAS
Papillon La Pature

In this butterfly the sexes are completely different. The male is black with silver-blue-green marks and a series of blue spots around the margin of the hindwing. The female is dull brown with white tracery around the margins of the hindwing. Both sexes have a stubby tail. It is endemic to the island of Réunion and has been protected by the French government since 1979. The butterfly breeds on citrus. It is classified as Vulnerable in the *Red Data Book of Threatened Swallowtail Butterflies of the World*.

PAPILIO PILUMNUS
Three-tailed Tiger Swallowtail

Typical of the tiger swallowtails with their tiger stripes, this migrant species can be distinguished from *P. multicaudata* by having one less stripe. The tails are unequal in length, and there is a series of metallic blue marks on the hindwing. The butterfly breeds on *Litsea* species which grow in woodland and which is a member of the *Lauraceae* family. It is not threatened.

PAPILIO POLYXENES ASTERIUS
American Swallowtail, Black Swallowtail, Parsnip Swallowtail

This butterfly has four subspecies, usually very black, although some lighter yellower forms exist. The butterfly is very successful over a wide range of habitats from Alaska to Central America. The caterpillars can defoliate vegetables such as carrot, celery and parsnip, hence the name parsnip swallowtail.

PAPILIO PHORCAS
Green-patch Swallowtail

The distinctive green patch is found mostly on the male, though the female, which is very slightly larger, may have either a yellow or green patch. The green covers a very broad area over the base of the hindwing. Both sexes are tailed. Butterflies fly in forested areas where they may be quite common. They are continuously brooded in some places, and the caterpillars feed on *Teclea* species, which are members of the *Rutaceae* family.

PAPILIO POLYMNESTOR
Blue Mormon

This is a quite magnificent butterfly with slightly curved forewings which are mostly black with a touch of silvery blue. The blue markings broaden out to cover the entire hindwing, which has two distinct rows of black spots. It is a wide-ranging butterfly of forests and woods, and it also visits gardens to feed on nectar. This species is relatively common and not threatened.

PAPILIO PTOLYCHUS

The butterfly is large and mostly black, with a patch of white behind the apex of the forewing and some white marks on the margin. The hindwing has a broad curved band of white which contrasts with the black ground. The hindwing is also scalloped with an orange eye-spot in the anal region. The butterfly is found on the Solomon Islands and Bougainville. It is not threatened.

PAPILIO REX
Regal Swallowtail, King Papilio

The sexes are generally similar with cream spots over a brown ground color and two flashes of orange at the base of the forewing. There are seven subspecies, and the butterfly is involved in mimicking danaids. The female has different forms which are thought to mimic either *Danaus formosa* or *D. mercedonia*. The butterfly lives in highland rainforest and breeds on *Calodendron*, a genus of the *Rutaceae* family. The butterfly is quite common and not threatened.

PAPILIO TOBOROI

The sexes look similar. They are dark with a touch of blue, and two blue-green bands cross the wings. The caterpillars are gregarious and feed at night on the leaves of *Litsea* and *Flintersia* species. Up to 700 have been found in one mass. People eat the caterpillars, which are easy to collect since they aggregate in the forks of trees, up to 300 of them at a time. This magnificent butterfly of the Solomon Islands is classified as Rare in the *Red Data Book of Threatened Swallowtail Butterflies of the World*.

PAPILIO RUMANZOVIA

The sexes are completely different. The male is mostly very dark with pale blue dusting on its hindwings. The female has red on the base of its forewings which is continuous with pale red which runs around the hindwings. Sometimes the red is replaced by yellow. Both sexes have well rounded forewings. The butterfly occurs in the Philippines and Indonesia, and is not a threatened species.

PAPILIO SCHMELTZII

This has large, curved forewings which are black. The tailed hindwing has a flash of white contrasting with the black ground color. The butterfly only occurs in Fiji, where it is common and not threatened.

PAPILIO TROILUS
Spicebush Swallowtail,
Green-clouded Swallowtail

This is a dark-colored swallowtail with smudgy green-yellow marks around the hindwings, and a row of off-yellow marks by the margin of the forewing. The butterfly mimics poisonous *Battus philenor*, and two subspecies are known. It is found in open wooded areas where it breeds on *Benzoin*, *Sassafras* and *Magnolia* species. It is common and not threatened.

PAPILIO VICTORINUS

The dark forewings are dotted with yellow, and the hindwings have two rows of red marks, chevrons toward the margin and dots to the inside. There are three subspecies. The butterfly lives in forested areas, spends much time on the canopy, and breeds on the native avocado *(Persea americana)*. It may visit gardens. Some specimens stray into the southern USA.

PAPILIO WOODFORDI

Although very similar to *P. ptolychus* in size, pattern and color, this species lacks the little eye spot in the anal region of the hindwing. The hindwing is heavily scalloped, and there is a suspicion of a blunt tail. Four subspecies are recorded. The butterfly occurs on the Solomon Islands and is farmed on Bougainville. It is not threatened.

PAPILIO ULYSSES
Ulysses Butterfly, Blue Mountain
Swallowtail, Mountain Blue, Blue Emperor

This is the flashiest of Australia's butterflies. The male is the brighter with its iridescent blue-green colors in strong contrast to the black ground color. The female is more subdued, but both sexes have black tails and irregularly scalloped hindwings. There are 16 subspecies recorded. Males are always curious about blue objects, even artificial ones, and this can be used to draw them closer for observation purposes. The species is protected in Queensland.

PAPILIO WEYMERI

This is a tailless swallowtail which has a band of large cream marks across the dark forewing and a slightly scalloped hindwing. The female is brown with radiating white marks on the forewing and a band of blue and yellow marks on the hindwing. This is a species of the virgin rainforest as well as secondary scrub areas. It is known to breed on *Micromelum*, a rutaceous plant. The butterfly is endemic to two islands in Papua New Guinea and is classified as Rare.

PAPILIO XANTHOPLEURA

The forewings are dull black with a faint dusting of green. The hindwings are black with a great deal of green dusting between the veins and a series of lunules around the wing. The ends of the veins are drawn out as tiny tails around the margin. Little is known about this uncommon species from the Amazon rainforests of Peru and Ecuador. It is likely to be designated as rare.

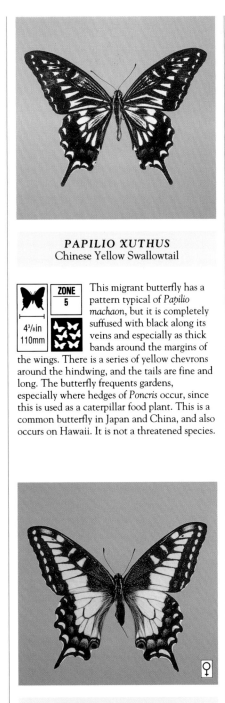

PAPILIO XUTHUS
Chinese Yellow Swallowtail

ZONE 5 — 4³⁄₈in 110mm — This migrant butterfly has a pattern typical of *Papilio machaon*, but it is completely suffused with black along its veins and especially as thick bands around the margins of the wings. There is a series of yellow chevrons around the hindwing, and the tails are fine and long. The butterfly frequents gardens, especially where hedges of *Poncris* occur, since this is used as a caterpillar food plant. This is a common butterfly in Japan and China, and also occurs on Hawaii. It is not a threatened species.

GENUS
PARIDES

A group of South American butterflies which have a black ground color. The sexes are usually different, and the male has an androconial fold. Females are used as models for a number of mimics. One unusual characteristic of *Parides* that distinguishes them from their mimics is that they do not mud-puddle. All *Parides* breed on poisonous *Aristolochia* species.

PARIDES AGLAOPE

ZONE 2 — 3¹⁄₄in 85mm — The sexes are slightly different, although both have a black background with a reddish-pinkish mark on the hindwing. The male has a bluish spot on the forewing, but in the female this is replaced by a white mark. The forewing shape is drawn out, rather like a heliconid butterfly. The butterfly occurs in Bolivia, Brazil and Peru, and, although uncommon, it is not threatened.

PARIDES ASCANIUS
Ascanius Swallowtail,
Fluminense Swallowtail

ZONE 2 — 2⁵⁄₈in 68mm — The sexes are similar with dark forewings broken by a large white flash. This continues onto the tailed hindwings, which are much suffused with pink. The butterfly lives in coastal swamps where its caterpillar food plants, *Aristolochia* species, occur. The butterfly is classified as Vulnerable in the *Red Data Book of Threatened Swallowtail Butterflies of the World*.

PARIDES EURIMEDES MYLOTES
Cattle Heart

ZONE 2 — 2in 52mm — The pattern and colors of this species are simple. The black ground color is interrupted on the forewing by a dash of white-cream and green, and on the scalloped hindwing by an accordion of magenta. The butterfly occurs in Central America and is a rare stray into the southern US. It occurs in open forested areas where it breeds on *Aristolochia* species.

PAPILIO ZELICAON
Western Swallowtail

ZONE 1 — 3¹⁄₈in 80mm — This is a *Papilio machaon*-type butterfly, but with much black over its wings, especially near the bases of the forewings. The outer parts have a band of yellow marks and the yellow chevrons around the hindwing margins. Reddish-orange pervades the undersides. This is a migrant butterfly with several forms. It breeds on a great variety of umbelliferous plants. Adults indulge in a lot of hill-topping to find a mate. The butterfly is common and not threatened.

PARIDES GUNDLACHIANUS
Gundlach's Swallowtail

ZONE 2

3¹/₈in
80mm

This is a stylish butterfly with pronounced scalloped hindwings and dominant tail. There is also a bright red band edged in white on each hindwing. The ground color is black, and there is metallic green-blue on the forewing of the male. The green-blue is lacking in the female, which has a tracery of white running across the forewings. The butterfly occurs in rainforests.

PARIDES HAHNELI
Hahnel's Amazon Swallowtail

ZONE 2

4in
100mm

The curious shape of the wings is a good identification guide. The forewings are long, and the hindwings are very reduced, scalloped, and with a long tail. Females are larger than males. The black wings have lighter patches giving a checked appearance. The habitats of this butterfly are the lush overgrown banks of the Amazon River, and it may well feed on *Aristolochia* species. The butterfly is classified as Rare in the *Red Data Book of Threatened Swallowtail Butterflies of the World.*

PARIDES ORELLANA

ZONE 2

4³/₈in
110mm

This is a fine-looking butterfly with dark forewings, larger, rounder and lighter in the female, with a large flash of rose-vermillion on the hindwing. The rose marks on the female form a row of tapering spots. The hindwing is also uniformly scalloped. The butterfly is found in the rainforests of the Amazon. It is uncommon, but not threatened.

PARIDES PHOTINUS

ZONE 2

3³/₄in
95mm

A delightful and attractive butterfly with just a suggestion of two unequal-length tails. It has black wings with two rows of red marks on the hindwing, the outer marks forming chevrons, the inner ones spots. The butterfly is found in lowland and highland rainforest from Mexico to Costa Rica, where it breeds on *Aristolochia* species. It is relatively common and not threatened.

PARIDES PIZARRO

ZONE 2

3 1/2 in 93mm

The black ground color of this butterfly is uniform on the forewing. The black hindwing is scalloped and interrupted by a group of three to four cream spots in the male, and three to six spots in the female. The butterfly occurs in lowland rainforest, but little is known about the biology of this species; even its food plant is unknown. It is classified as Insufficiently Known in the *Red Data Book of Threatened Swallowtails of the World*.

PARIDES STEINBACHI

ZONE 2

3 1/8 in 80mm

This is a black butterfly with a white-cream patch on the forewing and various red and white spots on the hindwing. Very little is known about the ecology of this species, but specimens have been taken in highland rainforest. It probably breeds on *Aristolochia* species. It is classified as Insufficiently Known in the *Red Data Book of Threatened Swallowtail Butterflies of the World*.

PARNASSIUS APOLLO
Apollo

ZONE 3·5

3 1/8 in 80mm

A white butterfly with extensive but variable black spots all over the wings. Red spots decorate the hindwings. In the female a special cap fits over the rear of the abdomen after mating – to stop any further copulation. The butterfly flies over alpine meadows where it breeds on *Sedum* species (stonecrops). Many factors have contributed to the decline of the Apollo in Europe, including habitat change combined with climatic change, acid rain, and collection of the species. It is classified as Rare in the *Red Data Book of Threatened Swallowtail Butterflies of the World*.

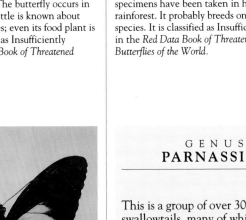

PARIDES SESOSTRIS
Southern Cattle Heart

ZONE 2

3 1/2 in 90mm

The black wings provide a contrast to the yellow-green metallic flash on the forewings of the male. The hindwings are uniformly scalloped, and in the male the scent fold is white and conspicuous. The female has a white spot on the forewing. Four sub-species are recorded. The butterfly occurs from Mexico to Bolivia and breeds on *Aristolochia* species.

GENUS
PARNASSIUS

This is a group of over 30 sedentary swallowtails, many of which live in mountain habitats, even at 44,300ft (13,500m) on Mt. Everest. The populations of several species have been extinguished by development of ski resorts, and other species are threatened.

PARNASSIUS AUTOCRATOR

ZONE 5

2 5/8 in 70mm

Unlike many other common parnassian swallowtails, this species does not have any red marks on its wings. The female has a wide yellow-orange patch on the hindwing which is absent in the male. The butterfly breeds on *Corydalis adiantifolia* and possibly *C. hindukushensis*, both of which could be threatened by over-grazing. Too little is known about the ecology of this rare butterfly which inhabitats Tadzhikstakaya and Afghanistan, regions seldom visited by lepidopterists. It is classified as Rare in the *Red Data Book of Threatened Swallowtail Butterflies of the World*.

PARNASSIUS CLODIUS
American Apollo, Clodius Parnassian

ZONE
1

2½in
64mm

The American Apollo has waxy white wings with red spots on the hindwing. The hindwing is indented on the inside edge. Twelve subspecies exist, including a dark form which occurs in Alaska. Females lay eggs on various species of *Dicentra*, including *D. uniflora*. Drought, logging and damming waterways are thought to cause problems to populations. However, the species is not threatened.

PARNASSIUS EVERSMANNI THOR
Evermann's Parnassian, Yellow Apollo

ZONE
1·5

2⅜in
60mm

This butterfly is named after the males, which are yellow; the females are white. Both sexes have red spots on the hindwing. There are 12 subspecies. The butterfly occurs in alpine areas, often near forests. Caterpillars feed on *Corydalis* species in North America and Asia, and *Dicentra* species in Japan. It is not threatened.

PARNASSIUS MNEMOSYNE
Clouded Apollo

ZONE
3·5

2⅜in
62mm

One of the smallest and daintiest of the Apollos, with no red spots and heavily indented hindwings dusted with pale gray marks to the inside. There are, incredibly, 125 subspecies so far described. The butterfly occurs in alpine meadows and among woodland, and breeds on *Corydalis* species. Several of its habitats continue to be threatened by afforestation and development of mountaintop ski resorts.

PARNASSIUS PHOEBUS SACERODOS
Small Apollo, Phoebus Parnassian

ZONE
1·3

3⅛in
80mm

Typical of many of the parnassians, this butterfly has a pronounced, indented margin to its hindwing. There are two red spots of unequal size on the hindwing and some smaller ones on the forewing. There are a number of subspecies recognized. Apollos live in mountainous regions and cope well with bad weather. Apollos have become collectors' prizes, and their numbers have declined due to habitat destruction plus the effects of acid rain. They are protected in France and classified as Vulnerable in Europe and in the USA.

71

GENUS
PROTOGRAPHIUM

Closely related to *Graphium* and *Eurytides*, this genus has one species.

PROTOGRAPHIUM LEOSTHENES
Four-bar, Four-bar Swordtail

	ZONE 6	The butterfly has four black bands which run back from the leading edge of the forewing. The long black tails are edged in white. There are two
2½in 64mm		

subspecies known. The butterfly frequents rainforests and breeds on *Rauwenhoffia* species, a member of the *Annonaceae* (custard apple) family.

TEINOPALPUS IMPERIALIS
Kaiser-I-Hind

	ZONE 5	The sexes are different. The male is green on the uppers with an orange flash on the hindwing. The larger female has a gray-brown forewing and five tails behind a flash of
5in 130mm		

orange on the hindwing. The long tails are pointed, and the margin of the hindwing is scalloped. The butterfly is a forest dweller of highland areas, and visits both the canopy and ground level. It probably breeds on *Daphne* species. The butterfly is classified as Rare in the *Red Data Book of Threatened Swallowtail Butterflies of the World*.

GENUS
TEINOPALPUS

There are two Asian species, about which little is known. They live in rainforests and are much sought by collectors. Both species are listed in the *Red Data Book*.

TEINOPALPUS AUREUS
Golden Kaiser-I-Hind

	ZONE 5	This is a rarity, not seen in its native China for a long while. The curved and indented forewings are mostly brown with a green line separating the green-dusted black base.
4⅜in 110mm		

The hindwing is mostly yellow, scalloped and tailed. Little is known of its ecology, but it does fly in highland rainforest. The butterfly is classified as Insufficiently Known in the *Red Data Book of Threatened Swallowtail Butterflies of the World*.

GENUS
TROGONOPTERA

There are two species which belong to this genus, and they are among the largest butterflies in the world. They live in virgin rainforest and are highly collectable. They are both listed by CITES.

TROGONOPTERA TROJANA

	ZONE 5
8in 200mm	

This is among the largest of the rainforest butterflies. The male has a broken line of metallic green crossing the wings; the female is dull brown with lighter areas toward the margins. It occurs in the Philippines where up to 50 males have been witnessed to every one of the elusive females, which probably spend much of their time on the rainforest canopy. The food plants have not been identified.

TROGONOPTERA BROOKIANA
ALBESCENS
Raja(h) Brooke's Birdwing

	ZONE 6
6⁷⁄₈in 175mm	

This magnificent species, which has a broad chevron of metallic green across its dark wings, is named after the British Rajah Brooke of Sarawak. There are five subspecies recorded. Although it is protected in Malaya, about 125,000 specimens are probably "legally" exported each year. It is a butterfly of the virgin rainforest and breeds on *Aristolochia* species. It is well-exploited; D'Abrera mentions seeing over 300 set specimens in a dealer's establishment in the Cameron Highlands.

TROIDES AEACUS
Golden Birdwing

	ZONE 5
6in 150mm	

The sexes are completely different. The smaller male has a dark forewing dusted with highlights. Its "golden" parts are on the hindwing, which is mostly a deep yellow with black scalloping around the margin. The female is smudgy black with windows of smudgy orange on the hindwing. This is the most poorly known of the birdwings: even its habitat and food plants are not fully described.

GENUS
TROIDES

This is a large genus of birdwing butterflies from Asia. They are characterized by having bright yellow on the hindwings and dark forewings. There are over 20 species, and they are all listed by CITES. They are highly collectable butterflies and are sold commercially for high prices.

TROIDES HALIPHRON
SOCRATES

	ZONE 5
5¹⁄₂in 140mm	

The male is jet black with a curved, bright yellow mark in the center of the hindwing. The female is very much larger and is dull brown on the forewings, which have a dusting of lighter scales. The hindwing has a widely dispersed yellow area. This butterfly is found on many of the Indonesian islands and, although protected, is not threatened.

TROIDES HELENA CERBERUS
Common Birdwing

ZONE
5·6

7in
180mm

Male and female share the same color scheme, though the female is much larger and duller. The female also has a row of black spots in the yellow hindwing patch, which are much reduced in the male. Up to 17 subspecies have been recorded for this common birdwing. The butterfly lives in rainforest areas, and will also visit urban habitats. It breeds on *Aristolochia* species. On the Malayan peninsula it is classified as Vulnerable.

TROIDES MAGELLANUS

ZONE
5

7½in
190mm

The male has black forewings with just a little light high-lighting along the veins. This highlighting is greatly emphasized in the larger female. On the male the yellow of the hindwing is distinct and cut only by the black veins, whereas on the female hindwing it is a dirtier shade and dispersed to outer chevrons and an inner patch. The butterfly is not threatened.

TROIDES PRATTORUM
Buru Opalescent Birdwing

ZONE
5

8in
200mm

This is one of the most spectacular birdwings, due to the marking on the hindwing which appears blue when seen from the side. This opalescent effect is responsible for its common name. It lives in highland rainforest on the island of Buru in the Moluccas. Little is known of its ecology, and the caterpillar food plants are unknown. The butterfly is classified as Indeterminate in the *Red Data Book of Threatened Swallowtail Butterflies of the World*.

TROIDES HYPOLITUS

ZONE
5·6

8in
200mm

This birdwing has a silvery appearance on the forewing. The forewings of both sexes are black and dusted with lighter scales along the main veins, though more so in the much larger female. The yellow marks are drawn out and staggered around the margin of the hindwing and those marks on the female hindwing contain a black spot. There are four subspecies which occur on a number of Indonesian and Moluccan islands. The butterfly is reasonably common and not threatened.

TROIDES MIRANDA

ZONE
5

7½in
190mm

The sexes are completely different. The male has the typical black forewing and yellow with black border on the hindwing. It also has a dusting of white toward the apex of the forewing. The larger female has uniformly dull brown forewings and dark hindwings, which have some dirty yellow toward the base. Two subspecies occur. This rainforest insect is not threatened.

TROIDES RHADAMANTUS DOHERTYI
Talaud Black Birdwing

ZONE
6

6½in
164mm

Named after one of two islands in Indonesia where this birdwing is found, the species, especially the male, is very black all over. The forewings of the female are slightly lightened-up, and there is a small flash of dirty yellow on the hindwing. The butterfly occurs in lowland and coastal habitats and probably breeds on *Aristolochia tagala*. The butterfly is classified as Indeterminate in the *Red Data Book of Threatened Swallowtail Butterflies of the World*.

TROIDES RHADAMANTUS
PLATENI

ZONE 5

6in
150mm

As birdwings go, this is one of the smallest, including the female. The basic birdwing color scheme is maintained, but the yellow on the male hindwing is rather smoky on the trailing edge. The butterfly is found in many islands in the Philippines, where it occurs in the rainforest. It is not threatened.

GENUS
ZERYNTHIA

A genus of rather sedentary butterflies which have small wings, very hairy bodies, and very complex color patterns on their wings. They breed on poisonous members of the *Aristolochiaceae*.

ZERYNTHIA RUMINA
Spanish Festoon

ZONE 3

1³/₄ in
46mm

Brightly colored in black and yellow, both wing surfaces have a lot of red marks which are key features. The zigzag marks typical of these festoons are evident, especially around the margins of the wings. The butterfly enjoys lush meadows where the *Aristolochia* species, their caterpillar food plants, occur. It is strongly resident and has a single generation each year.

ZERYNTHIA POLYXENA
Southern Festoon

ZONE 3

2in
52mm

A tailless swallowtail with characteristic zigzag marks over the wings and a series of black bands along the leading edge of the forewing. The overall pattern is reversed on the underside. The butterfly likes old meadows, especially those beside streams, where its caterpillar food plant, *Aristolochia* species, grow. It spends most of its life in the meadow in which it was born and is strongly resident.

PIERIDAE

The Pieridae, which include the whites and sulfurs or sulphurs, do not have tails and are named after their white, yellow, and orange colors. Orange tips are typical of the whites, the males of which have distinctive orange tips on their otherwise white wings. Because of their gregarious behavior, whites and sulfurs can be very numerous, especially around water sources in tropical climates. Many, such as the Large and Small white, are pests since they breed on members of the *Cruciferae*, or cabbage family, which includes several plants grown as crops.

Many whites and sulfurs migrate. This not only increases their uniformity through breeding, but also increases their potential as pests. The white colors are used as a form of advertisement, and the combined effect of black markings on a white background makes these butterflies obvious to predators.

(The butterfly above is *Appias nero*.)

GENUS
ANTEOS

This is a genus of three relatively large yellow butterflies called "mammoth sulfurs," which are found in Central and South America. They are powerful fliers, all migratory, and some fly north into southern USA. The butterflies live in open, flowery habitats, the males mud-puddle, and the females almost certainly breed on *Cassia*.

ANTEOS MAERULA
Yellow Brimstone, Yellow-angled Sulfur

	ZONE 1·2
3½in 89mm	

This is a large butterfly which is yellow on both surfaces of its wings. The forewings are hooked, and the hindwing has a slight "tail." It is a strong migrant which colonizes scrubby areas, where it breeds on leguminous shrubs such as sennas and cassias including *Cassia emarginata*. Like A. *clorinde*, this species occurs in lowlands up to about 3,000ft (900m).

ANTEOS CLORINDE NIVIFERA
Ghost Brimstone, White-angled Sulfur

	ZONE 1·2
3½in 89mm	

This is a beautiful migrant butterfly with white uppers, marked with an orange bar on the forewing, and lime-yellow undersides. The forewings are hooked, and the hindwing has a slight "tail" which is a mere bump. The butterfly breeds on various leguminous plants including those in gardens, such as *Cassia emarginata*. The adult visits all sorts of garden flowers including *Hibiscus* and *Lantana* for nectar. It flies in lowlands up to 3,000ft (900m).

ANTEOS MENIPPE
Mammoth Sulfur

	ZONE 2
2⅝in 68mm	

This is a large "orange tip" of Latin America. The forewing is uniformly curved with a large area of orange on the apex. The margin of the apex is black, and the overall ground color of the wings is yellow-lemon. It is a migrant species. Like other members of the genus, the butterfly is very active in open sunny areas, often beside water, and the males sometimes congregate and indulge in mud-puddling. The butterfly breeds on *Cassia* species.

GENUS
ANTHOCHARIS

A genus of relatively small "white" butterflies which have brightly colored marks inside the tip of the forewings. The colors are usually orange-red, as are the orange tips. They occur mostly in Europe and North America, where they exploit cruciferous plants.

ANTHOCHARIS CARDAMINES
Orange Tip

The male is distinguished by the orange tip on the forewing. Both sexes have an attractive green mottling on the underside of the hindwing which is partially visible on the upperside. The butterfly frrequents damp areas, roadside, and hedges and breeds on various common cruciferous plants. It is a wanderer, rather than a migrant, and can colonize areas away from where it emerged. There is a single generation a year and a long flight period from March to May.

ANTHOCHARIS MIDEA
Falcate Orange Tip

The characteristic feature is the hooked forewing combined with the black dotting around the margins of the wings. The orange spot is only present in the male. The underside of the hindwing has an undistinguished attempt at mottling. The butterfly breeds on a large number of cruciferous plants and has a single brood each year. It may be found in serveral different types of habitat including open forests, waysides and recently disturbed ground.

ANTHOCHARIS BELIA
Moroccan Orange Tip

A delightful butterfly with orange tips and a yellow background in the male, and a hindwing underside suffused in bold green and yellow marks. The female lacks the yellow background of the male. The butterfly breeds on various mustards of the *Cruciferae*, and there is a single generation a year. It is found along waysides, woodland margins and in flowery fields.

ANTHOCHARIS LANCEOLATA
California White Tip, Gray Marble

The butterfly is white and lacks the orange tip typical of males. The forewing is slightly pointed, and the underside of the hindwing is mottled with brown. It flies in disturbed areas and canyons, and breeds on various crucifers belonging to the genus *Arabis* as well as on *Sisymbrium officinale*. There is a single generation each year.

ANTHOCHARIS SARA
Western Orange Tip, Sara Orange Tip

This has typical orange-tip colors on the uppers with mottled green on the underside. The forewing tip is rounded. There are some subspecies recorded, including a yellow mountain form. The butterfly breeds on a wide variety of plants belonging to the *Cruciferae*, and lives in light woodland and in alpine meadows and pastures.

GENUS
APHRISSA

A genus of South and Central American whites, similar to *Phoebis*, which have shiny undersides.

APHRISSA STATIRA
Yellow Migrant, Migrant Sulfur, Statira

ZONE
1·2

2⅝in
70mm

The female is a uniform yellow and has a thin and wavy black border on the forewing tip. The male lacks the black border, but has strong yellow-orange at the base of the wings, and pale yellow toward the outside. This is a common species and a regular migrant, breeding on *Cassia* and *Calliandra*.

GENUS
APORIA

A large genus of butterflies found throughout Europe and Asia.

APORIA CRATAEGI
Black-veined White

ZONE
3·5

2⅝in
68mm

Black veins cross the white wings and give this butterfly its common name. The wings are rather papery, and the butterflies lose their scales rapidly during their courtship rituals. The butterfly became extinct in Britain in 1930, but it remains a pest in some parts of Europe, breeding on cultivated fruit trees.

GENUS
APPIAS

A very distinctive genus of butterflies with strongly curved wings, especially in the male; this makes them powerful fliers. Many dwell in virgin rainforest, and males are common mud-puddlers. They occur in Africa, Asia (mainly), and in the Australian region including Australia itself. The sexes are usually completely different in color, the females darker with more subdued colors than the flashy males.

APPIAS CELESTINA
Common Migrant

ZONE
5·6

2⅝in
70mm

This migrant butterfly has sturdy curved forewings and is a strong flier. At least two subspecies are known, one of which is silvery blue. The other is light orange in the center of its wings and dark brown-black to the outside. The male is more often seen than the female, which probably spends more time in the rainforest canopy.

APPIAS DRUSILLA
Tropical White, Florida White

ZONE
1

2³⁄₈in
60mm

The forewing has the characteristic curved leading edge typical of appias butterflies. The uppers are white in the male and pale yellow in the female. The underside is a rather dirty yellow. There is variation in color, with some forms having more yellow on the uppers. The butterfly prefers woody habitats and breeds on various members of the *Capparidaceae*. It is continuously brooded in the south.

APPIAS EPAPHIA
Diverse White

ZONE
4

2³⁄₈in
60mm

The sexes are completely different. The male is white with a black apex to the forewing; the female is mostly black with a white base to the hindwing and a white bar and spots on the forewing. The butterfly prefers open bush and open woodland areas, where it breeds on *Capparis*, *Boscia* and *Niebuhria* species, all members of the *Capparidaceae* family. It is a common butterfly and will sometimes be found in large numbers.

APPIAS HOMBRONI

	ZONE 6

2⁵/₈in
70mm

The male is a faded steely blue on the upperside, with darkened veins on the underside. The female is dark with lighter areas to the base of the wings. Males mud-puddle and frequent riversides and clearings. The butterfly is found in Sulawesi.

APPIAS LALASSIS

	ZONE 5

2⁵/₈in
70mm

The forewings are not elegantly curved as in the more typical *Appias* butterflies. The ground color is a blue-white, and the apex of the forewings has a wide margin of black. There are two small spots on the forewing which are more intense on the underside. This butterfly is found in southeastern Asia, including Burma.

APPIAS NERO
Orange Albatross

	ZONE 5·6

2⁵/₈in
70mm

This is one of the most spectacular *Appias* butterflies. The sexes are completely different. The male is bright orange to brick-red, the female a dull brown. There are several subspecies known. The male is more often seen than the female, which stays in the canopy and rarely descends to mud-puddle. Males stream off the canopy and follow rainforest rivers downstream. Swift fliers of the open areas of rainforests, this species breeds on members of the *Capparidaceae*.

APPIAS PHAOLA
Congo White

	ZONE 4

2³/₈in
60mm

The ground color is white in the male and grayish white in the female. Both sexes have a broad black apex of the forewing and a dainty row of lunules on the margin of the hindwing. The hindwing can sometimes be yellow. Little is known of the ecology of this butterfly, but it may breed on members of the *Capparidaceae*.

APPIAS PLACIDA

The forewings are curved and relatively pointed, which is typical of the genus. The coloration is unusual in being dark brown to black with no marking except for a fine cream border. This is a powerful flier, which inhabits sunny rainforest river edges and clearings. It probably feeds on members of the *Capparidaceae*.

GENUS
ARCHONIAS

A genus of five South American species which are relatively small, have flattened antennal clubs, and slightly scalloped hindwings. Very little is known about their biology, let alone their caterpillar food plants, but the butterflies appear to mimic *Parides* and *Heliconius* species.

ARCHONIAS TEREAS APPROXIMATA

This species looks like a mimic of a female *Parides* swallowtail. The black elongated forewings, which have a central white area, and the black hindwings with their flash of red, are quite unmistakable in the subspecies *approximata*. The early stages of these butterflies have yet to be described. The butterfly lives in the open parts of the rainforest.

APPIAS SYLVIA
Woodland White

The male has a white ground color, while that of the female is tinged with yellow. The margins of the forewing are black which verge into lunules toward the trailing edge. The lunules are more pronounced on the margin of the female hindwing. This butterfly is a mimic of the male *Mylothris rhodope*. It frequents forested and open woodland.

ARCHONIAS BELLONA

This butterfly shows a close resemblance to heliconids in the shape of the wings and the pattern. Radiating red lines give a fiery look to the hindwings. The black forewings have a yellow-cream splash of color. The early stages of the butterfly are still to be elucidated.

GENUS
ASCIA

A genus of whites from North and South America, which live on open areas.

ASCIA MONUSTE
Southern White, Great Southern White

The sexes differ in that the female has two different color forms, light and dark. The male is white, and the female can be either like the male or as a dark form covered in dusky scales. The butterfly is strongly migratory at irregular intervals. It flies in coastal areas where it breeds on maritime crucifers.

GENUS
BELENOIS

A genus of medium-sized African butterflies which have white and yellow colors, often with a dark forewing apex. Some are strong fliers and are migratory. They breed on members of *Capparidaceae*, the caper family.

BELENOIS CREONA REVERINA
African Common White

2³/₈in
60mm

ZONE
4

The sexes are different. The male is white with a dark border speckled with white dots. The ground color of the female is cream or yellowish, but the outer half of the wings is a fairly uniform dark brown. The spot in the forewing cell is much larger in the female. The butterfly is sometimes migratory.

It is common through much of Africa, as its common name suggests, and it breeds on *Capparis* species.

BELENOIS RAFFRAYI
Raffray's White

2¹/₈in
55mm

ZONE
4

The black colors of this mountain species are wholly appropriate to aid in heat-absorption. The sexes are similar with generous black forewing tips and a blue-white base. The hindwing is black on the outer part and blue-gray on the inside. The underside is black, too. The caterpillar food plants are probably among the *Capparidaceae*.

BELENOIS AUROTA
Brown-veined White

2³/₈in
60mm

ZONE
4

The sexes are different. The male is white with a brown border around its wings punctuated with white spots. The larger female may be white or yellow with a broader border; it also has a larger spot at the end of the cell on the forewing. The butterfly occurs along woodland edges and bush where it breeds on *Capparis* and *Boscia* species.

BELENOIS THYSA
False Dotted Border

The sexes have the same pattern but different ground colors, white in the male and ocher in the female. The undersides of the hindwing are orange, and this shows through faintly to the upper surface. Other key features are the lack of a black spot in the forewing, and the triangular marks around the margins of the wings. It is a butterfly of the rainforest and light woodland, and it probably breeds on plants of the *Capparidaceae*.

3in / 78mm · ZONE 4

BELENOIS ZOCHALIA
Forest White

The key feature is the two thin black lines on the underside of the hindwing. The black apex contains five irregular white spots, and a series of sharp black marks occur around the margin of the hindwing. There is a dumb-bell-shaped black mark in the forewing cell. The ground color of the female is cream or yellow compared to the white of the male; otherwise, the sexes are similar in pattern. The butterfly is found in forests and woods, where it breeds on *Maerua* species of the *Capparidaceae*.

2½in / 65mm · ZONE 4

GENUS
CATASTICTA

This South American genus has over 100 species of checkered butterflies.

CATASTICTA URICOECHEAE

The brown and white mottled forewing has a row of small white chevrons inside the margin. The hindwing is red with a broad dark band and dark margin. Males can land on rivers, drink, and then take off again. Little is known about this butterfly's ecology.

2in / 50mm · ZONE 2

GENUS
CATOPSILIA

A genus of butterflies from Africa, occasionally southern Europe, Asia, and Australia. They have broad wings, often bright colors, and some are strong migrants. The sexes are often sexually dimorphic, and their caterpillar food plants include the *Leguminosae*, the pea family.

CATOPSILIA FLORELLA
African Migrant, African Emigrant

This is one of the most successful butterflies in Africa. It has fairly simple colors and lines. The male is pale white with a touch of green, and the female is yellow. There is mottling over the wings, and the underside is a little richer in yellows. This migrant butterfly occurs in several different types of habitat from forest, savanna, scrub and gardens. It breeds on *Cassia* species.

2⅝in / 70mm · ZONE 4

CATOPSILIA POMONA
Lemon Migrant, Lemon Emigrant

This butterfly exists in many different color forms, from fresh yellow to dark female forms. The lemon color is at the base of the wings. There are two basic types of variation, one with pink antennae, the other with black antennae. Tips of the wings are usually dark; this carries on around the wings, but peters out in some cases. The butterfly is a migrant and a strong flier which visits open areas, clearings in rainforest, and villages in search of nectar sources. It breeds on *Cassia* species.

3⅛in / 80mm · ZONE 5·6

CATOPSILIA SCYLLA
Yellow Migrant, Orange Emigrant

ZONE 5·6

2¹⁄₂in
65mm

The forewing is white with dark margins and apex, the hindwing pale to egg yellow with a few dark blemishes around the periphery. Several subspecies and forms exist, but these often have the same sort of contrasting colors on the wings. The butterfly is found in forest clearings and in villages. It breeds on *Cassia fistula* and *C. obtusifolia*.

GENUS
CEPORA

This is a genus of slow fliers of the lowlands which are found in Asia and the Australian region.

CEPORA ASPASIA RHEMIA

ZONE 5

2³⁄₈in
60mm

The male has creamy forewings crossed by black veins, with dark margins and apex. The egg yellow hindwings have a black margin. The female is similar, but lacks the luster of the male. There are at least 17 subspecies in the *Iudith* group. They fly in lowland forests.

GENUS
COLIAS

A very large and successful genus of "yellows," "sulfurs," and "clouded yellows" which are found mostly in the Northern Hemisphere in North America, Asia and the Australian regions. Other species occur in Africa and South America. Sexes are often dimorphic, and many are strong migrants, which has contributed to their success. They also breed extensively on members of the *Leguminosae*, the pea family.

COLIAS ALEXANDRA
Alexandra Sulfur, Ultraviolet Sulfur

ZONE 1

2³⁄₈in
60mm

The sexes have much the same pattern, although the female is less strongly marked. The ground color of the male is canary yellow with a darker apex of the forewing which is suffused with lighter areas. There is a tiny dark dot in the cell of the forewing. The hindwing lacks any strong marks. The butterfly exists as three subspecies and flies in open flowery woods and grassland. Marking experiments show that, on average, the butterfly moves no more than half a mile, and lives no longer than two weeks. It breeds on various members of the pea family, *Leguminosae*.

COLIAS BEHRII
Sierra Green Sulfur

ZONE 1

1¾in 44mm

This is quite a small sulfur, with dull green colors and a restricted distribution. It is identified by the dark greenish bloom over the wings. The butterfly is found in southern California. It frequents flowery meadows where the male exhibits patrolling flights close to the ground on the look-out for females. The female lays her eggs on willow and blueberry, plants typical of wetter habitats.

COLIAS CROCEUS
Clouded Yellow

ZONE 3·5

2⅛in 54mm

One of the most common clouded yellows in Europe, this is easily recognized by its strong orange color (not yellow as its common name implies). There are strong black margins, and these are decorated with yellow blobs in the female. Like many *Colias* it has attractive pink legs and antennae. The Clouded yellow always visits wild flowers in meadows and along waysides, and is a fast mover from flower to flower. It is also a very powerful migrant and covers most of Europe in its spring migratory waves.

COLIAS ELECTO
African Clouded Yellow

ZONE 4

2in 52mm

Unusually, the male is larger than the female. It is certainly the brighter of the two, which is usual, with rich orange wings and a black border. There is a single, conspicuous dot in the forewing cell. The female has eight pale yellow spots dispersed in her dark border, but her colors are very dull in comparison with the male. This African migrant lives in grassy and flowery areas, and breeds on alfalfa and clover. It is also found in Arabia.

COLIAS BOOTHII
Arctic Green Sulfur

ZONE 1

1½in 40mm

This is a hybrid of the Arctic green sulfur which has three named subspecies. *Boothii* hybrids are orange as opposed to the variable yellow-green of the true species. The butterfly lives in alpine meadows and breeds on *Astragulus* species.

COLIAS DIMERA

ZONE 2

1¾in 44mm

This is an interesting species which departs from the usual *Colias* characteristics. The forewings are orange, the hindwings are yellow, both with a dark base to the wings and a dark body. The apex and outer margin of the forewings are black, and there is no spot on the wings. The butterfly flies in open meadows.

COLIAS ERATE
Eastern Pale Clouded Yellow

ZONE 3

2in 52mm

Pale yellow-orange pervades the wings, which have dark borders smudged with yellow spots in the female and well-defined borders in the male. This migrant butterfly flies in flowery meadows, but its life cycle and caterpillar food plants have not been described. It occurs in eastern Europe.

COLIAS FIELDI

ZONE 5

2¹⁄₈in
54mm

This is very similar to *C. croceus* with orange wings, deeper on the hindwings than forewings, and a dark border around the wings. The spot in the forewing is large and conspicuous. The border is suffused with yellow-orange spots in the female compared to the unmarked borders of the male. A migrant butterfly, it occurs in flowery meadows and probably breeds on members of the *Leguminosae*.

COLIAS HYALE
Pale Clouded Yellow

ZONE 3

2in
50mm

The male is pale yellow, the female white, both with a weak orange spot on the hindwing and a black spot on the forewing. The black margins of the male have yellow spots; those of the female have white spots. The butterfly is a regular migrant and visits flowery meadows, including clover fields for nectar. It breeds on clover.

COLIAS LESBIA

ZONE 2

1³⁄₄in
46mm

This species exists in several forms, and one of the most interesting is a dark form which is found in the Andes. The rich orange colors are distinctive. The dark margins are present, but the characteristic of the species is the dark scales running along the veins from the margin. The female has wider margins which contain pale yellow marks. The butterfly occurs in alpine meadows.

COLIAS HECLA
Northern Clouded Yellow

ZONE 1·3

1³⁄₄in
46mm

An orange butterfly which has strong black markings at the forewing tip and around the margins in the male; these areas are infused with yellow in the female. The butterfly breeds on alpine milk vetch, *Astragulus alpinus*. It is a migrant species and flies in alpine meadows. Its distribution is probably over most of arctic Europe and North America.

COLIAS INTERIOR
Pink-edged Sulfur

ZONE 1

1⁷⁄₈in
48mm

Pink edging of the wings, as well as pink antennae and pink feet, is fairly widespread among this genus. But this species has conspicuous pink suffusions which run over the underside of the wings and on the body. The butterfly is found extensively across North America in clearings where it breeds on blueberry.

COLIAS MEADII
Alpine Orange

ZONE 1·2

1³⁄₄in
44mm

The uppers are deep orange with dark borders typical of the genus, but the undersides are greenish-black toward the base of the hindwing. There are two known subspecies. The butterfly occurs in alpine meadows of Montana and New Mexico. Adults appear to live about a week and are rather sedentary. They breed on clover.

COLIAS NASTES
Arctic Green Sulfur,
Pale Arctic Clouded Yellow

ZONE 1·3

1⁷⁄₈in
48mm

This butterfly frequents the high arctic regions. It has a pale lemon-yellow ground color with a dusting of gray marks near the forewing tip. A number of subspecies have been described. The butterfly may be found on bogs, moors, and in tundra habitat where its food plant, alpine milk vetch, *Astragulus alpinus*, is found.

COLIAS OCCIDENTALIS
Golden Sulfur

ZONE 1

2in
52mm

The golden description comes from the underside of the hindwing, which is a rather rich yellow and has a distinct reddish spot in the center. The upperside is also rich yellow with a dark border, uncluttered by marks in the male, but diffused with yellow spots in the female. The butterfly delights in lowland meadows, and the male engages in patrolling behavior to locate females. The female lays eggs on various species belonging to the *Leguminosae*.

COLIAS PALAENO
Arctic Sulfur, Moorland Clouded Yellow

ZONE 1·3

1⁷⁄₈in
48mm

This is a large butterfly which has conspicuous black edges to its wings. The male is a rich lemon color, and the female is pale cream. Both have pink fringes to the wings, pink legs, and pink antennae. Subspecies are known to exist. As its common names suggest, the butterfly occurs on arctic moorlands, and on bogs where its caterpillar food plant, the whortleberry, may be found.

COLIAS PELIDNE
Blueberry Sulfur

ZONE 1

1⁵⁄₈in
42mm

The sexes are different. The male has a yellow ground color, the female white. Both have a dark band around much of the margins of the wings and pink fringes. The underside of the male is orangey, while that of the female is dark yellow. The butterfly lives in alpine meadows and bogs in the tundra where it breeds on blueberry, *Vaccinium* species, after its common name. Males indulge in patrolling behavior.

COLIAS PHILODICE
Common or Clouded Sulfur, Mud-puddle

ZONE 1·2

1⅞in 48mm

The ground color of the male is lemon yellow with a dark band infused with traces of yellow along the veins. The female is slightly larger with a much broader dark band smudged with yellow. This is one of the most common butterflies in North America, though it is also found in Central America. Contributory to its success is the fact that the caterpillars will feed on a wide selection of leguminous plants. It lives in many sunny and flowery habitats. Its name of Mud-puddle reflects the male's behavior of drinking at puddles and streams.

COLIAS SCUDDERII GIGANTEA
Willow Sulfur

ZONE 1

2in 50mm

This is a form of the Willow sulfur, *C. scudderi*, with larger black borders and more green on the underside of the hindwings. *Gigantea* is one of two named subspecies. It occurs in the northern part of the species range well above the Arctic Circle of northwestern North America. The butterfly lives in flowery meadows, and probably does not wander too far from these localities in which it probably breeds on wild leguminous plants.

GENUS
COLOTIS

A large genus of small butterflies found in southern Europe, the Ethiopian region of Africa, and Asia. Species are recognized by the large patches of color on the forewing and the seasonal forms. Many fly in open tropical savanna and breed on members of the *Capparidaceae*, the caper family.

COLIAS SCUDDERII
Willow Sulfur

ZONE 1

1¾in 44mm

The sexes are different, which is typical of many *Colias*. The male is pale yellow, the female white, both with a dark margin. The undersides are much darker, especially the hindwing which has a prominent pink-edged spot in the center. The underside of the forewing is pale yellow with a small black spot. There are two named subspecies. The butterfly lives in arctic bogs and tundra, and may breed on various acid-loving plants such as blueberries and willows. The life cycle has yet to be described.

COLIAS VAUTIERI

ZONE 2

2in 50mm

This is a deep orange butterfly. The base of the wings is dark. In the forewing cell there is a single black spot. The female is slightly larger than the male, with less defined markings, especially on the forewing tip. Little is known of the life history of this butterfly.

COLOTIS AGOYE
Speckled Sulfur Tip

ZONE 4

1¾in 45mm

The key characteristic is the pointed forewing. The sexes are fairly similar with white wings, speckled with dark scales in wet-season forms, and an orange-ocher apex to the forewing. The female is slightly larger, with a black rim around the orange forewing tip and a little black scaling on the inside edge of the orange. In wet-season forms, the female may have darker veins to the outside edge. The butterfly flies in open bushy countryside.

COLOTIS ANTEVIPPE GAVISA
Red Tip

ZONE 4

1½in
40mm

Named after the red tip on the forewing, this characteristic is displayed most strongly in the male. There are many variable seasonal forms. The male is mostly white, but around the margin of the hindwing there may be a series of amazing diamond-shaped black marks. The female has a yellow ground suffused generously with black marks. It is a very common butterfly, found throughout grasslands where it breeds on various members of the caper family, *Capparidaceae*.

COLOTIS AURIGINEUS
Veined Gold, Double-banded Orange

ZONE 4

2in
50mm

The two common names reflect the "veined gold" appearance of the underside, particularly the hindwing, and the orange of the uppers which is crossed by a wavy band of black producing two orange areas broken by black veins. Only the male has a silvery base to the forewings. The margins of the wings are black highlighted by thin orange lines. The butterfly flies in upland and open grassy habitats as well as woodland and probably feeds on members of the caper family.

COLOTIS CALAIS
Topaz Arab, Small Salmon Arab

ZONE 4

1¾in
45mm

The outer half of the wings are black, especially the hindwing which encloses a few pale orange dots. The forewing has a dull orange ground color which infuses the darker apex. The female is similar in pattern, but slightly paler. The butterfly flies in upland and open grassy areas where it breeds on *Salvadora persica*, a member of the *Salvadoraceae* family. It is a moderate migrant in Saudi Arabia.

COLOTIS CELIMENE
Lilac Tip

ZONE 4

1¾in
45mm

The lilac tip is only present in the male. The female has a black tip to the forewing which is continuous, with a black band around the hindwing. The ground color is creamy white in the female, and white in the male, which also has a black hindwing band. The butterfly flies in open bush and savanna and probably feeds on members of the caper family.

COLOTIS ERIS
Banded Gold Tip, Black-barred Gold Tip

ZONE 4

2¹⁄₈in
55mm

The black and white markings in both sexes are very similar, but the ground colors differ, white in the male and cream in the female. The black markings are strong along the trailing edge of the forewing and around the apex of the wing. The male has some brown marks, but these are reduced in size and colored cream in the female. The butterfly lives in savanna and open bush areas where it breeds on various members of the caper family.

COLOTIS DANAE
Scarlet Tip, Crimson Tip

ZONE 4·5

2in
50mm

The sexes are dissimilar and very variable, but both have a scarlet tip. The ground color of the male is white with wings edged entirely in black. The white on the female is covered with a loose row of black spots and the base of the wings are gray. The scarlet tip of the female also has a row of black spots, and black scales encroach from the margins. The butterfly lives along woodland edges, in bush and savanna country, and breeds on *Cadaba* species belonging to the *Capparidaceae* family.

COLOTIS ELGONENSIS
Elgin Crimson Tip

ZONE 4

1³⁄₄in
45mm

The male has the crimson tip, which is composed of a series of oblong crimson spots lying very close together over a black background. The ground color of the male is white, and there is a small spot at the end of the forewing cell. The female lacks the crimson tip and has an off-white ground. The butterfly is found throughout the year in highland areas. It probably breeds on members of the caper family.

COLOTIS HALIMEDE COELESTIS
Orange Patch White, White and Orange Halimede, Dappled White

ZONE 4

2¹⁄₈in
55mm

The large orange smudge crosses the middle of the wings where the trailing and leading edges of the wings meet. The base of the wings are gray. In the female the orange band may be duller in color or even absent. The female also has gray spots on the forewing. The butterfly lives in dry grassy habitats and probably breeds on species of the caper family.

COLOTIS HETAERA
Crimson Tip

ZONE 4

2¹/₂in
65mm

The male has a most distinct crimson tip set in a dark apex. The rest of the wings are white with dark veins. The female has more black in the apex and much less crimson, with dots dispersed about the wings. Dry- and wet-season forms of the female can look completely different. In the wet-season form the female has thick dark margins around all wings and yellow-green on the rest of the wings. The butterfly occurs in savanna and bush country, and probably breeds on various members of the caper family.

COLOTIS REGINA
Large Violet Tip, Regal Purple Tip,
Queen Purple Tip

ZONE 4

2⁷/₈in
74mm

An impressive butterfly with violet tips in both sexes, though this is interspersed with white and deep purple-red marks in the female. The ground color of the male is white, but cream in the female. The trailing margin of the hindwing has a series of black marks which creep up the veins in an attractive manner. The underside edges of the hindwing are tinged orange. The species flies in bush country and probably breeds on members of the caper family.

COLOTIS VESTA AMELIA
Veined Orange

ZONE 4

2³/₈in
60mm

The distinguishing mark of this species is the large white base to all the wings. The outer half of each wing is black with traces of orange near the margin. The female is similar to the male, but not so bright. The butterfly may be seen throughout the year and inhabits open grassy and arid habitats. It is a very variable species and probably breeds on members of the caper family.

COLOTIS IONE
Purple Tip, Violet Tip

ZONE 4

2⁵/₈in
70mm

Three specimens of the same species can look very different. The male has violet tips to its white wings, the dry-season form of the female has red tips to its yellow wings, and the wet-season form of the female has red tips and white marks set in a black ground color. The butterfly lives in open savanna and open woodland, and breeds on various members of the caper family.

GENUS
DELIAS

This is a group of 70 or more gaily colored butterflies from Asia and the Australian region. The bright colors of the undersides are thought to be a warning to predators, and some of the butterflies are involved in mimicry with zygaenid moths. *Delias* have gregarious caterpillars which live in silken webs on their food plants, members of the *Loranthaceae*, the mistletoe family.

DELIAS BAGOE

The uppers have a fawn ground color with an orange apex to the forewing and a small amount of black around the apex. The rear part of the hindwings have a thick black band. The butterfly lives in open sunny habitats.

DELIAS HARPALYCE

The underside of the hindwing is distinctive, with a kinked red line of spots crossing the wing and a row of irregular yellow-orange spots near the outer margin of the underside of the forewing. The uppers are gray to the center, with dark outer areas containing a row of dull orange marks. The butterfly can be abundant one year, scarce the next.

DELIAS ARUNA

This butterfly has a spectacular underside, since the lower half of the hindwing is mostly red in contrast to the rich brown ground color. There is a tiny white mark in each of the red areas. A line of brown cuts the red areas into two unequal parts. The underside of the forewing is also brown, with some of the white marks showing through in the cell region. The upperside is brilliant orange with black tips to the forewing.

DELIAS EUCHARIS
Common Jezebel

The underside is the most characteristic feature of this black-veined butterfly. The hindwing underside is bright with an egg-yellow base and a row of red wedge-shaped marks around the black margin. There is a touch of yellow on the apex of the underside of the forewing. The butterfly occurs in many habitats including garden areas.

DELIAS HENNINGIA

The forewings of both sexes are dark, but in the female they are smudged with a blue dusting to form two vague lines. In the male the bottom half of the wings has a distinct area of steel blue. The yellow on the black hindwing of the male is much more defined than in the diffuse female. There are various subspecies, and in *D. henningia ottonia* there is a flash of red at the base of the hindwing, as in this specimen.

GENUS
DERCAS

A genus of butterflies which occurs from India to China.

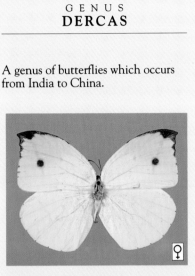

DERCAS LYCORIAS

| ZONE | 5 |
| 2³/₈in 60mm | |

The sexes are fairly similar in pattern and size, though the female forewing is more hooked and less colorful than the bright yellow male. The forewings are brown around the apex and have a very obvious brown spot. The hindwings are relatively unmarked.

GENUS
DISMORPHIA

These butterflies have no exceptional features, but they are a large and widely distributed genus in South America. Little is known about their populations or their caterpillar food plants, though *Inga*, a leguminous plant, may be used. Many of the dismorphids are involved in mimicry.

DISMORPHIA CORDILLERA

| ZONE | 2 |
| 2⁷/₈in 74mm | |

This is a particularly large dismorphid butterfly which looks distinctly like a heliconid, which it probably mimics. The long forewings are very dark with plenty of long yellow marks. The hindwing has a radiating red pattern, similar to that of *Heliconius erato*, with just a few yellow marks.

DISMORPHIA SPIO
Haitian Mimic

| ZONE | 2 |
| 2³/₄in 72mm | |

The color is very variable from yellow, orange to brown. The body is long and thin, and the forewing is strongly curved, almost making a hook-tip. This is clearly a mimic of another butterfly, almost certainly a heliconid with long forewings and similar color and pattern. The butterfly occurs in the Antilles, and in rainforest above 2,000ft (610m). Its caterpillar food plant remains unknown.

GENUS
DIXEIA

A genus of butterflies found in Africa and Madagascar. They are white or yellow and generally small butterflies. They live in forested areas as well as savanna and breed on members of the *Capparidaceae*, the caper family.

DIXEIA DOXO COSTATA
African Small White

| ZONE | 4 |
| 2in 50mm | |

This is rather like *Pieris rapae*, but with fewer spots. The male is white with a black apex and partial margin in black. The female has slightly more black at the margins and a single black spot on the forewing. The spot is prominent on the underside of the forewing. The butterfly occurs in many habitats and is widespread in Africa, breeding on *Capparis* species. A very similar species. *D. charina*, is also known as the African Small White.

DIXEIA SPILLERI
Spiller's Yellow

ZONE
4

1³/₄in
45mm

This has very simple features. The male is pure yellow, uncluttered with marks on the center of the wing, with a serrated black border and apex. The female is similar, but the shade of yellow verges toward ocher. The butterfly frequents woodlands and forests. It probably breeds on various members of the caper family.

GENUS
ELPHINSTONIA

A North African genus of small butterflies whose range extends eastward.

ELPHINSTONIA CHARLONIA
Greenish Black Tip

ZONE
3·4·5

1³/₈in
36mm

This is a little lemon-yellow butterfly with a mottled black tip and gray-black base to its wings. The yellows verge on greenish lines. There is a black spot in the forewing cell, and this is larger in the female. A number of subspecies exist throughout its range. It occurs in open flowery areas and breeds on *Matthiola tessala*.

GENUS
EROESSA

A genus with a single rare species found only high in the mountains of Chile.

EROESSA CHILENSIS

ZONE
2

2 in
50mm

Overall the wings are white with a black forewing which contains a broad band of orange. The underside is similar, but with yellow on the tip. Faint black dots run around the margin of the hindwing, the underside of which is yellow mottled with dark squiggles.

GENUS
ERONIA

A genus of African butterflies, found also in Saudi Arabia, breeding on *Capparis*.

ERONIA CLEODORA
Vine Leaf Vagrant

ZONE
4

2⁵/₈in
70mm

The undersides have a cryptic leaf-like pattern in brown, white and yellows. The uppersides are cream and black separated by a ragged line. A migrant with seasonal and regional forms, it flies in open woodland and breeds on *Capparis*.

GENUS
EUCHLOE

A genus found throughout Europe and Asia, with some species in North America and Africa. The butterflies tend to be small and white, with dappled undersides to the hindwing.

EUCHLOE AUSONIA
Dappled Marble, Dappled White,
Mountain Dappled White

ZONE
1·3
4·5

1⁷/₈in
48mm

The butterfly has light-colored uppers. The black spot on the forewing touches the margin and is dispersed along it a little way. The undersides are dappled in green. There are several subspecies recorded. The butterfly occurs in mountainous regions, breeding on a wide variety of members of the cabbage family. It does have some powers of dispersal over several miles.

EUCHLOE BELEMIA
Green-striped White

This butterfly is named after the way the white on the underside of the hindwing runs across the overall mottled green color to produce a striped effect. The uppersides are white with dark margins. The apex is suffused with white patches. The life cycle of this species has yet to be determined.

EUCHLOE HYANTIS
Pearl Marblewing

The marbling over the white underside of the hindwing is very evident. Another key feature is the almost rectangular black mark in the forewing cell, seen on both surfaces. The uppers are white with interrupted gray scales near the tip of the forewing. The butterfly flies in deserts and canyons, and breeds on a variety of crucifers including *Descurainia pinnata* and *Caulanthus* species.

EUREMA DAIRA
Barred Sulfur

The male is more heavily marked than the female, with brown markings obscuring most of the yellow on the forewing. The white hindwing is edged in brown. The female has much less brown on the wings, and more white than yellow on the forewing. The underside of the hindwing is slightly russet. This migrant butterfly lives in all sorts of open flowery habitats and breeds on *Aeschynomene* and *Stylosanthes* species, members of the *Leguminosae* family.

EUCHLOE CREUSA
Northern Marble, Northern Marblewing

The upperside is white with a small amount of darkening of the apex of the forewing and a small spot in the cell region. This forewing spot and dark apex are visible from below. The underside of the hindwing is marbled in green and white. The butterfly frequents alpine meadows and breeds on *Draba* species.

GENUS
EUREMA

This is a widespread genus of small butterflies which have a circumtropical distribution. They are usually lemon-yellow with black borders. Males often have a long scent patch on the forewing. The caterpillars feed on a wide variety of members of the *Leguminosae*, pea family.

EUREMA HAPALE
Pale Grass Yellow

This is a small butterfly of very pale yellow colors. There is a relatively large black apical mark, but otherwise the wings are unmarked. The sexes are similar. The butterfly is fairly well distributed in Africa and frequents moist habitats such as damp grasslands, marshes and streamsides.

EUREMA HECABE SOLIFERA
Common Grass Yellow

ZONE 4·5	
1½in 40mm	

The roundness of the hindwing and the bulging nature of the margin of the forewing are distinctive. The male has a yellow ground with an extensive wavy-edged brown-black apical mark. The female is slightly larger with similar markings. This is a common migrant butterfly found in a variety of habitats from savanna to scrub and gardens. It breeds on several members of the pea family.

EUREMA PROTERPIA
Little Jaune

ZONE 1·2	
2in 52mm	

Like many of the *Eurema*, this butterfly has an angled hindwing. The sexes are different. The male is bright orange with or without black scales running along the veins, and with a bar of black on the leading edge of the forewing. The female is a duller orange with dull black around the hindwing margin. This butterfly occurs from sea level to mountains, and breeds on *Desmodium* species.

EUREMA LISA
Little Sulfur

ZONE 1·2	
1½in 38mm	

This is a small butterfly which has a distinctive brown forewing apex in contrast to the yellow ground. There is a little brown around the yellow hindwing, the underside of which is covered with faint brown spots. The butterfly is migratory and may be very common. It enjoys open flowery areas, often disturbed by man, and breeds on members of the pea family including *Cassia* species.

EUREMA MEXICANA

ZONE 1·2	
2in 50mm	

This is a dainty butterfly. The male has continuous irregular-sized patches of black around the wings, whereas the female only has black patches on the forewing. Yellow is present on the leading edge of the hindwing. The ground color in both sexes is palest yellow. There is a faint protuberance, or tail, on the hindwing. The butterflies are found in open areas of forest up to 6,550ft (2,000m) and breed on *Diphysa robinoides* and *Cassia* species.

GENUS
GANYRA

A genus of North and South American butterflies which are powerful fliers, and some are strong migrants. They live in open areas and breed on members of the *Capparidaceae*, *Cruciferae* and *Tropaeolaceae* – caper, crucifer or cabbage, and nasturtium families.

GANYRA JOSEPHINA
Giant White

	ZONE 1
2³/₄in 73mm	

The wings are white to cream, somewhat curved and drawn-out, and relatively unmarked. The female often has a few gray marks in the cells and toward the apex of the forewing. The butterfly occurs in southern Texas. Its caterpillar food plant is unknown.

GANYRA BUNIAE

	ZONE 2
3¹/₈in 80mm	

This butterfly is rather like a blue form of the Cabbage white, *Pieris brassicae*, particularly in the male which has a dark margin, but is otherwise completely blue-white on the uppers. Much darker female forms which are smudged along many of the veins with brown scales sometimes occur. There is an interesting difference between two color forms: those that migrate are gray, while the non-migratory ones are yellow-white with dark margins.

GONEPTERYX CLEOPATRA
Cleopatra

	ZONE 3·4
2¹/₂in 65mm	

This is slightly larger than *G. rhamni*, and the male has a large area of orange in the middle of its forewing which is not always easy to see from the underside. The female is a typical weak green color. Easy to identify on the wing, it is more difficult to recognize when feeding. It flies in wooded and rural areas where it breeds on buckthorns, *Rhamnus* species.

GENUS
GONEPTERYX

A genus containing a few species of large yellow and pale green butterflies which extends from Europe to Asia. The wings are broad and slightly hooked, and the underside is fairly cryptic to help the adults during their hibernation.

GONEPTERYX RHAMNI
Brimstone

	ZONE 3·4·5
2³/₈in 60mm	

The sexes are different colors. The male is bright lemon-yellow, the female lime green, each with a single small orange spot in the center of the wings. The wings are strongly curved, which helps to disguise the insect among the ivy leaves where it probably hibernates. The butterfly lives along waysides, scrubby areas and light woodland where its food plants, the buckthorns, *Rhamnus catharticus* and *R. frangula* occur.

GENUS
HEBOMOIA

This is a genus of three species with orange tips and wings, two are found in Asia and one in South America. They are all strong fliers which frequent watercourses, trails and forest edges. Many subspecies are recorded for the Asian species.

HEBOMOIA LEUCIPPE DETANII

This differs from *H. glaucippe* in having most of its forewing bright orange, instead of simply the tip. The forewing is crossed by black veins with a definite serrated black border. The hindwing is yellow. The butterfly travels along open valleys, clearings, streams and river banks where it settles to mud-puddle. It probably breeds on the caper family.

HEBOMOIA GLAUCIPPE
Great Orange Tip

The flight of a male alongside a rainforest river or track is most impressive, the bright orange tips of the wings easing identification. Both sexes have these orange tips, but the female is seen less often than the male. There are a number of subspecies known. One of the most impressive is *H. glaucippe vossi* with bright yellow hindwings. The underside is dull and mottled, and rather leaf-like. This is the largest pierid butterfly in Asia, and it can be quite common in lowlands, breeding on members of the caper family.

GENUS
HESPEROCHARIS

A genus of ten South American species, whose biology is mostly, as yet, unknown.

HESPEROCHARIS GRAPHITES

The underside of the creamy hindwing is attractively covered with a tracery of black marks with yellow toward the base of the forewing. The hindwing is slightly scalloped. The butterfly frequents open places in rainforest and drinks nectar. The caterpillar food plants are unknown.

GENUS
ITABALLIA

A genus of four South American species, whose biology is mostly, as yet, unknown.

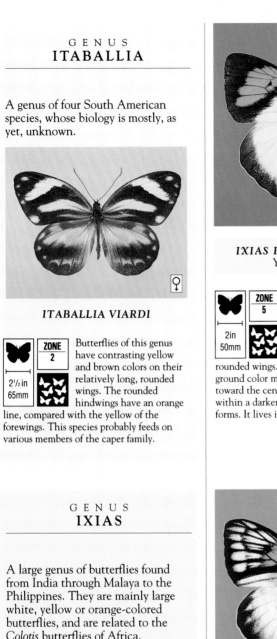

ITABALLIA VIARDI

Butterflies of this genus have contrasting yellow and brown colors on their relatively long, rounded wings. The rounded hindwings have an orange line, compared with the yellow of the forewings. This species probably feeds on various members of the caper family.

	ZONE 2
2½in 65mm	

GENUS
IXIAS

A large genus of butterflies found from India through Malaya to the Philippines. They are mainly large white, yellow or orange-colored butterflies, and are related to the *Colotis* butterflies of Africa. Caterpillars feed on *Capparis* species.

IXIAS PYRENE PIRENASSA
Yellow Orange Tip

This species appears to exist as an hitherto unsorted complex of species and forms. The general form and pattern are fairly constant, a neat, compact butterfly with rounded wings. However, the colors vary. The ground color may be yellow, orange or white toward the center, with yellow or orange tips within a darker margin. There may be darker forms. It lives in hills up to 3,000ft (900m).

	ZONE 5
2in 50mm	

IXIAS REINWARDTI PAGENSTECHERI

This pretty butterfly has a bold, net-like forewing with contrasting black veins against a pale lemon ground color. The male has an orange blotch toward the base of the forewing, but this is absent in the female. The hindwing is pale yellow with a dark margin. Fairly restricted in its range, this butterfly is only found on a few of the eastern islands of Indonesia.

	ZONE 5·6
2⅛in 55mm	

IXIAS UNDATUS

The differences between the male and female of this species are striking. The male is rich egg-yellow on its uppers with a thin dark margin around the wings. On the tip of the forewing there is a generous flash of orange set in a dark apex. The female is less extravagantly colored, in palest blue with a dark apex and margins. The butterfly frequents open clearings along rainforest rivers and in secondary vegetation.

	ZONE 6
3in 76mm	

GENUS
LEPTOSA

A genus of Asia and Africa which are white and medium-sized with rounded wings.

LEPTOSA ALCESTA
African Wood White

The sexes are similar, and there may or may not be a small dot on the forewing and a dark patch on the apex. This feeble flier frequents shady woods and forests and breeds on *Richea* species.

	ZONE 4
1¾in 45mm	

GENUS
MELETE

There are about ten species in this genus, but there is some doubt about these generally colorful South American butterflies being pierids. They are identified by their long antennae and the black bar which runs through the forewing cell. They may breed on members of the mistletoe family, *Loranthaceae*, and may also be migratory, for they are powerful fliers.

MELETE POLYMNIA

ZONE 2

2½in 65mm

The strong, slightly pointed forewings of this species are typical of this genus. The ground color is a rich lemon-yellow with a dark apex to the forewing, and a black band with some yellow spots around the trailing edge of the hindwing. It flies in forest margins and clearings.

MELETE LYCIMNIA

ZONE 2

2⅝in 70mm

The undersides are brighter than the uppers, yellow on the hindwing with a clear-cut thick band of brown to the outside. The forewing is light on the inside with dark and yellow marks at the apex. The uppers are mostly white with a dark margin and a thin brown rim to the hindwing. Subspecies exist, and yellow hindwings in the female are sometimes found. The butterfly frequents forest margins and clearings.

MYLOTHRIS CHLORIS AGATHINA
Dotted Border, Common Dotted Border

ZONE 4

2¼in 56mm

This common butterfly is very variable and takes its name from the dotted border around all the wings. Both male and female have at least two color forms, which are regional in distribution. The male exists in creamy white or with a white ground color strongly tipped in black. The female may be strong orange or white with half the hindwing black, the other a sandy color. The butterfly is found in many different types of habitat, from gardens to savanna, where it breeds on various members of the mistletoe family.

GENUS
MYLOTHRIS

A genus of over 50 species found in Africa. They are generally white or yellow. *Mylothris* butterflies are poor fliers and generally fly slowly. They are often seen in the foliage of forest trees.

MYLOTHRIS RHODOPE
Tropical Dotted Border, Rhodope

ZONE 4

2½in 65mm

Both sexes have the familiar dotted border typical of the genus, but the ground color varies considerably. The male is usually white with a black tip to the forewing. The female forewing may be white, yellow or strongly orange, and the off-white hindwing has larger spots around the margin than the male. The butterfly lives in rainforest areas. Both the male and female are mimicked by various species of *Appias*, *Belenois* and *Dixeia*.

GENUS
NEOPHASIA

A small genus of butterflies found in Central America and reaching into the southern USA. They are closely related to the genus *Catasticta*.

NEOPHASIA TERLOOTII
Chiricahua Pine White, Mexican PineWhite

ZONE 1·2

2¼in 57mm

The sexes look completely different. The males are black and white with a distinctive black area filling the forewing cell around the apex of the wing, and heavy black veining throughout. The female is deep orange with reddish marks, but also has the dark veins and black areas. Named after the Chiricahua Mountains of Arizona where the butterfly may be seen, it lives in forested areas and breeds on *Pinus ponderosa*.

NEOPHASIA MENAPIA

ZONE 1

2in 51mm

This is a beautiful white butterfly with an orange margin around the underside of the hindwing and heavy black veining. The ground color is white with irregular black marks sculptured around the apex of the forewing. A guide to identification is that this species is only found among pine trees, often fluttering high among the branches. It breeds on the pine and may be a pest.

GENUS
NEPHERONIA

Mostly an African genus, but with a species in the Indian subcontinent. The butterflies are relatively large, and white or yellow with black margins. They are strong fliers and generally powerful migrants.

NEPHERONIA ARGIA
Large Vagrant

ZONE 4

3⅛in 83mm

A highly variable migrant species which not only varies between sexes and within sexes, these butterflies also have different seasonal and regional forms. Males are often pale white or blue-white-green. Females are more variable, being pale yellow, deep yellow, or orange-yellow with a reddish flush on the base of the forewings. The butterfly is a powerful flier and lives in forests, woods and scrubby areas. It is the largest member of the white family of butterflies in South Africa.

NEPHERONIA THALASSINA
Cambridge Vagrant

ZONE 4

2⅜in 60mm

The key feature is the underside which has a pearly gloss lacking in *N. argia*. The male has a greenish hue, while the female can be any color from white, yellow to orange on its hindwings, and even on its forewings. The female has more black around the apex of the white forewing than the male. The female also has larger spots around the trailing edge of the hindwing. This migrant butterfly is a swift flier usually associated with woods and forests.

GENUS
PARERONIA

A genus of Asian and Australian butterflies with polymorphic females.

▲

PARERONIA VALERIA HIPPIA
Wanderer

 | ZONE 5 | 3¹/₈in 80mm

Males are light blue with black veins and a thick black margin around all wings. Females are black with blue veining and speckling. There are several subspecies. It is found up to 3,000ft (900m) in clearings in secondary vegetation. It breeds on *Capparis*.

PARERONIA TRITAEA

 | ZONE 6 | 4in 100mm

This species is dull brown with a tracery of yellowish markings all over its wings, radiating out from the center between the dark veins and as a row of spots behind the margin of the wings. It is very variable with many subspecies. The butterfly is found on the equatorial island of Sulawesi in Indonesia.

GENUS
PEREUTE

A genus of South American butterflies with a black ground color and strident yellow or red bands.

PEREUTE LEUCODROSIME

 | ZONE 2 | 2⁷/₈in 74mm

The soft blue dusting over the base of the wings is typical of several of this genus of butterflies. This species has a substantial red bar across the otherwise black forewings. The butterfly only occurs west of the Andes from Venezuela to Peru.

GENUS
PHOEBIS

A genus of butterflies found entirely in North and South America. They are large and fast flying, and all are migrants. They exploit areas where forest has been cleared, and some breed on members of the *Leguminosae*, the pea family. The sexes are dimorphic.

PHOEBIS AVELLANEDA
Red-splashed Sulfur

	ZONE 2
3¹⁄₂in 90mm	

The red splashing occurs on both sides of the butterfly, though it is more extensive in the female. The smaller male is mostly splashed with red on the uppers with a little area of yellow on the forewing. The underside is dull orange with a few short dark lines. The female uppers are mostly red, but with lots of black spots, particularly on the forewing. The underside is strongly marked in red, with a collection of white spots in the cell of the forewing. The life cycle of this particular butterfly is unknown.

PHOEBIS AGARITHE
Large Orange Sulfur

	ZONE 1·2
2³⁄₄in 72mm	

Males are rich yellow with unmarked uppers. The underside is slightly less bright, but there is a faint line crossing the forewing. The female may have different forms, either pale orange-brown or a mottled shiny gray, both with a forewing spot and line. This migrant butterfly lives in lowland forest and takes nectar. It breeds on various members of the pea family.

PHOEBIS ARGANTE
Apricot Sulfur, Argante Giant Sulfur

	ZONE 1·2
2⁷⁄₈in 74mm	

The sexes are different. The male has an unbroken line across the forewing, and the underside has less red-brown compared with the female. Females may be yellow or whitish, with a spot and a black apex to the forewing and brown checks around the hindwing. The butterfly is migratory and likes open areas of cleared forest, where it breeds on a variety of opportunist leguminous scrub species including *Cassia* and *Inga*.

PHOEBIS PHILEA
Orange-barred Sulfur, Yellow Apricot

ZONE
1·2

3½in
90mm

The sexes are different. The male has a uniform yellow ground color smudged with orange on the forewing and on the trailing edge of the hindwing. The female has at least two forms, one yellow with a prominent rosy trailing edge to the hindwing, and another mottled grayish pink with a dark margin. The butterfly is a strong migrant. Males are aggressive maters. In 15 to 30 seconds a male will roughly apprehend an overflying female, knock her to the ground, and copulate. The butterfly breeds on members of the pea family.

PHOEBIS SENNAE EUBULE
Cloudless Sulfur

ZONE
1·2

2¾in
72mm

The sexes are different in this migrant species. The male is yellow and unmarked. The female is the palest yellow with an edging of undulating black-brown marks and a conspicuous forewing spot. The underside is variously mottled with brown marks arranged in broken lines. The butterfly can be abundant in both lowland and highland. It prospers in open land and breeds on species of *Cassia*.

PIERIS BRASSICAE
Large White, Cabbage White

ZONE
1·2·3
4·5

2½in
65mm

This is one of the most successful butterflies in Europe. The female is usually a little larger than the male, with more spots on the forewing. Several subspecies exist, including one on the Azores. The butterfly occurs in many types of habitats, especially urban and horticultural. It has been found breeding on over 100 food plants, and it can be a pest. It is a powerful migrant and can top up failing populations by immigration. It has been introduced to South America and may spread north.

GENUS
PIERIS

A widespread and successful genus found in North America, Europe, Asia, with introductions into South America (as well as North), and into the Australian region. Part of the success of *Pieris* is due to the fact that they have fully exploited members of the *Cruciferae* as caterpillar food plants. Some species are strong migrants; others have become pests on *Brassica* crops.

PHOEBIS RURINA

ZONE
2

3⅛in
80mm

The male is a uniform rich yellow and very attractive. There are at least two types of female; pale white-cream with an orange trailing edge to the hindwing, or pale white. Both forms have a small forewing spot. The characteristic drawn-out hindwing tail is present in both sexes. A strong migrant, this butterfly inhabits lowland and highland and breeds on *Cassia fruticosa*.

PIERIS NAPI
Green-veined White, Sharp-veined White

ZONE
1·3·5

2in
50mm

The veins are suffused with green, especially on the underside of the hindwing and more so in later generations. The female has more spots on the forewing than the male. There are a number of sub-species which exist including yellow and dark forms. The butterfly prefers damp habitats such as meadows, fields and waysides where its caterpillar food plants exist. Unlike its relatives, it tends to be resident rather than migratory.

PIERIS RAPAE
Small White, Sharp-veined White

ZONE 1·3·5

2¹/₈in
55mm

This is a smaller version of the Large White, *P. brassicae*, in pattern, size and color. It is a migrant, too, and covers much of Europe with its invasions. It breeds on crucifers like the Large White and can be a pest. Unlike the Large White, whose white caterpillars live on the leaves, those of the Small White live inside the plants, such as in the heart of a cabbage. The butterfly was introduced to Quebec in about 1860 and to California possibly in 1866. Since then, it has colonized most of the US.

♀

PIERIS VIRGINIENSIS
Diffuse-veined White

ZONE 1

1³/₄in
45mm

As its common name implies, the markings on this butterfly are diffuse instead of sharp, and the underside hindwing markings are scattered with gray-green scales. It is a migrant found in various northeast-coast states of the US and flies in slightly drier habitats than the Sharp-veined White, *P. rapae*.

GENUS
PINACOPTERYX

A small genus of African butterflies with alternating light and dark bands.

PINACOPTERYX ERIPHIA
Zebra White

ZONE 4

2¹/₂in
65mm

Both sexes have thick and uniform bands of black and white, cream, or yellow. However, there is variation among seasonal forms, those of the dry season being paler. The butterfly is found in grassy and open scrubby areas. It breeds on *Capparis oleoides* and *Maerua triphylla*, both members of the *Capparidaceae* family.

GENUS
PONTIA

A genus of butterflies from Europe, Africa and Asia. They are small white butterflies with mottled green undersides, and they breed on members of the *Cruciferae*. Some species are strong migrants.

PONTIA CHLORIDICE
Small Bath white, Great Basin white

Like other whites the female has more spotting, and is slightly bigger than the male. It takes its British common name from the town of Bath in Avon where its representation was first recognized in a tapestry. The American common name is from one region where the butterfly occurs, though it is found in much of the western United States. It breeds on various cruciferous plants.

PONTIA BECKERII
Sagebrush White

The large black, somewhat squarish spot in the forewing cell is characteristic, and the sexes are fairly similar. The undersides of the hindwing and the tip of the forewing are both mottled in green-white. This is a butterfly of the desert, foothills, sage hills and canyons where the familiar sagebrush grows. It breeds, however, on the cruciferous plants which occur along streamsides and canyon bottoms.

PONTIA CALLIDICE
Peak White

The female has more black markings on the forewings and forewing tips than the male, and the gray-green markings on the underside of the hindwing show through more in the female. The butterfly flies in mountainous areas in flowery meadows where it find its caterpillar food plants *Erysimum pumilum* and *Reseda* species. Up to two generations occur in Europe and three in North America.

PONTIA HELICE
Mustard White, Meadow White

This is a relatively small white, which is more strongly marked with black in the female. In other respects the sexes are similar. The black tip has a few characteristic white marks, and there is a rectangular mark in the forewing cell. The trailing edge of the hindwing has a row of black dots. As its common name suggests, the butterfly flies in meadows, in highland areas, and on grassy plateaus in particular. It breeds on various members of the cabbage family such as *Sisymbrium* species.

▲

PONTIA OCCIDENTALIS
Western White

The uppers are white, but sprinkled with lots of gray marks toward the apex of the forewing and the trailing edge of the hindwing. There is a gray rectangular spot in the forewing cell. The underside of the hindwing has green-yellow veins, and the dark markings of the forewing upper show through on the underside. Females are more heavily marked. The butterfly occurs in lowland as well as upland, including alpine meadows. It breeds on crucifers or *Cleome* species.

PONTIA PROTODICE
Common White, Checked White

The checked appearance of the uppers gives this migrant butterfly its name. The forewings appear mostly black with white spots in the female, and white with black spots and marks in the male. The undersides can be rather smudgy yellow-green with indistinct marks. The butterfly enjoys open areas, especially those associated with man, and breeds on all sorts of opportunist crucifers as well as *Cleome* species.

PONTIA SISYMBRII
Spring White

The sexes are rather similar with a forewing spot and dark markings on the apex of the forewing, and the undersides are variously mottled with gray-black along the veins. The butterfly enjoys the arid countryside of steppe, desert and rocky slopes. It is one of the earliest butterflies to take wing each year, hence the common name. Its specific name refers to one of the common crucifers on which a number of whites breed.

GENUS
PRESTONIA

The distinguishing feature of this genus is the shiny undersides of the wings.

PRESTONIA CLARKI

This species has rich mottled orange over its wings and a black spot in the cell of the forewings. This butterfly is generally quite common, and success is due to having several leguminous caterpillar food plants on which it breeds. It lives in open areas and visits gardens for nectar sources.

PRIONERIS

A small genus of butterflies from India to Malaya which breeds on *Capparis*.

PRIONERIS CLEMANTHE
Redspot Sawtooth

ZONE 5

3⅛ in
80mm

The uppers are gray-blue on the forewing, pale yellow on the base of the hindwing. The basal half of the underside of the hindwing is bright orange with a tiny red mark. It is found in the forest canopy with other pierids at damp drinking stations.

ZERENE

A genus of North and South American species which have very distinctive markings on the uppers. The butterflies live in many sorts of semi-natural habitats and breed on various members of the *Leguminosae*, the pea family.

ZERENE CESONIA
Dog-face Butterfly

ZONE 1·2

2⅝in
68mm

Named after the characteristic dog face present on the forewing. This feature is best seen in the male, since the female is somewhat mottled and lacks the dark marks on the hindwing. Both sexes have a spot on the forewing. This is a common butterfly whose distribution corresponds to cattle ranching, since the leguminous plants on which the butterflies breed are promoted for cattle.

ZERENE EURYDICE
Californian Dog Face, Flying Pansy

ZONE 1

2½in
64mm

The male shows the typical dog-face characteristic, with its black apex markings indented to the inside around the violet-tinged base of the wing. The hindwing is orange. In the female the ground color is pale lemon with little trace of the dog face. The butterfly is found in the California foothills.

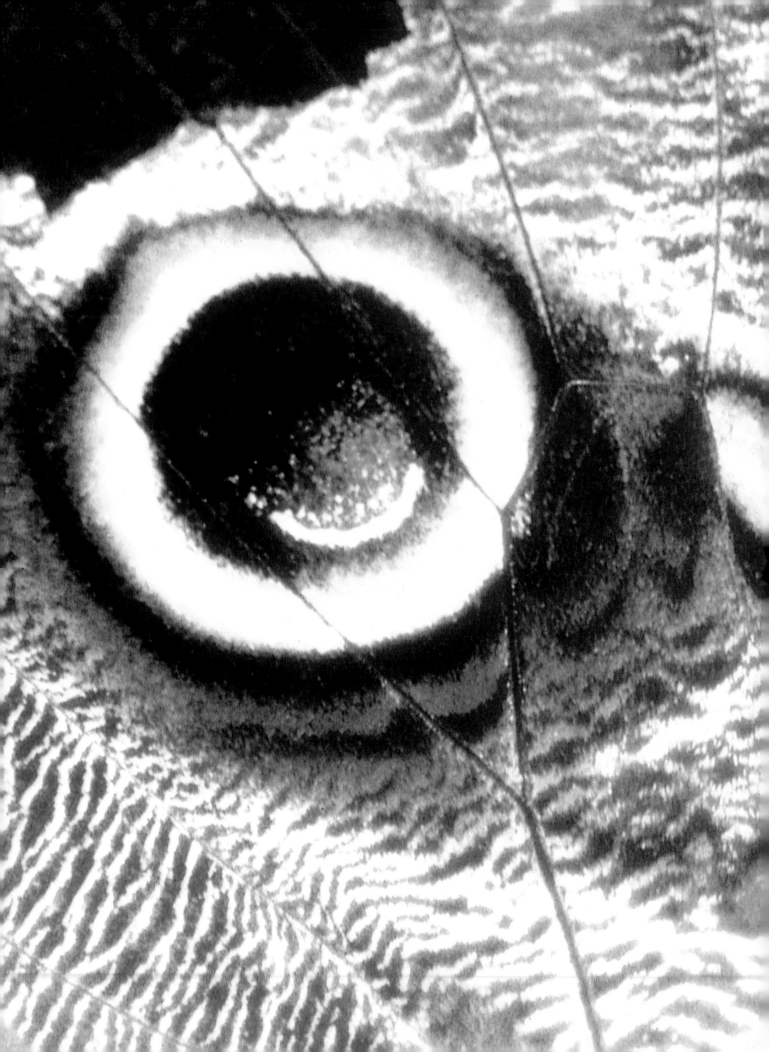

NYMPHALIDAE

This is the largest family of butterflies, an amalgamation of several groups which were once deemed separate families, such as the monarchs or danaids, the browns or satyrids, the snouts or libytheids, and the metalmarks, riodinids or nemeobiids, which are closer to the lycaenids. The characteristics which bring them together are the possession of two pairs of functional legs (instead of the usual three pairs), the first pair being much reduced. The nymphalids have stout, rather large bodies in comparison with their wing size, with strong legs. They often have brown colors (as in the browns or monarchs) and are powerful fliers. Iridescent colors, caused by the diffraction of light on wing scales, are often found in nymphalids, but this is not an exclusive characteristic.

(The butterfly above is *Caligo memnon*.)

GENUS
ACRAEA

This genus is one of the largest in Africa with over 150 species. They occur throughout the continent and in most habitats. They are brown, yellow, orange, or red and have poison in their bodies. These poisons make the butterflies chemically distasteful to birds, a necessary protection as they are slow fliers. Larvae feed on various members of the daisy and passion flower family, *Compositae* and *Passifloraceae*.

ACRAEA ANDROMACHA
Glasswing, Glass Wing, The Small Greasy

ZONE 5·6 | 2³/₈in 60mm

It is named after the transparent forewings. The sexes are similar, with a light yellow and black-spotted hindwing which has a black border. The wings are elongated as in other acraeas. The butterfly flies in open woodland and scrubby country, and its gregarious caterpillars feed on members of the genus *Passiflora*. This is the only member of this genus found in Australia.

ACRAEA CALDARENA
Black-tipped Acraea

ZONE 4 | 2¹/₈in 55mm

The black tip is prominent and larger than that possessed by other acraeids. There is also a black marginal band with pink spots around much of the hindwing. The ground color of the male is pink; that of the female is less bright and may be brown. The butterfly lives in open scrub and savanna.

ACRAEA ACRITA
Fiery Acraea

ZONE 4 | 2¹/₂in 65mm

True to its common name, this butterfly has a really fiery color, especially on its uppers. The forewing tip is black, and there are small black dots on all the wings. The undersides are less intense red. The female may be similar, but is very variable, even to brown. The butterfly occurs in open savanna and bush, and is found throughout most of the year.

ACRAEA ANEMOSA
Broad-bordered Acraea

ZONE 4 | 2⁵/₈in 70mm

The sexes are similar, with the broad black border very evident on the trailing edge of the hindwing. However, the key feature is the lack of tiny spots on the hindwing. The base of the wings is dark. There are black forewing marks and a black tip. The underside of the hindwing has a lighter central area. The butterfly flies in open savanna and bush country, and is present throughout most of the year.

ACRAEA ENCEDON
Common Acraea, White-barred Acraea

ZONE 4 | 2¹/₈in 55mm

This is a mimic of *Danaus chrysippus* in size, color and pattern. The red-brown color, fairly pointed wings, and a contrasting white and black border help to convey the mimicry message. Both sexes can be very variable, and may or not have a dark forewing apex. Even white forms occur which mimic *Amauris*. The caterpillars eat members of the genus *Commelina*. Widespread in Africa, the butterfly also occurs in Arabia.

ACRAEA MIRANDA
Desert Acraea

 ZONE 4 · 2⅛in 55mm

The wings are quite long, and the ground color is orange-red. There is no black tip to the forewings, as in other acraeas but there are two curved bands on the forewing. The unspotted hindwing has a dark band around the trailing edge. The sexes are similar, but the female may have a yellow-orange or gray ground color. The butterfly flies in the desert, keeping close to the ground, near scrubby vegetation.

GENUS
ADELPHA

This is a genus of North and South American butterflies with 70 species and 250 forms and races. They are all very similar and are therefore difficult to identify: small differences in spots, angles of lines, and colors are crucial. Caterpillars are more easily differentiated, but few life histories of individual species are known. The butterflies are found in most habitats, from sea level to the upland rainforest, and they exploit a wide range of plant families as caterpillar food plants.

ADELPHA LEUCERIA

 ZONE 2 · 2⅜in 62mm

The orange band which crosses both wings and breaks up near the apex of the forewing is a useful guide to identification. The ground color of the wings is brown. At the anal part of the hindwing, there is a small false eye. The butterfly frequents rain and cloud forest, and will even fly in mist. Mostly males are encountered, as females remain in the canopy. The life cycle has not been described.

ACRAEA ZETES
Large spotted Acraea

 ZONE 4 · 3in 75mm

Black spots of different sizes on all the wings characterize this butterfly. The sexes are very similar with a reddish ground color, although the female may be a little duller. The apex of the forewing is dark with a row of five russet spots at the margin and a light patch near the tip. There is great variation within this species. The butterfly lives in savanna, alongside forests and wooded scrub where it breeds on *Passiflora* species.

ADELPHA BREDOWII
California Sister

 ZONE 1·2 · 3⅛in 86mm

The key features are the orange spot on the apex of the forewing and an unbroken white band across the wings, both visible on the underside where there is a pale blue band around the inside of the margins, and pale blue marks by the base. The butterfly is a native of the southwestern US and is found in Central America where it occurs in oak woodland on foothills. It breeds on a wide range of native oaks. Adults are attracted to sweet things, even to grape juice spilled at wineries.

ADELPHA MELONA

 ZONE 2 · 2in 50mm

The underside is characteristic of the species, with a broad white band which runs across the wings, and a thinner white band across the base of the wings. The slightly scalloped margin of the hindwing also has a thick white band. The white is broken by orange-brown marks. Butterflies frequent open, sunny flowery areas.

GENUS
AGLAIS

This genus of butterflies have exploited much of the world well, and have more species in Europe and Asia than in North America. They are relatively small butterflies, with orange, yellow and black markings, and some species are migratory. Larvae breed on members of the nettle family. Adults hibernate.

AGLAIS URTICAE
Small Tortoiseshell

	ZONE 3·5
2in 50mm	

The sexes are similar, with three black bars on the leading edge of the forewing, and a series of variable blue marks inside the margins of the orange-red wings. The outer edges of the wings are sculptured to a point, and the underside of the wings are dark, especially toward the base. The butterfly is very common in all sorts of habitats from gardens to upland, and it hibernates as an adult. It breeds on the ubiquitous nettle *Urtica* species, and it is a strong migrant.

AGLAIS MILBERTI
Milbert's Tortoiseshell, Fire-rim Tortoiseshell

	ZONE 1
2in 51mm	

The name of "fire-rim" is very appropriate, since the outer orange band is highlighted with the darker basal area by a suffusion of bright light orange. The undersides are very dark and somber, which is typical of tortoiseshells which hibernate, as this one does It is a migrant and breeds on various members of the nettle family. There is a great similarity between this species and A. *urticae*, and perhaps they share the same ancestry.

GENUS
AGRIAS

These are striking tropical rainforest butterflies from South America, which have bright primary colors. They are eagerly sought by collectors. The larval food plants are not at all clear, perhaps kept secret by breeders. Members of the *Erythroxylaceae* appear to be utilized.

AGRIAS AMYDON

	ZONE 2
3³⁄₈in 88mm	

This is a powerful flier which has a number of subspecies and is very variable. The uppers may be blue, red, or orange; the hindwing may be mainly blue, have only a small touch of blue, or be mostly brown. The undersides of the forewings may be brown or mostly orange. The underside of the hindwing is a little more consistent, with convoluted curves of yellow and pale blue marks. The butterfly lives in the rainforest, the male on the canopy, often visiting fruit for sugars. It breeds on members of the genus *Erythroxylum*.

AGRIAS NARCISSUS

	ZONE 2
3¹⁄₂in 90mm	

This is a variable species like most of the *Agrias*. The underside of the forewing is red at the base, and dark toward the tip with a light line passing through it. The hindwing has convoluted marks of yellow and brown with a row of blue spots around the inside of the margin. The upperside of the forewings have a red band with blue to the inside and black on the apex. The hindwing is mostly blue. The male, as illustrated, has hair-tufts on the hindwing. The butterfly flies in the rainforest and may breed on *Erythroxylum* species.

GENUS
AMATHUXIDIA

Large winged, tropical butterflies of the jungles of India and Southeast Asia.

AMATHUXIDIA AMYTHAON
Koh-I-Noor Butterfly

	ZONE 5
4¹⁄₂in 113mm	

Of ten subspecies recorded, the most common form has a dark brown ground with a blue flash on the forewing, orange in the female. The hindwing is drawn out into a stubby tail. Undersides vary from pinkish blue to brown with four large eye-spots and at least five thin lines crossing the wings.

GENUS
AMAURIS

This is an African genus of 25 species which are speckled brown, orange, or black, rather similar and related to members of the *Danaus* genus. They fly in open forested areas and breed on plants such as *Cynanchum* and *Tylophora* species.

AMAURIS ELLIOTI
Ansorge's Danaid

	ZONE 4
3¹⁄₈in 80mm	

In this species the sexes are similar with black and white or yellow ground colors. However, there is a bright flash of golden yellow at the base of the hindwings. White or yellow spots cover the forewing and make a ring around the hindwing. In some forms the white areas are replaced by bright orange. Butterflies are found in highland rainforest and are sometimes gregarious.

AMAURIS HECATE
Dusky Danaid, Black Friar

	ZONE 4
3¹⁄₈in 80mm	

Black Friar is a most appropriate name for this dark-colored species. There is a white bar and a scattering of tiny white spots on the forewing. The mainly dark hindwing also has a few white spots and a small light area at the base. The sexes are similar. The butterfly flies in rainforest, but its caterpillar food plants have not been identified.

AMAURIS NIAVIUS
Friar

ZONE 4

4in
100mm

There are two large patches of white on the forewing, one, which is on the trailing edge, continues on from the large white patch on the hindwing. Although this species is variable throughout its range in terms of the amount of white on its wings, the sexes are similar. The black and white color scheme of this butterfly is used as a model for female forms of *Papilio dardanus* and *Hypolimnas dubius* (not described).

AMAURIS OCHLEA
Novice

ZONE 4

3¼in
85mm

The sexes are similar in this black and white butterfly. The key features are the large white mark on most of the hindwing, and two unbroken white marks on the forewing. There are a few tiny white spots on the uppers. The butterfly may be found in suitable shady areas among light woodland and along forest glades, where it breeds on *Tylophora* and *Cyanachum* species.

GENUS
AMNOSIA

A genus of a single variable species restricted to the Indonesian Islands.

AMNOSIA DECORA EUDAMIA

ZONE 5

2⅞in
74mm

Males are very dark or black with a pale blue-white band across the forewing. Females are brown with more white in the band and also have a white band on the underside of the forewing. Subspecies exist, but little is known of its life cycle.

GENUS
ANAEA

This is a genus of Central and South American butterflies which are similar in behavior to the African genus *Charaxes*. They are called leaf-wing butterflies since the undersides of the wings are leaf-like and help to disguise the butterfly when it settles on the ground. Some species are sexually dimorphic. The larvae feed on members of the *Euphorbiaceae* (spurges), *Piperaceae* (peppers), and *Lauraceae*.

ANAEA ANDRIA
Goat-weed Butterfly, Goatweed Butterfly

ZONE 1·2

2½in
65mm

The leaf shape of the wings is a key identification feature. The forewings are curved, and the hindwings are extended as a tail. The male is brighter, with its orange colors, but these are suffused with lots of brown marks and lines in the female. The undersides are very drab and well suited for camouflage during hibernation. It breeds on various members of the spurge family, *Euphorbiaceae*.

ANAEA CUBANA
Leaf Wing

ZONE 2

3½in
90mm

This is the largest *Anaea* likely to be found. It is distinguished by its bright orange, almost red, colors on the upper surfaces. The forewing is hooked and the hindwing partially scalloped with a substantial tail. Females are larger than males. The undersides are relatively dull, so when it rests on twigs in open wooded country it resembles some of the leaf butterflies of Asia. It is migratory and occurs only on Cuba. The butterfly breeds on members of the spurge family, such as crotons, often grown in gardens.

GENUS
ANARTIA

A small genus of four species which are found from the southern US to Central America, including the West Indies. Common butterflies of the tropics, they are swift fliers and bear some resemblance to members of the *Cynthia* genus. They breed on members of the *Acanthaceae* and, perhaps, also on the *Verbenaceae* and *Scrophulariaceae*.

ANARTIA JATROPHAE SEMIFUSCA
White Peacock

ZONE 1·2

1⁷⁄₈in 48mm

The butterfly has a characteristic coloration and fairly complicated pattern. The ground color is pale white-gray, and there are alternate bands of relatively light and dark shading over the wings, with three key black spots. The hindwing is partially scalloped with a suggestion of a tail. There are a few subspecies known. This migrant butterfly is frequently seen along waysides and roads and in open country where it breeds on water hyssop, *Bacopa monnieri*.

ANARTIA CHRYSOPELEA
Huebner's Anartia

ZONE 2

2¹⁄₄in 56mm

The sexual difference is the background color, which is brown in the female and black in the male. Both sexes have a fairly uniform white band crossing the forewing and a white patch crossing the hindwing. The pattern is repeated on the underside. The hindwing is scalloped, and there is a short tail. There is also a red-circled eye-spot on the trailing edge of the forewing. The early stages of this butterfly have not yet been described.

GENUS
ANTANARTIA

A genus of mostly tailed African butterflies found both on the continent as well as on the islands of Madagascar and Mauritius. They breed on various plants including *Urtica*, *Acalpha*, and *Boehmeria* species.

ANTANARTIA ABYSSINICA
Ethiopian Admiral

ZONE 4

1¹⁄₂in 40mm

The sexes are similar, with a black-brown ground color crossed by an orange-brown band. There is no tail. The black tips of the forewing contain a few white spots, and there is an orange-brown band around the margin of the hindwing. The butterfly is found near forests and woods in highland areas, where it breeds on stinging nettle, *Urtica* species.

ANTANARTIA SCHAENEIA
Long-tailed Admiral

ZONE 4

2³⁄₈in 60mm

Although similar to the European *Vanessa atalanta*, this species lacks the large amount of white on its wings and has two tails of unequal length. It has an open circle of tiny white dots on the black apical patch of the forewing. The butterfly is found in highland areas, where it breeds on various members of the nettle family, including *Boehmeria*, *Fleurya*, and *Pouzolzia* species.

GENUS
ANTIRRHAEA

A group of about 20 species of the rainforests of South and Central America. They have angular hindwings. The adults frequent deep shade. Males have tufted patches on the upperside of the forewings and brushes on the overlapping parts of the wings and on the male claspers. Most species probably breed on members of the palm family.

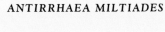

ANTIRRHAEA MILTIADES

 | ZONE 2

4in
100mm

This is a very dark and somber-looking butterfly, with curved wings typical of the antirrhaeas. The key feature of the male is a flash of white on the hindwing. This is absent in the slightly larger female. Undersides are rich dark brown crossed by a white band. The butterfly occurs in swamp forests, along streams and trails. It perches a lot and feeds on rotting fruit and fungi. The butterfly breeds on *Geonoma longivaginata*, a member of the palm family.

ANTIRRHAEA AVERNUS

 | ZONE 2

3½in
93mm

This is a very dark brown butterfly with a scalloped hindwing drawn out to a short tail. The shape of the forewing is unusual in that it has a distinctive kink on the outer edge. A row of blue marks crosses the hindwing. The butterfly lives in the rainforest and probably breeds on a species of palm.

ANTIRRHAEA GERYON

 | ZONE 2

3½in
93mm

This is a large brown butterfly which has a distinctive short tail which points to the side, and a row of large false eyes around the margins of the wings. The underside is russet-gray with a line crossing both fore and hindwings. The butterfly lives in the rainforest and probably breeds on a species of palm.

▲

ANTIRRHAEA PTEROCOPHA

	ZONE 2	
4¼in 108mm		

The sexes are different, the male being brighter and smaller than the female. The blue on the hindwing of the male is distinctive. The underside is dark gray-blue with one thin line crossing the wings, a feature also seen in the more orangey underside of the female. The female uppers are dark brown toward the center, and light brown at the margin of the hindwing. There is a faint violet band on the forewing. Both sexes have hooked wings. The butterfly occurs deep in virgin cloud forest. It breeds on *Calyptrogyne* species, members of the palm family.

GENUS
APATURA

Large and powerful butterflies which occur in Europe, Asia, and the Australian region.

APATURA IRIS
Purple Emperor

	ZONE 3·5	
2⅞in 74mm		

The metallic purple color of the male is only seen from certain angles, so it appears to flash in flight. Both sexes have white bars across the wings. The butterfly is territorial and defends woodland paths, glades and "master oaks," and breeds on willows.

GENUS
APATURINA

A genus from New Guinea, which have large bodies and stout wings.

APATURINA ERMINIA

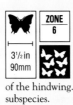

	ZONE 6	
3½in 90mm		

The dark brown forewings have an interrupted orange band across the wing and two small white spots near the apex. There is a small eye-spot near the anal part of the hindwing. There are a number of subspecies.

GENUS
APHANTOPUS

A group of brown butterflies, found in Europe and Asia, which breed on grasses.

APHANTOPUS HYPERANTUS
Ringlet

	ZONE 3·5	
1⅞in 48mm		

This very dark butterfly has a series of eye-spots, each one highlighted by a yellow ring, conspicuous on the undersides. The butterfly successfully exploits rough grassland, including sea cliffs and highway edges, and enjoys a wide distribution despite being rather sedentary.

GENUS
ARASCHNIA

Characterized by their map-like patterning, these butterflies are found in Europe and Asia.

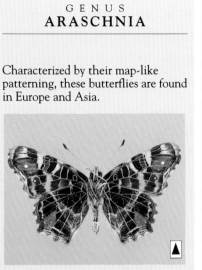

ARASCHNIA LEVANA
Map Butterfly

	ZONE
1½in 38mm	**3·5**

The smaller and brighter male is tawny and black. The dark brown female has a yellow band crossing the wings and a partial red band toward the hindwing margins, with white spots near the apex of the forewing. They fly in open woodland and breed on nettles.

GENUS
ARGYNNIS

Collectively known as fritillaries, this genus of woodland butterflies occurs in Europe and Asia. Butterflies are large, orange, and speckled with black spots. The males have large black sex brands on the forewing. Adults regularly visit woodland and wayside blossoms, and many species breed on violets.

ARGYNNIS ADIPPE
High Brown Fritillary

	ZONE
2⅜in 62mm	**3·4·5**

Females are always larger, and more heavily covered with black spots, than males. The forewings have a certain squarish look to them, and the base of the wings is covered with brown-green hairs. The undersides of the hindwings have silver marks. The butterfly flies in open woodland areas, especially in clearings, and breeds on violets. It has become less common in recent years, probably due to habitat destruction. A number of nature reserves have been set up to protect this species.

ARGYNNIS AGLAJA
Dark Green Fritillary

	ZONE
2¼in 58mm	**3·5**

A large orange and black butterfly with a green suffusion over the underside of the hindwing, especially near the base. The underside has a series of distinct large light-colored spots. The markings on the uppers are very variable. This butterfly breeds on violets in clearings and in woods. It may also be found flying over open countryside. There is usually only one generation each year. It has declined in recent years in England.

ARGYNNIS PAPHIA
Silver-washed Fritillary

	ZONE
2⅝in 70mm	**3·5**

The most impressive of the three butterflies in this genus. The male is very attractive with its long dark marks along the veins on the upper forewing. There are prominent spots all over the uppers of the female, which is very slightly larger. A dark form of the female exists. Unlike other fritillaries which lay eggs on violets, this species lays eggs on a nearby tree trunk so the freshly-emerged larvae have to walk to their food plants. This species has declined in England.

GENUS
ARGYROPHENGA

A brown butterfly with a characteristic elongated wing shape and large eye-spots.

ARGYROPHENGA ANTIPODUM

	ZONE
2⅛in 54mm	**6**

Occupying most of the forewing is a large eye-spot made up of at least two white pupils set in a black area and contrasting with a nearby reddish orange patch. The hindwing contains a much smaller eye-spot. The forewing spot on the underside is much reduced. The underside of the hindwing is streaked with 7-8 silver lines.

GENUS
ARGYROPHORUS

A genus of two South American species which have silver marks on the uppers.

ARGYROPHORUS ARGENTEUS
Silver Butterfly

ZONE 2

2¹/₈in 55mm

Shiny silver covers the uppers of this species. The undersides are also silvery, but there is a little orange at the base of the forewing and a distinctive black eye-spot near the tip of the forewing. The underside of the hindwing has an overall wavy pattern.

GENUS
ASTEROCAMPA

These are the hackberry butterflies, which are named after their larval food plant, the hackberry, *Celtis* species, native to North America. The butterflies are relatively large, with a mottled pattern. The females are larger than the males.

▲

ASTEROCAMPA CELTIS
Hackberry Butterfly, Hackberry Emperor

ZONE 1·2

2³/₈in 60mm

The female has a pale orange ground color, compared to the white-orange of the male. The forewing of the male is much suffused with black, especially near the tip, and in both sexes there is a characteristic series of black spots around the margin. The butterfly flies in woods and forests, particularly where hackberries grow.

ASTEROCAMPA CLYTON
Tawny Emperor

ZONE 1

2¹/₂in 65mm

Tawny in color, tawny in name, this species has fairly sharp-angled wings with orange marks and spots over most of the forewing. The hindwing has an undulating row of black spots around the margin. The female is paler than the male. There are a number of subspecies. The butterfly is widespread in North America, and it flies in open wooded areas and forest margins, where it breeds on hackberries.

ASTEROCAMPA LEILIA
Desert Hackberry

ZONE 1·2	
2½in 65mm	

There are more similarities between hackberry butterflies than differences, but the key features to look for in this species are the two white bars on the leading edge of the forewing, the two black spots on the outer edge of the forewing, and the more elaborate eyespots on the underside of the hindwing. The desert habitat is also a useful clue to its identity. It breeds on the hackberry, *Celtis pallida*.

GENUS
ATERICA

A small genus of widespread African butterflies also found in Madagascar.

ATERICA GALENE
Forest Glade Nymph

ZONE 4	
3⅛in 80mm	

The black forewings have pale yellow marks in the male, white in the female. The male hindwings have a pale yellow patch, the female has white wing bases with radiating black veins. The butterfly frequents rainforest clearings and shady river banks, and breeds on *Quisqualis*.

GENUS
ATHYMA

A genus of Asian and Australian butterflies with powerful wings; similar to *Neptis*.

♀

ATHYMA DAMARIS

ZONE 5	
3⅛in 80mm	

The butterfly looks speckled with an ocher-yellow ground and dark brown veins. There is a reddish-orange flash at the forewing base. A few subspecies exist over the butterfly's range from India to Burma. It lives in open habitats and appears not to venture higher than 6,500ft (2,000m).

GENUS
BAEOTUS

A genus of two species with black and white undersides and toothlike edges to the hindwings.

BAEOTUS BAEOTUS

ZONE 2	
3¾in 95mm	

The butterfly is very attractive, with its scalloped hindwing and a blue band crossing both fore and hindwings. The undersides are black and white checks. This rare butterfly is found in virgin rainforest in the Amazon basin and Costa Rica. Its caterpillar food plant is unknown.

GENUS
BASILARCHIA

A genus of large "admiral" butterflies found in North America, and closely allied to *Limenitis*. *Basilarchia* live in woodlands and in open scrubby areas.

BASILARCHIA ARCHIPPUS
Viceroy

ZONE 1·2	
3in 76mm	

This is the mimic of the Monarch and Queen butterflies (*Danaus plexippus* and *D. gilippus* respectively). Its distinguishing feature is the black line which traces across the black veins on the hindwing. The model butterflies do not have this line, but otherwise, the Viceroy is roughly the same size, shape, color and pattern, and flies in the same places as the mimic. It breeds on a wide variety of tree species belonging to the willow and rose families.

BASILARCHIA ARTHEMIS
White Admiral, Banded Purple

The broad white band which crosses the upper sides of the wings is distinctive, and this is repeated on the undersides. The ground color of the uppers is deep velvet brown, that of the undersides is light brown. Blue marks run around the wing margins. The butterfly breeds on various species of willow and birch (*Salix* and *Betula*).

BASILARCHIA LORQUINI
Lorquin's, Orange Tip Admiral

The orange tips are highly contrasted on the uppers, and there is a distinctive white band across the dark velvety uppers. The band is repeated on the lighter undersides. It takes its name from the Frenchman, Pierre Lorquin (1797-1873), who collected this butterfly in California. It is fiercely territorial and has even been known to attack seagulls which get too close. The butterfly breeds on various trees and shrubs belonging to the willow, rose and buckthorn families.

GENUS
BASSARONA

A genus of butterflies found from Assam, via Malaya, to Indonesia. The forewing is characteristically well curved, and the veins nearest the leading edge are very close together.

BASSARONA DUDA

It is a large, strong butterfly which has a dark brown ground color suffused with a white and a blue band across the hindwing, and a disjointed band across the forewing. There are two white spots near the leading edge near the tip of the forewing. This is a variable species, and a number of subspecies are known. The butterfly occurs from northern India to Burma, but little has been written about its life cycle.

BASSARONA PATALA

ZONE 5 · 4¾in 120mm

It is a large butterfly with a greenish-brown ground color and strident yellow marks on the forewing. The main yellow bar is made up of five major spots, and there are two more yellow spots nearer the tip. On the hindwing, three small yellow marks run back from the leading edge. There are also three black-edged "watermarks" toward the base of the forewing. This butterfly exists as a number of subspecies from Northern India to China. Little is known on the ecology of this species.

BASSARONA SAHADEVA

ZONE 5 · 3¾in 95mm

The ground color is a greenish-brown, slightly lighter to the outside. On the forewing is a bar of five major yellow spots which spreads out toward the margins. Two unequal-sized yellow spots are near the tip. The wings are scalloped, and there are some black "watermarks" near the base of the forewing. The butterfly occurs in Sikkim.

BASSARONA HIKARUGENZI

ZONE 5 · 4in 100mm

This is attractive in its uniformity. The butterfly is black-brown with a curved band of white around the inside of the margin of the hindwing, and another, like a mirror image, around the forewing. There are just a few other marks on the forewing. Overall the appearance is black with scalloped hindwings. Other similar species have the addition of metallic blue. The butterfly is found in the Philippines.

GENUS

BIBLIS

A South and Central American genus with a single species breeding on *Tragia*, a species of spurge.

BIBLIS HYPERIA
Red Rim

ZONE 2 · 2½in 65mm

The red rim around the trailing edge of the hindwing may act as a warning as it is shown off during the butterfly's relatively slow flight. The hindwing margin is scalloped, and the brown forewing has light brown margins. The butterfly flies in open scrubby areas.

GENUS
BICYCLUS

An African genus of brown butterflies with round wings. Species live in woody areas and breed on grasses.

BICYCLUS SAFITZA
Common Bush Brown

	ZONE 4
2 in 50mm	

The uppersides are velvety brown. Toward the forewing apex is a lighter brown or yellow patch and a small white eye-spot in the center of the wing. The undersides have eye-spots around the margins. There are darker wet-season forms, and lighter dry-season forms.

GENUS
BOLORIA

A genus of relatively small butterflies known as fritillaries. Examples occur in the tundra, taiga, and mountains of the Arctic region. They are found around the Northern Hemisphere in Europe, Asia, and North America. Many feed on bog plants such as *Polygonum*, *Vaccinium*, and *Viola* species.

BOLORIA AQUILONARIS
Cranberry Fritillary

	ZONE 3·5
1⁵/₁₆in 34mm	

The black-speckled appearance of the orange wings is typical of many of the fritillaries, but the key features here are the two bands of V-shaped black marks toward the base of the forewing. The underside of the hindwing is maroon with yellow and white. The butterfly is found on bogs and moors where it breeds on cranberry, *Vaccinium oxycoccus*.

BOLORIA EPITHORE
Western Meadow Fritillary

	ZONE 1
1⁵/₈in 41mm	

The forewing tip is rounded, and there is more orange on the wings than in other bolorias. There are two subspecies recognized which share the characteristic yellow band which crosses the wings. The butterfly flies in mountainous regions in meadows and clearings, in the west of North America reaching into Canada. It breeds on violets and has a single brood each year.

BOLORIA BELLONA
Meadow Fritillary

	ZONE 1
1⁷/₈in 48mm	

The characteristic feature is the squared-off margin on the outer part of the forewing. The ground color varies from light brown to dark brown. Black spots cover the underside of the forewing, but the hindwing is devoid of well-defined marks. At least two subspecies have been recorded. The butterfly is found throughout much of northern America and breeds on violets.

BOLORIA EUNOMIA
Ocellate Bog Fritillary, Bog Fritillary

	ZONE 1·3
1³/₄in 46mm	

The ground color is rich orange on the uppers, with orange and yellow on the underside. There is rather more darkening of the base of the hindwing than anywhere else, and the underside of the hindwing has various distinguishing yellow marks drawn together as an irregular band. The butterfly occurs throughout much of North America and Western Europe, breeding on bistort, *Polygonium bistorta*. In North America the caterpillar uses other bog-plant species as food plants.

BOLORIA EUPHROSYNE
Pearl-bordered Fritillary

ZONE
3·5

1¾in
46mm

The "pearl borders" are seven pearly-looking marks around the trailing edge of the underside of the hindwing. Another key feature is the pair of much larger pearly spots also on the hindwing. The upperside, which is similar in the sexes, is deep orange with plenty of black spots. The base of the upper side of the wings is black. The butterfly lives in woods, glades and forest edges, and breeds on violets.

BOLORIA NAPAEA
Mountain Fritillary

ZONE
1

1⅝in
42mm

A small orange butterfly with dark bases to its wings and small black marks on the uppers. The undersides are mottled with greenish-purple marks on the hindwing and orange with black marks on the forewing. The butterfly lives in small groups in arctic regions, usually above the tree line. It breeds on alpine bistort.

BOLORIA PALES
Shepherd's Fritillary

ZONE
1·3

1½in
40mm

The rich orange background color of the uppers is covered with lots of black marks, and the base of the wings is dark. The hindwing edge has a slight kink on the leading edge. The undersides are lighter, especially the forewing, and the hindwing has purple-brown marks and bands. The butterfly breeds on violets like many of its relatives.

BOLORIA SELENE
Silver Meadow Fritillary,
Small Pearl-bordered Fritillary

ZONE
1·3

1⅝in
42mm

Strongly marked with dark spots, the rich orange uppers are distinctive. The underside is also strongly marked in black, and on the hindwing there is a band of very sharp pointed marks. This specimen illustrated (from Germany) lacks many black marks. A number of subspecies are known. The butterfly is found well inside the arctic regions and frequents woods, forest edges, alpine meadows and bogs. It breeds on violets.

GENUS
BRENTHIS

Small-sized fritillaries found in Europe and Asia which breed on a variety of plants.

BRENTHIS INO
Lesser Marbled Fritillary

ZONE
3·5

1½in
40mm

A small variable fritillary whose fairly rounded wings lack strong spotting. The black spots inside the margin of the hindwing are irregular in size and the base of the hindwing is dark. The butterfly lives in boggy and marshy areas, and also frequents drier ground.

GENUS
BRINTESIA

A genus of browns which have brown and black coloration with white marks. They tend to live in light woodland, but fly in sunny glades and between trees, laying their eggs on grasses. There are many species which occur widely in Europe and Asia.

BRINTESIA BRAHMINUS WAHMINOIDES

ZONE 5

2½in
65mm

This is a very dark brown butterfly which has its margins scalloped in pale cream lunules. There is a prominent cream band stretching across the wings, starting as an imperfect circle around an indistinct eye-spot on the forewing tip, and passing to the rear in a more consolidated band. The undersides are much lighter, and the cream band is more pronounced, especially around the forewing eye-spot.

BRINTESIA CIRCE
Great Banded Grayling

ZONE 3

2⅝in
68mm

The easy way in which this brown woodland butterfly, whose wings are crossed by a definite white band, flits between the trees is unmistakable. Once disturbed, it will fly to another tree trunk and try to hide, using its underside colors and patterns as camouflage. At rest, the forewing can be moved to be within the hindwing, typical of many browns. The butterfly breeds on grasses such as the bromes (*Bromus*), patches of which occur in oak woods.

GENUS
BYBLIA

A genus of African butterflies occurring in woodland and scrubby habitats.

BYBLIA ILITHYIA
Joker

ZONE 4

2⅛in
55mm

The most prominent feature is the black band which crosses the uppers. The row of deep orange dots around the margins is distinctive, as are the little dots on the inside of the hindwing. The butterfly is widespread in Ethiopia and flies in woodland and scrub habitats.

GENUS
CAEROIS

A genus of two species from South and Central America, they both have a very elongated forewing which is strongly curved and pointed. The hindwing has a tail. This genus is very closely related to the *Antirrhaea* and is recognized in the male by the tufts of androconial scales on the inside edge of the underside of the forewing. Butterflies apparently breed on members of the palm family and possibly on sugarcane.

CAEROIS CHORINAEUS

ZONE 2

4in
100mm

The profile of this butterfly is a key identification feature, since the hooked forewings are particularly long in proportion to the hindwings. The hindwing is angular with a curved tail. There is an orange band across the forewing, but otherwise the ground color is a dull brown.

CAEROIS GERDRUDTUS

ZONE 2

4⅛in
104mm

The wings have a distinctive shape, the leading edge of the forewing is strongly curved, and the hindwing is very angular with a substantial tail. The upperside is suffused with a violet-blue. On the tip of the forewing is a large eye-spot, with two much smaller ones on the hindwing. The undersides are very pale and crossed by lines. The butterfly is not very common. It lives in the rainforest and breeds on the palm, *Socratea durisima*.

GENUS
CALIGO

This is a genus of 17 species from the lowland rainforest of South and Central America. They are called owl butterflies because of the large false eyes on the underside of the hindwing. The butterflies are big and fly mostly at dusk and dawn. Larvae grow relatively slowly and feed on members of the *Heliconiaceae*, *Marantaceae* and *Cylanthaceae*. Fully-grown larvae are spined and appear to be unpalatable to ants. The presence or absence of androconial tufts on the inner margin of the hindwing is critical in identifying species.

CALIGO BELTRAO
Owl Butterfly

	ZONE 2
5¹⁄₂in 140mm	

The wings are very rounded and relatively long from front to rear. The margins are very gently wavy. On the upper surface, most of the wing is blue at the base, with black to the outside and a key orange band on the forewing tip. The undersides are much lighter and include the huge typical "eye," hence the common name Owl Butterfly.

CALIGO MEMNON
Owl Butterfly

	ZONE 2
6¹⁄₈in 156mm	

This is recognizable from the other owl butterflies by the large patch of pale orange-yellow covering most of the forewing. The outer margin of the forewing and most of the hindwing is very dark. The butterflies live in agricultural areas and breed on *Heliconia* species and the related banana. The early stages in the wild have not been described, but this species is reared easily on banana in butterfly houses.

GENUS
CERCYONIS

This is a North American genus of browns which have relatively large eye-spots on the forewing on both surfaces, and smaller spots on the hindwing. They live in grassy woodland habitats, and all species probably breed on grasses.

CERCYONIS MEADII
Mead's Wood Nymph, Red Wood Nymph

ZONE 1

2¼in
56mm

This is a dull-looking butterfly with brown on its upperside, suffused in brown-red and with two eye-spots on the forewing. The underside is mottled brown-white on the hindwing, and orange on the forewing with a repeat of the two eye-spots. The butterfly enjoys grassy habitats in light woodland, where it is a resident species. Not a lot is known about its early stages in general, but it probably breeds on grasses such as *Bouteloua gracilis*.

CERCYONIS STHELENE OKIUS
Great Basin Wood Nymph,
Scrub Wood Nymph

ZONE 1

2in
51mm

Females are larger than males, with two prominent eye-spots on the forewing tip, and these are repeated on the underside. The underside of the hindwing is drab and well marbled, and, like the upper surfaces, the outer part of the wing is lighter than the inner. This is a very variable species which has three subspecies. The butterfly is a resident, prefers fields, meadows and woods, and breeds on a variety of grass species.

CETHOSIA CHRYSIPPE CLAUDILLA
Red Lacewing

ZONE 6

4in
100mm

This is a large butterfly with a prominent scalloped margin on all wings. The ground color is very dark, but is highlighted with a white flash on the forewing. All the wings have an orange-red base with a slight rosy blue bloom. There are other races and forms known, and some authorities place this species as a subspecies of *C. cydippe*.

GENUS
CETHOSIA

A large genus of large and elegant butterflies, with species found in both the Asian and Australian regions. The larvae breed on members of the passion flower family, *Passifloraceae*. Adults are often bright orange-red and are apparently distasteful to predators. Variegated colors are found on the undersides of the wings.

CERCYONIS PEGALA
Blue-eyed Grayling, Goggle Eye,
Wood Nymph

ZONE 1

2⅞in
74mm

"Goggle eye" describes the large pair of eye-spots on the forewing, which are some of the largest seen in this genus. "Blue-eyed" refers to the pale blue in the center of the eye-spots, which are repeated on the underside of the forewing in the female. The underside of the male hindwing has a series of eye-spots. The butterfly is a resident species which lives in grassy habitats by streams, in light woodland, and in meadows, where it breeds on a wide variety of grasses.

CETHOSIA CYANE

ZONE 5

4in
100mm

The *cyan* in the name refers to the blue-violet which is suffused over the base of the underside of the forewing, with a little on the underside of the hindwing. The underside is an attractive mixture of white zigzag lines around the margin, and white and mustard color on the inside. The uppers are rich orange to the inside with a generous black forewing tip containing a white band. This species inhabits lowland and upland rainforest.

CETHOSIA HYPSEA
Malay Lacewing

3³⁄₈in 88mm	ZONE 5

This is a common butterfly which has mostly dark forewings containing a reasonably large creamy white mark in the central area. The hindwing is mostly a rich red-orange with thick dark margins which are strongly scalloped around the end of each vein. Fresh males have a rosy bloom over the main orange area. The butterfly is common along roadsides, where it breeds on *Adenia*, a climbing member of the passion flower family.

GENUS
CHARAXES

A large genus of over 100 species of butterflies which are typically African, with one species in Europe. They are strong and powerful fliers, which enjoy feeding on fruit and dung, and engage in hill-topping. Butterflies are strongly colored, and the hindwing often has one or two pairs of tails.

CHARAXES BOUETI
Red Forest Charaxes

3¹⁄₈in 80mm	ZONE 4

This charaxes has two tails, and a conspicuous indented forewing. The male is much richer in color than the female with its pale yellow band across the wings. The forewing tip is dark, and there is a pair of silvery blue spots on the anal region of the hindwing. The butterfly lives in both savanna and highland forest, and breeds on certain bamboo species.

CETHOSIA NIETNERI

4¹⁄₈in 104mm	ZONE 5

This is an attractive butterfly which has a very strong zig-zag pattern on the upper and lower surfaces. The uppers have a blue suffusion; the underside is pale with an orange margin. The black markings are heavy on the uppers and reduced to spots on the lowers. There are a number of subspecies. The butterfly is found in open forested areas, such as the highland areas of Sri Lanka and in India.

CHARAXES BOHEMANI
Large Blue Charaxes

4¹⁄₈in 105mm	ZONE 4

The prominent feature of this butterfly is the large expanse of metallic blue over most of the hindwing and on the base of the forewing. The remainder of the forewing is black, with two irregular-sized white marks near the tip. There are two modest-sized tails. The resident butterfly flies in bush and scrubby areas and breeds on various leguminous *Afzelia* trees.

CHARAXES CANDIOPE
Green-veined Charaxes

3¹⁄₂in 90mm	ZONE 4

The forewings are strongly curved and indented on the outer margin. The base of the wings is a rich orange, while the outer parts are black. There is a row of orange spots which runs across both wings in the black area. The body is also rich orange. The larger female has longer tails. The butterfly flies in many habitats including woods, forests and savanna and breeds on *Croton*, a member of the spurge family.

CHARAXES CASTOR
Giant Charaxes

ZONE 4

4³/₈in
110mm

This is a giant among the African charaxes. The female is by far the larger, with impressive long, curved tails. Both sexes have blue around the tail region, more on the female than the male, and on the underside. There is a distinctive yellow-orange band which comes across the wings, mostly across the dark brown forewing. The butterfly is widespread and lives in many different types of habitat including woods, forests, bush and coastal areas. It breeds on a variety of leguminous plants.

CHARAXES DRUCEANUS
Silver-barred Charaxes

ZONE 4

3¹/₄in
85mm

The ground color is a rich orange which pervades most of the wing. Toward the margin is a thick black band interrupted at the forewing edge by a series of orange spots. There is an orange band on the hindwing. The sexes are alike, but the female has slightly broader wings, more blue on the anal region and longer tails. The butterfly flies in forested areas and breeds on *Eugenia* and *Syzygium*, members of the myrtle family.

CHARAXES HANSALI
Cream-banded Charaxes

ZONE 4

3¹/₄in
85mm

This is essentially a black charaxes which has a prominent white band running across the wings. The sexes are similar. There is a row of very small white dots around the margins and some blue-violet spots near the tail. The tails are longer in the female. The profile of the butterfly is somewhat more streamlined than other "fatter" charaxes. It occurs in bush and scrub country, and breeds on *Salvadora persica* and *Osyris* species.

CHARAXES CITHAERON
Blue-spotted Charaxes

ZONE 4

3¹/₂in
90mm

This is one of the several blue-sheened charaxes that have an all-blue male and a brown female which has most of its blue restricted to the hindwing. The forewing of the larger female is brown, with a white band that turns blue as it reaches the trailing edge. The female has much larger tails. The butterfly frequents forests where it breeds on various members of the pea family.

CHARAXES EURIALUS

ZONE 5

4³/₈in
110mm

Very dark green to black is the ground color of this butterfly. The forewings are strongly curved and indented on the outer margin. The hindwing is scalloped with a short but firm tail. There is a flush of blue-green inside the margin which contains some black spots set against an orange border. The butterfly flies in open woodland and alongside forests.

CHARAXES JASIUS
Foxy Charaxes, Two-tailed Pasha

ZONE 3·4

3¹/₈in
83mm

A big and impressive butterfly with two unequal-length tails on each hindwing and dark uppers with light orange toward the margins. The underside is maroon with red-brown toward the outer part and a central white band. The female is slightly larger than the male. An elusive butterfly, it flies around mountaintops where it engages in hill-topping, in clearings and in scrubby areas, and breeds on the strawberry tree, *Arbutus unedo*. It is a very local butterfly.

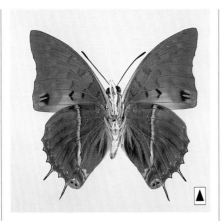

CHARAXES LASTI
Silver-striped Charaxes

This species is similar to *C. boueti*, but with less of the yellow-cream band across the wings. Otherwise, the sexes have fairly similar colors and patterns, emphasized more strongly in the male. The female is slightly larger, with longer tails, and slightly more blue at the base of the wings than the male. The butterfly occurs in coastal woods of Kenya and Tanzania, and breeds on the leguminous *Afzelia*.

CHARAXES PELIAS
Protea Charaxes

This species looks a little like *C. jasius*, but its key features are shorter tails and a grayer underside, not red-brown. The base of the wings are rich brown and separating this from a black margin is an orange band which crosses the wing. Blue spots are present at the base of the tail. This is a species of the mountains, where it breeds on plants such as the camels'-foot, *Bauhinia*, a member of the pea family.

CHARAXES VIOLETTA
Violet-spotted Charaxes

This is one of the blue-sheened charaxes. The male has violet-blue over most of its dark uppers, while the female is black with a white band on the forewing, which gives way to a violet bloom on the hindwing. There are two tails in both sexes, but they are longer in the female. The butterfly lives in forests and woodlands. It breeds on *Deinbollia*, a member of the *Sapindaceae*.

CHARAXES NITEBIS

This is an oriental charaxes in which there are distinct sexual differences. The smaller male is black with a yellow-green basal area to the wing, and small yellow spots in the black forewing tip. The female is light to dark brown, with a row of black spots on the margin of the hindwing and some yellow chevrons on the forewing. Subspecies exist. The butterfly is found in open forested areas on Sulawesi and Sula Island, Indonesia.

CHARAXES PROTOCLEA
Flame-bordered Charaxes

The sexes are completely different. The male is covered mostly in a very attractive black with a wide margin of orange mostly around the hindwing. There are two little blue spots on the hindwing margin. The female, which is slightly larger, has a big band of white crossing the wing and breaking up near the black tip of the forewing. The base of the forewing is brown. There is a faint tracing of green along the veins. The butterfly flies in forests and woods and breeds on *Afzelia* and *Syzygium* species.

GENUS
CHAZARA

A genus of browns which have gray-brown colors and zigzag marks.

CHAZARA HEYDENREICHII

This is dark brown on the uppers with various smudges of pale cream-yellow loosely arranged as a band across the wings to enclose two dark unpupilled eye-spots. The undersides are light fawn, very cryptic for camouflage on the ground. The butterfly occurs in the Himalayan foothills.

GENUS
CHLOSYNE

A genus of North and Central American, relatively small fritillary butterflies collectively called checkerspots. Their patterns are very variable, which is typical of fritillaries generally. Butterflies are found in meadows, plains and waysides. Some species are migratory.

CHLOSYNE DEFINITA
Definite Patch, Coahuila Checkerspot

	ZONE 1·2
1³⁄₈in 35mm	

The uppersides are a medley of yellow and orange spots against a dark brown ground color. A series of orange spots goes around the margin of the hindwing. The undersides are checkered with four rows of white spots over an orange ground on the hindwing. The butterfly lives in scrubby desert areas and thorny areas, and breeds on the acanthus, *Stenandrium barbatum*.

CHLOSYNE PALLA
Creamy Checkerspot

	ZONE 1
1³⁄₄in 46mm	

This has the typical checkerspots appearance, but there is a sexual difference in that the male has the brighter display. The hindwing, on both surfaces, has two rows of cream spots crossing the wing, and the underside of the forewing is mostly orange with a little checkering on the apex. There are a number of subspecies. The butterfly lives in woody and scrubby areas, and breeds on various members of the daisy family, *Compositae*.

CHLOSYNE CALIFORNICA
California Patch

	ZONE 1
1⁵⁄₈in 41mm	

The base and margins of the wings are black, but there is a row of orange spots in the margin and a thick orange band which crosses the wings. The undersides are much brighter and lighter with more little white spots. The butterfly lives in deserts and canyons, and breeds on *Viguiera deltoides* and *Helianthus annuus*. Males are gregarious and engage in hill-topping. Although it does occur south into Mexico, the butterfly is conserved in the Joshua Tree National Monument.

CHLOSYNE GORGONE
Great Plains Checkerspot

	ZONE 1
1¹⁄₂in 40mm	

The underside of the hindwing has some distinctive white zigzag marks, and the margin of the forewing has a white-barred appearance. The gregarious caterpillars have been recorded on at least eight members of the daisy family, *Compositae*. The distribution of this butterfly is over the central area of the US, coincident with the Great Plains, from which it derives its common name.

CHLOSYNE THEONA
Mexican Checkerspot

	ZONE 1·2
1³⁄₄in 44mm	

The pattern on the underside of the hindwing is very uniform and distinct. There is a row of beautiful creamy marks across the wing. The ground color is orange. A number of subspecies exist. This is a Central American species, but it also occurs north into the southern parts of the US. The butterflies, which engage in hill-topping, live in foothills and woodland where they breed on members of the *Scrophulariaceae* and *Verbenaceae*.

GENUS
CIRROCHROA

A genus of relatively large Asian and Australian butterflies. They are found from India to New Guinea. One useful guide to identification is the antennal club, which is poorly defined. At least one species (not described here) is known to migrate.

CIRROCHROA THAIS LANKA

ZONE 5

2⅝in 70mm

The ground color is a rich brown over most of the wings, with a little white dot on the leading edge of the hindwing. The forewing tip and around the edges of all wings is a thin dark margin. The undersides are pearly purple-orange, with or without a white line. There are several subspecies. The butterfly occurs in lowland rainforest in India and Sri Lanka.

GENUS
CITHAERIAS

This is a genus of about ten species found in South and Central America. They are browns, but they have transparent wings and thin bodies, and they fly in the dark recesses of the rainforest. Red, yellow, or blue-violet colors may be evident on the forewing, and a false-eye on the hindwing. Caterpillar food plants are unknown, and life cycle data is completely lacking.

CIRROCHROA REGINA

ZONE 6

3⅛in 83mm

The undersides are more beautiful than the uppers, since the base of the wings are pink-violet edged in white. The outer parts of the wings are very dark and contain chevrons of blue with black spots. On the upper surface the marks are more heavily presented, orange at the bases, dark brown outers. The butterfly occurs in lowland rainforest on various islands of Indonesia and on New Guinea.

CIRROCHROA THULE

ZONE 6

4in 100mm

The upperside is a rich orange. Around the margins are two distinct wavy black lines, and inside these are a row of black dots. The base of the wings is marked as a darker area. The undersides are completely different. They are silvery white with a distinct row of black dots and wavy orange lines around the margins. A number of subspecies occur. The butterfly occurs on some of the eastern Indonesian islands and on New Guinea, in lowland rainforest.

CITHAERIAS PHILIS

ZONE 2

2½in 63mm

With elongated forewings and very rounded hindwings, this butterfly has transparent wings. The veins are faintly etched in light brown. On the hindwing there is a distinctive eye-spot on the outer margin, and a large area of the wing is suffused with violet. Butterflies live in the deep shade of rainforest, but their caterpillar food plants have yet to be discovered.

CITHAERIAS SONGOANA

2⁷⁄₈in 74mm	ZONE 2

This is a delicate-looking transparent butterfly with large cell areas in all wings. The hindwing has a smudge of pink on the trailing edge and a gold-ringed, pupilled eye-spot on the outer margin.

GENUS
CLOSSIANA

A large genus of medium-sized fritillaries which occur in North America, Europe and Asia. Many are associated with arctic habitats and occur within the Arctic Circle, where some spend two years in the larval stage. Typically the butterfly may be found in meadows, both lowland and alpine. They breed on bog plants, including violets, *Viola*, and *Vaccinium*, where their food plants are known.

CLOSSIANA CHARICLEA
Arctic Fritillary

1³⁄₈in 36mm	ZONE 1·3·5

A small butterfly with rounded forewings and dark markings set against a rich orange ground. The underside of the hindwing is orange-purple with silver spots. The butterfly has adaptations to cope with living in the high arctic, such as surviving intense cold and freezing conditions. Its caterpillar food plants have yet to be identified. It is one of a few butterflies which are found around the entire coastal area of Greenland.

CLOSSIANA DIA
Violet Fritillary

1⁵⁄₁₆in 34mm	ZONE 3·5

The violet tinge which covers the outer parts of the underside of the hindwing gives this fritillary its common name. The leading edge of the hindwing is strongly angled, and not rounded as in other related species. The ground color on the upper surface is rich orange, covered in black spots. The base of the wings are dark. The butterfly flies in light woodland and breeds on violets.

CLOSSIANA FREIJA
Zigzag Fritillary, Frejya's Fritillary

ZONE
1·3·5

1¾in
44mm

A good identification feature is the black zigzag band on the underside of the hindwing. Otherwise, the butterfly is like many other fritillaries of this size, with a dark base to the hindwings. The butterfly breeds on typical moorland and tundra plants such as cloudberry and whortleberry (*Vaccinium*), but it has been little researched.

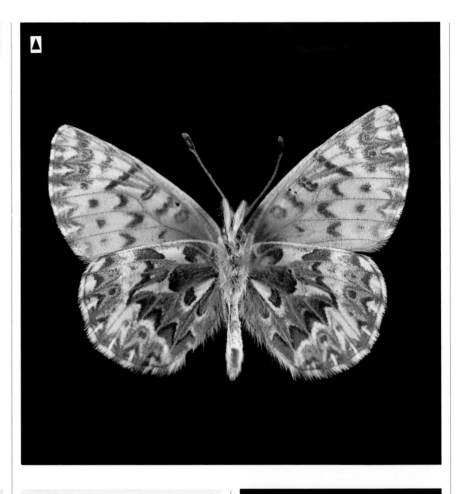

CLOSSIANA FRIGGA
Willow-bog Fritillary, Frigga's Fritillary

ZONE
1·3·5

1¾in
46mm

The bases of the uppers are very dark, but toward the margins is a row of black spots running around the fore and hindwings. The sexes are similar. The underside of the hindwing is variously colored in purple, red-brown, yellow and white. The butterfly occurs on bogs and moors, and breeds on cloudberry, *Rubus chamaemorus*.

CLOSSIANA IMPROBA
Dingy Arctic Fritillary, Dusky-winged Fritillary

ZONE
1·3·5

1⁵⁄₁₆in
34mm

Dingy aptly describes the dull appearance of this small butterfly. The underside is only marginally more exciting than the uppers, with some dull reddish-brown marks mixed with some dirty white marks. It is a circumpolar butterfly that is used to living in harsh arctic conditions. It is not known on which food plant it breeds.

CLOSSIANA POLARIS
Polar fritillary

ZONE
1·3

1½in
38mm

The dull orange background is suffused with dark spots and marks all over the wings, and the base of the hindwing is dark. The underside of the hindwing is the key identification feature with its many tiny white marks distributed over the entire wing. The butterfly occurs in the high arctic and breeds on mountain avens and whortleberry.

CLOSSIANA TITANIA
Purple bog Fritillary, Titania's Fritillary

ZONE
1·3·5

1⁷/₈in
48mm

A substantial fritillary with bold black markings over its uppers, including a ring of well-defined black spots around the inside of the margin. There is a row of black triangular marks on all margins. The underside of the hindwing has some rather pointed light-colored marks edged in black. A number of subspecies exist. The butterfly occurs on arctic meadows and in the tundra, where it breeds on violet.

GENUS
COELITES

A genus of two species which inhabit the lowland rainforest of Asia and the Australian region. They occur from Burma to Sulawesi where they fly in the dark of the forest understory. Nothing is known about their life cycle or caterpillar food plants.

COELITES EPIMINTHIA

ZONE
5·6

3¹/₈in
84mm

A highly characteristic wing shape helps to identify this species. The forewing is curved, hooked, and indented on the outer margin. The hindwing is elongated, scalloped, and drawn-out into a stubby tail. The uppers are violet-blue with a black male sex brand on the inside edge of the hindwing. The undersides are silvery brown with a series of eye-spots on the hindwing. There are at least three subspecies known. Nothing is known about the life cycle except that it, like C. *euptychioides*, lives deep in the dark lowland rainforest.

COELITES EUPTYCHIOIDES

ZONE
6

3¹/₈in
80mm

The blue is confined to the trailing edge of the hindwing in this species. The rest of the upper surface is a uniform light brown. The undersides are much lighter, but the surprise here is the very large eye-spot on the trailing edge of the hindwing with three much smaller ones at the margin. The profile of the wings is not curved, hooked, and drawn-out in a tail as in C. *epiminthia*. Subspecies are known, but the life cycle is not.

GENUS
COENONYMPHA

This is a genus of browns which are widely distributed in the European and Asian regions, with examples in North America. Collectively, they are called "heaths." They have exploited grassy areas, including heaths, since they breed on grasses. Generally, the butterflies have light brown colors which match the terrain in which they live.

COENONYMPHA ARCANIA
Pearly Heath

ZONE
3·5

1¹/₂in
40mm

This is a very pretty butterfly with a pale white-yellow patch highlighting a series of eye-spots on the underside of the hindwing. There is another closely related but smaller species, called Darwin's Heath, which has a small white patch in the same place. The butterfly lives in light woodland and grassy areas, where its caterpillar food plants, *Melica*, a genus of grass, occur.

COENONYMPHA CORINNA
Corsican Heath

ZONE 3

1⅛in
30mm

This is one of the smallest and daintiest heaths. The upper surfaces are orange with darker borders. The undersides are lighter, and there is a small white patch on the underside of the hindwing. The butterfly is restricted to the Mediterranean islands of Corsica and Sardinia, where it lives in grassy areas. Its caterpillar food plants remain unknown.

COENONYMPHA HAYDENII
Wyoming Ringlet, Yellowstone Ringlet

ZONE 1

1⅞in
48mm

This is a very dark brown butterfly on both surfaces. The underside of the hindwing has a series of pupilled eye-spots around the margin, and in fresh specimens there is a faint bronze-green metallic hue over the wings. Early stages have not been described, but it is thought that the butterfly breeds on grasses and sedges. It has a very restricted distribution and is protected within the Yellowstone National Park and the Absaroka Wilderness Area.

COENONYMPHA IPHIOIDES
Spanish Heath

ZONE 3

1½in
40mm

The male is darker than the female and has a dark brown ground suffused toward the base of the forewing and around the margin of the hindwing with a thin orange line. The forewing of the female is yellow-orange, and the hindwing is brown. The undersides are striking with their series of black eye-spots around the margin of the hindwing. This species is found only in Spain. The caterpillar food plants are unknown.

COENONYMPHA GLYCERION
Chestnut Heath

ZONE 3·5

1³⁄₈in
36mm

This butterfly takes its common name from the chestnut color which suffuses the leading edges of the forewing. The ground color is normally dark brown on the uppers, and light brown on the lower surfaces, especially on the forewing. The hindwing underside has a neat row of black eye-spots. The butterfly lives on open grassy areas and breeds on various grasses such as *Melica* and *Brachypodium*.

COENONYMPHA HERO
Scarce Heath

ZONE 3·5

1⁵⁄₁₆in
34mm

This butterfly is a uniform brown with a faint orange tint to the leading edge of the forewing and a series of four orange spots around the margin of the hindwing. On the undersides the hindwing eye-spots are very conspicuous, and to the inside is a thin line of white. The butterfly flies in grassy meadows and moors, where it breeds on wild iris as well as various grasses such as *Lolium* and *Carex*.

COENONYMPHA PAMPHILUS
Small Heath

ZONE 3·5

1¼in
32mm

These butterflies have a very uniform, pale straw ground color. The female is slightly larger than the male and has a thin dark marking around the wings. There is a very small dark spot in the apex of the forewing. The base of the underside of the hindwing is very dark, while the base of the underside of the forewing is russet. This is a very widespread species which lives in fields, meadows, and along roadsides. It breeds on various species of common grass.

GENUS
CORADES

This genus of South American butterflies flies in highland rainforests.

CORADES IDUNA

ZONE 2

3in
76mm

The elongated hindwing is drawn out as a tail. The forewings are black with white spots; the hindwings are chestnut to the outside, dark brown to the inside. The undersides are very dull except for the white forewing spots. The dull appearance serves the butterfly well as camouflage.

GENUS
CYLLOPSIS

This is a genus of 25 species of browns from Central and South America. Some of the six species which occur in Costa Rica are found in montane areas, living in sunny sites. They are generally small butterflies, brown on top with gold and silver marks below. All species may breed on grasses, including bamboo.

CYLLOPSIS PERTEPIDA
Canyonland Satyr, Arroyo Satyr

ZONE 1·2

1³⁄₄in
44mm

The reddish-brown color is typical of both the upper and lower surfaces, but the underside of the hindwing is the key to identification. On the trailing edge there are two small pairs of eye-spots set in an area of silver-blue. The butterfly lives in some of the hottest habitats in deserts and canyons, but always around shady scrub. Its life cycle is undescribed, but its caterpillar food plants are almost certainly grasses.

CYLLOPSIS PYRACMON
Nabokov's Satyr, Mexican Arroyo Satyr

ZONE 1·2

1³⁄₄in
44mm

This little brown butterfly has two small pairs of eye-spots on the margin of the underside hindwing. There is a little line which runs straight behind these eye-spots; in related species the line bends. The butterfly lives in grassy glades in woodland where it probably breeds on grass, though its life cycle has yet to be ascertained.

GENUS
CYMOTHOE

This is a genus of exclusively African butterflies which exhibit sexual dimorphism and polymorphism. They have rather large and curved forewings, and the hindwings are often rounded, scalloped, and tailed. Butterflies live in woody areas and are often scarce.

CYMOTHOE CAENIS
Migratory Glider

ZONE 4

2⁵⁄₈in
68mm

The sexes are usually completely different. The male is white with various black zigzag marks around the margin of the wings. The larger female is white, black, or gray with a large white band crossing the wing. The undersides are drab for camouflage. The butterfly lives in forested areas and sometimes migrates in large numbers.

CYMOTHOE FUMANA
Gold-banded Glider

ZONE 4

3in
79mm

This butterfly takes its common name from the large gold bands on the hindwing and huge expanse of gold-yellow on the male forewing. The base of the male hindwing is black-brown. The female is brown with an orange-brown margin and also has a peppering of white dots on the forewing. The butterfly lives in the rainforest in much of central Africa.

CYMOTHOE SANGARIS
Red Glider, Blood Red Cymothoe

ZONE 4

2⅜in
70mm

The male is blood red all over the uppers; hence *sangaris*. The larger female has rich red-orange in the center of its wings, with dark margins splashed with white, especially on the forewing, and zigzags on the hindwing. There is much regional variation in the female. The butterfly frequents forest areas.

GENUS
CYNANDRA

A genus of African butterflies which live in the forest understory; males have flashy colors.

CYNANDRA OPIS
Shining Blue Nymph, Blue Banded Nymph

ZONE 4

2⅛in
55mm

The iridescent blue male has dark bands running through the wings and white spots near the forewing apex. The female has a brown ground and a yellow band on the hindwing, becoming thinner on the forewing.

GENUS
CYNTHIA

A genus of butterflies which has representatives in North America, Europe, Asia, and Australia. Many are powerful migrants, including *C. cardui*. This genus is sometimes regarded as a subfamily of *Vanessa*.

CYNTHIA CARDUI
Painted Lady

ZONE 1·3 5·6

2⅝in
70mm

The most widespread of the world's butterflies and a very powerful migrant. The forewing has dark tips and bold white marks. The rest of the wings are orange with gray and black marks, and blue spots near the margin of the hindwing. The undersides are mottled. This butterfly is very uniform in its pattern and coloration, although some sub-species do exist. One reason for its success is that it breeds on a wide variety of plants. These include common members of the mallow and daisy families, especially thistles.

CYNTHIA VIRGINIENSIS
American Painted Lady

ZONE 1·2·3

2⅜in
60mm

Identified by the unique pattern on the underside of the hindwing, which shows two large eye-spots against a white-cream cobweb patterned background. The butterfly occurs through most of North and Central America, and migratory strays turn up in the Azores, southern-western Europe, Britain, and Hawaii. It breeds principally on members of the daisy family.

GENUS
CYRESTIS

A genus of map-wing butterflies named after the fine transverse lines which cross the forewing. The sexes are alike, but there is one (not described here) which is dimorphic. They are typically of Asia and the Australian regions, and probably feed on *Tetracera sarmentosa* and *Ficus* species.

▲

CYRESTIS CAMILLUS
African Map Butterfly

 ZONE 4 2¹⁄₈in 55mm

Map butterflies are mostly found in Asia, but this is the only representative of its genus in Africa. It rests with its wings wide open, so its clear map-like pattern is very plain to see. The cream ground is interspersed with bands of orange, some edged in black. There is a definite tail and a pair of blue spots on the inside edge of the hindwing. The butterfly flies within forests.

CYRESTIS ACHATES
Map Butterfly

 ZONE 6 2¹⁄₈in 54mm

The amount of white on the wings and the proportion of orange around the margins of the hindwing are key identification features of this species. The forewings are crossed by three major lines as well as by the darkened veins. The butterfly is found alongside streams in lowland rainforest.

CYRESTIS MAENALIS

ZONE 5 2³⁄₈in 60mm

This is a very dark map butterfly with three major bands of white separated by thin lines crossing its wings. There is a small tail and a distinctive orange-red patch on the inside edge of the hindwing, and a small orange dot on the outside trailing edge of the forewing. Butterflies occur by streams in lowland rainforest.

CYRESTIS TELAMON

	ZONE 5
2in 50mm	

This is intermediate in color between *C. achates* and *C. maenalis*. There is one strong band of white which crosses the wings and terminates at the characteristic red-orange mark on the trailing edge of the hindwing. The outer parts of the wings are all very dark, with a thin tracery of white marks running around the edge. Butterflies inhabit lowland rainforest.

GENUS
DANAUS

A genus known as the "tiger butterflies" which has representatives in all geographical regions. More species occur in the Old World, but a typical danaid is the New World *D. plexippus*. Larvae of this genus feed on members of the milkweed and dogbane families, *Asclepiadaceae* and *Apocynaceae*, and render themselves poisonous to predators by storing plant poisons. There are many other butterflies that mimic toxic members of this genus.

DANAUS AFFINIS

	ZONE 6
2⁷⁄₈in 74mm	

The butterfly is mainly chocolate brown with prominent white patches in the center of each wing. Toward the tip of the forewing, there are a number of irregular-sized white spots, some of which may be fused. There is a certain amount of checkering around the margin of the hindwing. The upper pattern is repeated on the underside, but it is heavily infused with red-orange arrows. Butterflies are found in forest margins and open areas. They probably breed on members of the *Asclepiadaceae*.

DANAUS ASPASIA

	ZONE 5
3¹⁄₈in 81mm	

The key feature is the area of lemon-yellow mostly at the base of the hindwings, which may be more or less extensive. The rest of the wings are white with brown veins, giving them a very speckled appearance. The white marks are more like spots to the outside of the wing and form distinct windows towards the base.

DANAUS CHRYSIPPUS AEGYPTIUS
Plain Tiger, African Monarch,
Lesser Wanderer, Golden Danaid

	ZONE 4
3¹⁄₈in 82mm	

This lacks the black veins present in other similar species, but there is a pair of black spots on the usual dull orange hindwing. The apex of the forewing is black with some consolidation of white marks, and there is a white-spotted black band around the hindwing. The butterfly is a migrant and breeds on *Asclepias curassavica* and *Calotropis gigantea*. It is usually found in lowland areas where its caterpillar food plant occurs.

DANAUS ERESIMUS
MONTEZUMA
Soldier

	ZONE 1·2
3¹⁄₈in 80mm	

The ground color is dusky brown with a pronounced black margin around the wings, broader on the hindwing. The veins are black, and there is considerable white speckling on the black areas. The butterfly is migratory and breeds in southern Florida. It occurs in the Antilles and Mexico, and penetrates into several southern states of the US. It breeds on members of the poisonous *Asclepiadaceae*.

DANAUS GILIPPUS
The queen

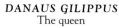

ZONE
1·2

3½in
90mm

This differs from *D. eresimus* in having more white spots on the forewing and white borders to the black veins on the underside of the hindwing, and it is often slightly larger. The Queen often flies in company with *D. plexippus*. It is a migrant which penetrates north into the US exploiting a wide range of habitats, but it cannot survive cold winters. It breeds on members of the *Asclepiadaceae*. Males possess reversible hair pencils for courting females.

DANAUS MELANIPPUS
Common Tiger

ZONE
5·6

3¾in
95mm

The distinctive feature is the white ground of the hindwing which is traversed by black veins; otherwise, it is similar to *D. plexippus* and *D. genutia* (not described). It is more common than the latter, especially on the lowland plains. The butterfly occurs from India to Burma, including Sulawesi.

DANAUS PLEXIPPUS
Milkweed, Monarch

ZONE
1·3
5·6

4in
100mm

A large and powerful butterfly which has established itself around the world through its great powers of dispersal. Its patterns and colors are not very variable, and, with the black and white spotting over the rich orange background, it has all the brightly colored characteristics of a toxic butterfly. It feeds on milkweed and utilizes the poisons in the plant in its own body for defense.

GENUS
DIAGORA

An Asian genus of butterflies whose color and patterns are similar to the danaids.

DIAGORA MENA

ZONE
5

3½in
93mm

The wing shape, pattern, and color are all typical of danaids, but the ground is light brown. The veins are etched in black, and the dark outer part of the forewing contains cream spots. There are faint red marks on the trailing edge of the hindwing.

GENUS
DIONE

This is a genus of four species from Central and South America, and the southern US. Typically, they have orange uppers with stunning silver marks on the undersides of the wings. They breed on many species of passion flower, *Passiflora*. They exploit secondary vegetation, and butterfly numbers increase dramatically in areas where there has been rainforest destruction.

DIONE MONETA POEYI
Mexican Silverspot,
Mexican Silver-spotted Fritillary

ZONE
1·2

2⅞in
74mm

The underside of the hindwing and the tip of the forewing are both generously endowed with silver spots. The uppersides are orange with black veins. Some heavy veining occurs near the base of the forewings and around the trailing edge of the forewings. The caterpillars are gregarious; so too are the adults, which rest in grass at night. The butterfly is found mostly in Central America. It is a migrant which rarely enters the southern US.

DIONE VANILLAE INSULARIS
Gulf Fritillary

The diagnostic features are the one to three black-ringed white spots near the base of the forewing. The wings are bright orange, and the veins marked in black. There are some larger blobs of black toward the margins, and a few small black marks between the veins on the forewing. The hindwing underside and forewing tip are covered in silver spots. The migrant butterfly flies in open, flowery, wayside, and garden habitats. This widespread and familiar butterfly visits gardens to drink nectar.

GENUS
DOLESCHALLIA

A genus of powerful butterflies which occur on New Guinea.

DOLESCHALLIA DASCYLUS

This has a very rounded hindwing ending in a stubby, in-turned tail. The forewing is indented on the outer edge. The male has a broken blue-green band on the dark forewing. The female has a small white-blue bar on the forewing with russet toward the base.

GENUS
DOXOCOPA

A genus of about 30 sexually dimorphic species whose males are all iridescent blue, green, or purple.

DOXOCOPA LAURENTIA
CHERUBINA

The male has an attractive band of iridescent green in the middle of the wings. The ground color is dark brown. The much larger female has a paler brown ground and a pearly blue band in the center of the wing. In both sexes the margins are scalloped. The butterfly lives in forest clearings.

GENUS
DRUCINA

This is a genus of three South and Central American butterflies which live in cloud forest habitats. Caterpillar food plants for all species will probably be found to be bamboos.

DRUCINA CHAMPIONI

The shape of the wings is characteristic. The hindwings are much broader and appear larger than the forewings. The ground color is dark brown, almost black. The most conspicuous markings are on the hindwing, which has a series of large blue blotches. The forewing has a row of very insignificant pale orange marks inside the margin. The butterfly flies in highland cloud forest. Caterpillar food plants are unknown.

DRUCINA LEONATA

The forewings are strongly curved, a useful identification feature, and the hindwings are very rounded. The hindwing has a very large patch of orange which covers most of the area. The forewing has a row of uniform yellow marks inside the margin. The female markings are less precise than those of the male. The undersides are dull for camouflage. A butterfly of the cloud forest, its caterpillar food plants are unknown.

GENUS
DRYAS

A single migratory species represents this South American genus.

DRYAS IULIA
Julia

ZONE 1·2

3½in 92mm

The uppersides of the elongated wings are orange, unmarked save for a conspicuous black blob or band in the cell area of the forewing. The undersides are very pale brown with small white flashes. Butterflies frequent open sunny and flowery areas, and breed on passion flower.

GENUS
DULCEDO

A genus with a single South American species which has rounded transparent wings.

DULCEDO POLITA

ZONE 2

2⅝in 70mm

There is a conspicuous eye-spot on the outer edge of the hindwing, and a pale orange map-like line on the upper surfaces. The veins are conspicuous, and wing margins are edged in black. The butterfly lives in shady forests and breeds on palms.

GENUS
ELYMNIAS

Members of this large genus of brown butterflies are called "palmflies" since they breed on palms, including the thorny rattan climber. They occur extensively in Asia and in the Australian region, and live in rainforest areas, preferring shade to sunshine.

ELYMNIAS AGONDAS
Palmfly

ZONE 5·6

3½in 90mm

This is a black and white butterfly with clear sexual differences. The male is mostly black with cream marks inside the margins of its wings, and a large cream band on the hindwing tinged blue at the edge. The female has white flashes on both wings and a group of black-ringed eye-spots on the hindwing. The patterns and eye-spots are repeated on the underside.

ELYMNIAS CASIPHONE
MALELAS

ZONE 5

4in 100mm

The outer part of the long forewings tend to be covered with white blotches and a suffusion of blue. The ground color may be rich brown or liberally peppered with white. The margin of the wings are somewhat irregularly scalloped. There are a number of subspecies.

ELYMNIAS CERYX

ZONE 5

4in 100mm

The sexes are dissimilar. The female has longer wings and more muted colors compared to the sky blue on the forewing of the male. The ground color of the male is black; that of the female is brown. On the hindwing there is a pattern of radiating vein marks with a row of dots near the margin. In both sexes the veins are marked in the ground color, and the white dots in the row around the margin of the forewing are much larger than those on the hindwing.

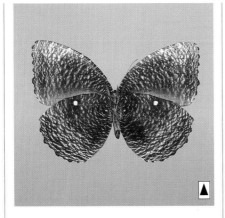

ELYMNIAS CUMAEA

ZONE 6

4in
100mm

The broad forewings, rounded hindwings, and irregularly scalloped margins are characteristic. Males are much brighter than females, usually with bright sky blue around the margins against a black ground. The slightly larger females have muted colors and a subdued ground color; the undersides are strongly mottled. At least six subspecies are recorded. The butterfly is found on Sulawesi, Indonesia, and other islands.

ELYMNIAS HYPERMNESTRA
Common Palmfly

ZONE 5

3⅛in
80mm

The female mimics danaid (*Danaus*) and euploeid (*Euploea*) species and is brown, white and black. There are two distinct forms of the female, orange and blue. In the blue form there are blue spots around either the forewing or hindwing. The undersides are mottled brown and drab, darker to the base of the wing. This is a most variable species, both sexually, seasonally, and in its subspecies. It is also the most widespread of this important genus. The butterfly occurs in coconut groves, where it breeds on the coconut palms.

ELYMNIAS NELSONI

ZONE 5

3⅛in
80mm

The male has bright blue on the outer half of its wings, and black on the inner half. The margins are irregularly scalloped and black. The undersides are dark. It occurs in Indonesia. Few of these butterflies have been collected until recently.

ELYMNIAS DARA BENGENA

ZONE 5

2⅝in
70mm

Males tend to have a black ground with a blue or pale blue band inside the margins of the wings. The females are usually duller with a brown ground. In both sexes the margins are irregularly scalloped, and there is a series of spots enclosed in the blue band on the hindwing. The undersides are brown with a pale band on the hindwing enclosing black spots. Six subspecies are recorded for this widespread butterfly. The butterfly occurs in both lowland and highland virgin rainforest.

ELYMNIAS MIMALON

ZONE 6

4in
100mm

This is a stunning butterfly, the male of which has a bright blue suffusion over its broad, rounded wings (not shown in this photograph). The female has a brown ground with a pale milky blue suffusion to the outside enclosing some white spots on the hindwing. The species is variable, and the female may be brown, or with just the tips of the scalloped margins black in contrast to the blue. At least two subspecies are known.

ELYMNIAS NESAEA LIONELI
Tiger Palmfly

ZONE 5

3¾in
95mm

There are several subspecies known from Sikkim to Malaya, and they vary in size as well as in the amount of brown on the wings. The pattern may be greenish, yellow-green, or pale cream. The general pattern is a dark brown ground color which also runs along the veins, the intervening spaces filled with color except at the margins, which are dark. The butterfly occurs in lowland and highland virgin rainforest.

ELYMNIAS PATNA
Blue-striped Palmfly

Unusually for this genus, the sexes are similar. The ground color is black with whispers of blue radiating out from small points on the forewing, with just a touch of blue on the hindwing. There is a row of faint white dots on the hindwing, usually four, and these are repeated more boldly on the brown underside. This delightful butterfly occurs in highland rainforest.

ELYMNIAS PENANGA

At least two subspecies are known in Malaya. They are rather similar to *E. patna* in the presence of whispers of blue on the forewing, but in addition they have an overall blue tint to the wing. The hindwing tends to have a brown ground color. Unlike *E. patna*, the female is very variable. The butterfly occurs in lowland virgin rainforest, as well as in secondary growth areas.

GENUS
ELZUNIA

A South and Central American genus of six species with a black ground color.

ELZUNIA BONPLANDII

The forewing, crossed by a bright green band, also has a small pale apical line. The hindwing has a green rim along the trailing edge and is orange-brown beneath. The forewing underside has a reddish base with black, green, and a pale brown tip.

GENUS
EREBIA

A large genus of browns which has over 100 species. Most of them live at high elevations, especially in arctic regions, although there are representatives in Europe, Asia, North America, and the Australian region. These butterflies are of medium size and have dark red colors. Some breed on various coarse grasses. However, there are several erebias in Europe whose larval food plants are still unknown.

EREBIA AETHIOPS
Scotch Argus

The rosy red flashes on the forewings contain a series of eye-spots, which are more pronounced in the larger female. The male is a rich brown with a black suffusion over the central area of the forewing; the female is a lighter brown. This is a mountain butterfly typical of many parts of Europe and east to Asia. It flies in alpine areas and around woods, and breeds on *Molinia* grass.

EREBIA CALLIAS
Colorado Alpine, Relict Gray Alpine

The upper sides are dark brown with a greenish tinge in fresh specimens. The underside of the hindwing is mottled gray, and the forewing is orange toward the base and gray at the tip. There are two small eye-spots on both sides of the forewing tip. The butterfly lives in alpine grasslands, where it probably breeds on meadow grasses and sedges. It is of conservation interest because of its relic distribution in various mountain ranges in western US, China, and the Middle East. This reflects the geographical separation of these areas caused by the Ice Age.

EREBIA DISA STECKERI
White-spot Alpine, Arctic Ringlet

	ZONE
	1·3·5
2in 50mm	

Rather a large and unmarked butterfly dressed in uniform pale brown on the uppers, with a modest row of orange-highlighted spots on the forewing. The underside of the hindwing is two-tone brown. Two subspecies are known, but the caterpillar food plants are unknown. It flies over bogs and moors, and takes two years to go through a single generation.

EREBIA DISCOIDALIS
Red-disked Alpine

	ZONE
	1·5
2in 51mm	

The key features are the lack of eye-spots and the red disk or flash of color on the forewing. The color is repeated on the underside. The ground color is brown-black, which becomes slightly lighter to the outside on the underside. The butterfly lives in open, wooded and grassy areas within the Arctic Circle and probably breeds on meadow grasses and sedges, spending two years as a caterpillar.

EREBIA EMBLA
Lapland Ringlet

	ZONE
	3
2in 52mm	

This is quite a large ringlet, and it has very rounded wings. On the forewings there are two sets of eye-spots, and one pair, which may or may not be pupilled, is fused. On the hindwing, a series of four blind eye-spots is found inside the margin. The eye-spots of the female are usually a little more emphasized than those of the male, but the overall colors are muted. The butterfly flies over boggy areas near trees, but its caterpillar food plants are unknown.

EREBIA EPIPHRON FAUVENI
Mountain Ringlet

	ZONE
	3
1⅝in 42mm	

This dainty-looking ringlet has rather expanded forewings, considerably larger toward the outside in some specimens. The ground color is a dark brown, and there is a dull orange-red flush on the forewing in which some very small black dots occur; this is repeated on the underside. There are several subspecies recorded from various mountain haunts in Europe. In one locality in the Harz Mountains in Germany, the butterflies have become extinct. The butterfly flies in grassy alpine meadows and breeds on tufted hair grass, *Deschampsia cespitosa*

EREBIA FASCIATA
Banded Alpine, White-band Alpine

ZONE
1·5

2¼in
57mm

This butterfly has a conspicuous whitish band which runs around the undersides of the wings. The male is black on the uppers, but the female is reddish brown over its wings. Both sexes lack any spotting. The butterfly lives in tundra and tussocky areas in the high arctic. It may breed on sedges or meadow grasses, though its life cycle has not yet been determined.

EREBIA LIGEA
Arran Brown

ZONE
3·5

2¼in
56mm

The markings on this ringlet are very precise. The male is the more strident, with a rich orange band across the wings containing relatively large pupilled eye-spots on the forewing, and small ones on the hindwing. The rich nutty color of the male is replaced with pale brown in the female, which has more strongly emphasized eye-spots. The pattern on the forewing is repeated on the underside, but the hindwing is dark and drab, and required for camouflage. The butterfly lives on grassy slopes and breeds on species like wood millet grass, *Milium*.

EREBIA MEDUSA
Woodland Ringlet

ZONE
3·5

1⅞in
48mm

A variable species, but the key feature is the four pupilled spots set out neatly on the hindwing. The forewing has a few large eye-spots set in an orange band. All these spots are repeated on the underside. There are a number of subspecies. The butterfly flies in lowland bogs as well as high in mountains, depending on the region, and breeds on finger grasses, *Digitaria*, and wood millet, *Milium*.

EREBIA HERSE

ZONE
5

2¼in
56mm

The ground color is sooty black and on the forewing is one large pupilled eye-spot and two other smaller and unpupilled ones, all set in a faintly lighter area infused heavily with black. All the orange brightness of other more colorful members of the genus is lost in this blackened butterfly, typical of many erebias found in high mountains. It occurs from Tibet to China.

EREBIA MAGDALENA
Magdalena Alpine, Rockslide Alpine

ZONE
1·5

2½in
64mm

Both sexes are strongly dark brown with a faint green dusting only when very fresh. Named "rockslide" after the stony habitat in which this butterfly lives, the female spends a lot of time basking and not on the wing. The caterpillars probably take up to two years to reach maturity, feeding on meadow grasses. The butterfly is conserved within Rocky Mountain National Park, a part of its widespread distribution.

EREBIA PANDROSE
Dewy Ringlet

ZONE
3

2in
50mm

The underside of the hindwing is the key to identification. It is gray with a wiggly black line and two other paler lines, as well as two small dots. The uppers have a rectangular flash of orange in which some small black spots reside. The hindwing is uniform brown with a row of small spots. The butterfly lives on alpine slopes, often in excess of 6,000ft (1,800m), and breeds on grasses, *Poa* and *Festuca* species.

EREBIA POLARIS
Arctic Woodland Ringlet

ZONE
3·5

1³/₄in
44mm

The wings are rounded, particularly in the female, which has much stronger markings on the underside of the hindwing. The upperside is a uniform warm brown with very small reduced spots in the male. The butterfly lives in Lapland and various points eastward, and its dark coloration enables it to warm up quickly in the northern sunshine. It frequents open woodland grassland, but its caterpillar food plant has not yet been discovered.

EREBIA THEANO
Theano Alpine, Banded Alpine

ZONE
1·5

1¹/₂in
38mm

This species is easier to identify than many of the *Erebia* as the key features are a little more obvious. There is a band of yellow-cream marks around the inside of the margin of the hindwing. The uppersides are crossed by reddish marks, and there are no eye-spots present at all. The butterfly lives in alpine meadows and pastures where it probably breeds on meadow grasses.

A New Zealand genus related to *Erebia*, they have map-like marks on the wing bases.

EREBIOLA BUTLERI

ZONE
6

2¹/₂in
64mm

The undersides are distinctive with a series of different-sized chevrons on the hindwing. The spots may be ringed in gold, and there are pale gold lines around the wing margins. At least two subspecies are recorded.

EREBIA ROSSII
Arctic Alpine, Ross's Alpine, Two-dot Alpine

ZONE
1·5

1⁷/₈in
48mm

Its "two-dot" common name comes from the pair of eye-spots on the forewing which may be large or small, but usually they are fused. The hindwing is a little mottled toward the outside. Overall this is a dark butterfly, which befits a species from the high arctic. The butterfly lives over a large area of the tundra and barren country. It probably breeds on various species of sedge.

EREBIA ZAPATERI
Zapateri's Ringlet

ZONE
3

1¹/₂in
40mm

The easily identifiable feature is the bright flash of orange-yellow on the forewing, within which is a pair of eye-spots. The rest of the wing is a rich brown color. The undersides are paler, especially on the hindwing, and the orange markings appear diminished near the apex of the forewing as do the eye-spots. The butterfly is only found in central Spain, and its caterpillar food plants are unknown.

A genus of six species with "owl-eyes" from South and Central America; they breed only on bamboo.

ERYPHANIS AESACUS

ZONE
2

5in
128mm

The male has blue uppers and a conspicuous white oval on the hindwing. The blue on the female is restricted to the wing bases, the outer areas being dark with a faint orange line on the forewing. The butterfly lives in cloud forest.

GENUS
ETEONA

A South American genus which has elongated and indented forewings.

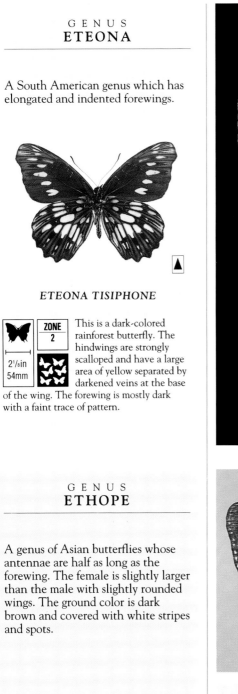

ETEONA TISIPHONE

	ZONE 2
2¹/₈in 54mm	

This is a dark-colored rainforest butterfly. The hindwings are strongly scalloped and have a large area of yellow separated by darkened veins at the base of the wing. The forewing is mostly dark with a faint trace of pattern.

GENUS
ETHOPE

A genus of Asian butterflies whose antennae are half as long as the forewing. The female is slightly larger than the male with slightly rounded wings. The ground color is dark brown and covered with white stripes and spots.

ETHOPE DIADEMOIDES

	ZONE 5
3¹/₈in 84mm	

This butterfly is distinguished by the series of creamy-white marks which "hang" around the wing margin like a necklace or diadem. The spots are small near the apex of the forewing, but become larger and form five large "pearls" on the hindwing. There are at least two subspecies recorded. The butterfly occurs in rainforest in Burma, Thailand, and Malaya.

ETHOPE HIMACHALA

	ZONE 5
4in 100mm	

The sexes share the same colors and patterns, but the female is almost ¹/₄in (20mm) larger. On both surfaces around the margin, there is a series of gold-ringed black eye-spots, each of which is pupilled in white. The markings on the underside tend to be larger than on the uppers. There is also a single eye-spot twice as large as the others on the outer leading edge of the underside of the hindwing. The butterfly occurs from northwestern India to Thailand, in rainforest.

GENUS
EUNICA

A genus of 60 species from South and Central America which live in primary forest.

EUNICA NORICA

	ZONE 2

2³/₈in
60mm

The male is dark brown-black, flushed blue inside the margin of the hindwing. The larger female is flushed white over the central region of the forewings; the hindwing is relatively unmarked. Butterflies live in cloud forest, but their caterpillar food plants are unknown.

GENUS
EUPHYDRYAS

A genus of butterflies called checkerspots in North America and fritillaries in Europe. Examples are found also in Asia. These medium to large butterflies have typical orange-spotted patterns and are frequently found in the open in grassy areas, especially meadows.

EUPHYDRYAS CHALCEDONA
Chalcedon or Western Checkerspot

	ZONE 1

2in
50mm

The spotting over the wings is rather more white and pale yellow against a black ground than yellow against an orange ground color as in related species. This is one of the most variable butterflies in North America with 17 subspecies. The butterfly occurs in various habitats from tundra to woods, open areas within live-oak woods, and chaparral. It breeds on plantain, honeysuckle, and snowberry.

EUPHYDRYAS EDITHA
Edith's Checkerspot, Ridge Checkerspot

	ZONE 1

1⁷/₈in
48mm

Checkerspots are very variable, and this one is true to form. The upperside is patterned with orange and yellow spots which are often enclosed with brown marks. In some individuals the orange markings are much reduced and replaced with black. The butterfly breeds on members of the figwort family. One of the subspecies – the Bay Checkerspot – which occurs on Jasper Ridge, California, is listed as a threatened butterfly by the federal government.

▼

EUPHYDRYAS GILLETTII
Gillette's Checkerspot,
Yellowstone Checkerspot

	ZONE 1	
1³/₄in 44mm		

This species can be identified by the two prominent orange bands which cross the hindwing, both separated by a pale yellow band. The uppersides are brown with yellowish spots. The butterfly lives in forest clearings and breeds on snowberry, *Symphoricarpos albus,* and honeysuckle, *Lonicera involucrata.* Within Yellowstone National Park, the butterfly is protected.

EUPHYDRYAS PHAETON
Baltimore

	ZONE 1
2¹/₂in 64mm	

This is one of the largest checkerspots. It has a distinctive orange band around the margins of all wings and several orange blobs near the base of the wings. Elsewhere on the underside and on the upperside, the ground color is black with white spots. The butterfly lives in wet meadows where the native turtlehead, *Chelone glabra,* grows. It breeds on this turtlehead as well as on other native plants. It is named after Lord Baltimore, an early colonist, whose heraldic shield color-matched this butterfly.

GENUS
EUPLOEA

This is the largest genus within the subfamily *Danaidae.* They have light and dark markings which are sometimes iridescent and, for this reason, are commonly called crow butterflies. Species are found in lowland and upland areas. They breed on members of the *Asclepiadaceae, Apocynaceae,* and *Moraceae,* and become poisonous to predators by incorporating chemicals into their bodies from the larval food plants. Some species exhibit sexual dimorphism. Males often have strong smells associated with their scent apparatus.

EUPLOEA ALCATHOE EICHHORNI
Striped Black Crow

	ZONE 5·6	
3¹/₄in 85mm		

The sexes have slightly different ground colors. The male is dark brown with a blue iridescence on the forewings, and the female is brown with a series of white spots on the forewing. While the male has two rows of white spots on the hindwing, the female has a series of longer marks. The butterfly is found from Burma to Borneo and in Australia. It breeds on *Ficus eugenioides, Hoya australis,* and *Nerium oleander.*

EUPLOEA BATESI

	ZONE 6	
4in 100mm		

This is a large butterfly with rounded wings. The brown and white coloration is reminiscent of the danaids, and on the underside of both wings there is an open series of white dashes. The brown color becomes lighter toward the margins.

EUPLOEA CLIMENA

	ZONE 5·6	
3¹/₈in 80mm		

The forewing is long and very dark, almost black. The hindwing is a russet brown and, like the forewing, is completely devoid of any markings. This rarity of northwestern Australia has also been found on Christmas Island south of Java, Indonesia.

EUPLOEA CORE GODARTII
Common Indian Crow, Australian Crow, Oleander Butterfly

ZONE
5·6

3³/₄in
96mm

The sexes are fairly similar, with a rich brown ground and a series of white marks around the wings. The male has a conspicuous sex brand on the forewing. There are a number of subspecies recognized. This is one of the most common butterflies in Australia, probably due to the caterpillars' acceptance of a wide range of food plants, such as oleander, mandevillea, stephanotis, fig, trachelospermum, and hoya.

EUPLOEA MULCIBER
Striped Blue Crow

ZONE
5

4in
100mm

The male is a little brighter than the female with a purple sheen over a black ground splashed with blue milky marks. This is a very variable species with several known subspecies. The butterfly flies along tracks cut through rainforests and along rainforest rivers, where it breeds on oleander, fig, and *Aristolochia* species.

EUPLOEA PHAENARETA CALLITHOE

ZONE
6

4³/₈in
110mm

This is an attractive subspecies of *E. phaenareta* in which the forewing is black, but the leading edge and the area toward the base of the wing is suffused with blue. The brown hindwings have a yellowish or brownish base, and a tiny blue spot. This spot is mirrored on the forewing. The butterfly lives in mangrove swamps.

EUPLOEA EURIANASSA

ZONE
6

3¹/₂in
92mm

This is a distinctive butterfly with a fairly uniform, pale halo around the margins of the dark brown wings. On the male there is a conspicuous light brown sex brand on the forewing. The butterfly occurs in New Guinea.

EUPLOEA PHAENARETA CASTELNAUI

ZONE
5

4³/₈in
110mm

A number of forms of this butterfly occur, and one of them, *E. phaenareta unibrunnea*, is chocolate brown over most of its wings with just a faint highlighting along the veins. The leading edge of the hindwings is white. The butterfly lives in mangrove swamps.

EUPLOEA SYLVESTER
Two-brand Crow, Double-branded Crow

ZONE
6

3¹/₈in
80mm

This is named after the pair of sex brands which appear on each of the forewings of the male. The forewings are elongated with a few white marks near the tip and a conspicuous band of white chevrons around the margin of the hindwing. There are a number of subspecies, but these are difficult to separate since they do not have very precise differences in their markings.

EUPLOEA TULLIOLUS KOXINGA
The Dwarf Crow

2½in 66mm	ZONE 5

The tips of the forewings are deep blue containing a few white spots. The rest of the wings are soft brown.
This is the smallest euploeid in Malaya – a good identification guide. There are a number of subspecies. The butterfly lives in clearings and waysides, and breeds on *Mikania cordata*, a member of the *Compositae* (daisy family).

GENUS
EUPTYCHIA

At least 15 species occur in lowland rainforest, and many breed on members of the moss family, *Selaginellaceae*.

♀
▲

EUPTYCHIA GERA

1¾in 44mm	ZONE 2

This is a very pale-looking butterfly with a dark border around all but the trailing edge of the forewing. There are two well separated eye-spots on the hindwing. The uppers are crossed by a faint pair of dark lines. The butterfly occurs in the Amazon basin.

GENUS
EURODRYAS

A genus of European and Asian fritillaries with orange and black-speckled patterns. Several species fly in upland, hilly, and mountainous regions, others in the arctic and tundra. The caterpillar food plants of some are unknown.

EURODRYAS AURINIA
Marsh Fritillary

1¾in 46mm	ZONE 3·5

This is a pretty little fritillary in which the female is larger than the male and has more rounded wings. The juxtaposition of the orange, yellow, and black marks on the wings, repeated on the underside without too much black, make this butterfly very colorful. At least four subspecies are recorded. Despite its color, it often lives in very drab places such as bogs, moors, and marshes. It breeds on devil's bit scabious, *Succisa pratensis*, and plantain, *Plantago* species.

▼

♀

EURODRYAS CYNTHIA
Cynthia's Fritillary

ZONE 3

1⁵⁄₈in
42mm

The sexes are dissimilar in this alpine species. The male has white highlighting the red spots on the wings and providing contrast to a row of red marks inside the margins of all wings. The female is red and orange, but drab all over, with a repeat of the pattern on the underside. Like several members of this genus, the caterpillars are gregarious and feed on lady's mantle, *Alchemilla*, of which there are several species, and plantain, *Plantago* species.

EURODRYAS IDUNA
Lapland Fritillary

ZONE 3

1¹⁄₂in
38mm

This Scandinavian species is rather like a smaller, but less brightly colored example of *E. cynthia*, although the sexes are the same. The underside is fairly bright on the hindwing with one definite band of orange and a squiggle or two near the base. The butterfly may be encountered in the open on moors and bogs, but its caterpillar food plant has not yet been ascertained.

GENUS
EUTHALIA

A large genus of browns found in the forests of the Australian region.

EUTHALIA AEETES

ZONE 5

3¹⁄₈in
83mm

The wing margins are all scalloped, and there is a white bar toward the apex of the forewing divided by dark veins. Pale orange rippled marks may cross the uppers. Slightly different color forms have been found on Sulawesi, Indonesia.

GENUS
FABRICIANA

This genus of large fritillaries occurs in Europe and Asia and is related to *Argynnis*.

FABRICIANA NIOBE
Niobe Fritillary

ZONE 3·5

2³⁄₈in
60mm

The key features are on the hindwing undersides: the green toward the base and the silver spots. The orange uppers have a marginal row of black chevrons and some disjointed marks across the wings. The butterfly lives in meadows and pastures, and breeds on violets.

GENUS
GEITONEURA

A genus of butterflies from the Australian region which are similar in size and pattern to the European genus *Pararge*. They breed on grasses.

GEITONEURA ACANTHA
Eastern Ringed Xenica

ZONE 6

2in
52mm

This is an orange-brown butterfly with speckled wings. The ground color is orange, with dark markings crossing the forewing tip and dark marginal lines. There is a small pupilled eye-spot on the forewing tip and one much larger on the hindwing. The margin of the hindwing is somewhat scalloped. The female is significantly larger than the male, with more pronounced eye-spots.

GEITONEURA KLUGI

ZONE 6

2in
50mm

The speckled nature of the wings is pronounced. The ground color is rich orange with thick margins and bands of dark brown on all wings. There is a small eye-spot on each wing. The rounded hindwings are gently scalloped and edged in fawn.

GENUS
GYROCHEILUS

A genus of South American butterflies, about which little is known.

**GYROCHEILUS PATROBAS
TRITONIA**
Red-bordered Brown, Red-rim Satyr

ZONE 1·2

2³/₄in
73mm

This is a large, dark brown butterfly which is named after the red rim around the margin of the hind-wing. The undersides are lighter, and the red rim is still present. The butterfly lives in forestry areas, but its life cycle is unknown.

GENUS
HAMADRYAS

This genus of butterflies are commonly called "calico butterflies," or "crackers." The mottled calico pattern is seen on the uppersides of the wings. The crack refers to the sound that the males produce from their abdomens while in flight during interactions with other males and during courting. The butterflies breed on members of the spurge family, *Euphorbiaceace*, and possibly the mulberry family, *Moraceae*.

HAMADRYAS AMPHINOME
Red Cracker

ZONE 2

1³/₄in
45mm

This butterfly is recognized by the brick-red color of the underside of the black-bordered hindwing. The forewing has a considerable amount of white inside the dark apex. A number of subspecies are known. The butterfly lives in rainforests and breeds on members of the spurge family. Like *Gyrocheilus patrobas* and *Hamadryas atlantis*, it is a casual vagrant into the southern US, from populations in Central America.

▼

HAMADRYAS ATLANTIS
Dusty Cracker

 | ZONE 2 | 2⅝in 70mm

The key identification feature is the series of five black lines of irregular length toward the base of the underside of the forewing. The upper surface is similar to other crackers and has a complicated pattern of mottles, spots, and eye-spots. The butterfly lives in open dry valleys.

▲

HAMADRYAS FERONIA FARINULENTA
Blue Cracker, Cracker

 | ZONE 1 | 2¾in 72mm

This is a darker-colored cracker than *H. februa*, with more intense markings and a suffusion of palest blue. The lack of red rings around the eye-spots on the hindwings is a key feature. A number of subspecies are recorded, and the butterfly is known to be a vagrant, even into the southern US. It occurs in various parts of the rainforest and breeds on *Dalechampia*, a member of the spurge family.

HAMADRYAS FORNAX
Yellow Cracker, Yellow-skirted Cracker

 | ZONE 2 | 1¾in 45mm

Smaller than the other crackers, this one has a number of subspecies. The one found in Costa Rica, *H. fornax fornacalia*, has a russet underside of the hindwing like the specimen illustrated, while the forewings reflect the strong patterning of the uppers. The butterfly occurs in moist rainforest and along trails and rivers, and breeds on *Dalechampia scandens*.

HAMADRYAS FEBRUA
Gray Cracker, Haitian Cracker

ZONE 2 | 3⅛in 80mm

The color pattern is complicated, but, like the other crackers, it is made up of a strong marbling of white and gray all over the wings. The underside of the hindwing loses some of the pattern at the base. The butterfly flies in woods and forest, where it may be common and present throughout the year. It breeds on various spurge species. Found in Central America, this species ventures into the southern US.

HAMADRYAS LAODAMIA

ZONE 2

2⁷/₈in
74mm

This hamadryas has delightful colors which are completely different from its allies. The wings are rounded and black, and the blue starry markings are distinctive. The blue-black iridescent markings on the undersides are edged in red inside the margin. The butterfly flies in the canopy and in sunny clearings of the rainforest. Like many of its allies, it breeds on *Dalechampia triphylla*.

GENUS
HAMANUMIDA

A genus of very speckled "guineafowl" butterflies found in Africa and Saudi Arabia.

HAMANUMIDA DAEDALUS
Guineafowl

ZONE 4

2³/₈in
60mm

An amazing speckly pattern, just like that found on the feathers of a guineafowl, gives this butterfly its common name. The butterfly is common throughout Africa and is present in Saudi Arabia. It inhabits savanna and scrubland, and breeds on *Combretum* (family *Combretaceae*).

GENUS
HELICONIUS

Commonly called "longwings" because of their very long wings, these heliconids are found principally in Central and South America reaching into the southern US. There are 15 species in Central America. The larvae feed on members of the passion flower family, *Passifloraceae*. The adults are gregarious and have communal roosting spots. Adults feed on pollen, from which they derive amino acids, enabling them to live up to nine months. Adults stay very much in the same localities, but these heliconids are very noticeable butterflies found in all types of habitats.

HELICONIUS ANTIOCHUS

ZONE 2

2⁷/₈in
74mm

This is a very black heliconid, with variable forewing features. The marks on the forewing, when present, may be white, yellow, or blue, while the hindwings remain uniformly black. The butterfly occurs in open areas within the rainforest and along sunny riversides and tracks where flowers grow.

HELICONIUS AOEDE

ZONE 2

3¹/₈in
80mm

This has a pattern fairly typical in several heliconids, but the yellow marks on the forewing are well dispersed, and there are bright red flashes on the forewings. The radiating marks on the hindwings continue to the margin of the wing. Overall, the ground color of this butterfly is black. It frequents open flowery parts of the forest and waysides.

HELICONIUS BURNEYI

ZONE 2

3³/₈in
88mm

This is very similar to *H. aoede*, but the yellow marks on the forewing are more organized into three main blocks, and there are flecks of yellow near the apex. The radiating red marks on the hindwing peter out well before they reach the margin. The red marks on the base of the forewing are elongated. The butterfly flies in open flowery areas.

HELICONIUS CHARITONIUS TUCKERI
The Zebra

ZONE 1·2

3³/₄in
94mm

The butterfly is recognized by the three long yellow stripes which cross the forewing and the thicker yellow stripe crossing the hindwing. There is also a distinctive yellow beading of spots inside the margin of the hindwing. Butterflies are common in the wild along flowery waysides. They roost communally and breed on *Passiflora adenopoda* and *Tetrastylis lobata*. This is a very familiar butterfly to visitors of butterfly houses since it is easy to rear.

HELICONIUS HECALE

ZONE 2

3³/₄in
94mm

A typical form of this highly variable species has a lot of orange over the wings, particularly around the base of the wings. Some forms have orange over most of the hindwing. On the forewings the orange blends into a suffusion of yellow, and there are other yellowish marks near the apex. Other forms have yellow spots on the forewing, and there is yet another variation which has large expanses of blue on the forewing. The butterfly is found in many types of habitat and has been found breeding on at least four species of *Passiflora*.

HELICONIUS DORIS
Doris Butterfly

ZONE 2

3¹/₂in
90mm

Three color forms of the butterfly occur, all of which can arise from one batch of eggs. The hindwing markings may be red, blue, or green, or any combination of these. The forewings are dark with yellow-green markings. This variable butterfly has several subspecies. It lives in open flowery habitats and breeds on *Passiflora ambigua*. Large numbers of pupae may be found on tree trunks, which is unusual for butterflies generally.

HELICONIUS ERATO
The Small Postman

ZONE 1·2

2⁷/₈in
74mm

This is a very variable species, with several well-known subspecies. The black forewings may have a large yellow mark, or a red mark, and the hindwings may have radiating red lines or simply a yellow band. One of the subspecies has blue all over the uppers. The undersides are variable, too, and are similar in their variation to *H. melpomene* with which this species flies. The Small Postman has been recorded as migratory. It breeds on several species of *Passiflora*. The one illustrated is from French Guiana.

HELICONIUS HERMATHENA

ZONE 2

3¼in
85mm

The key feature is the yellow-green band on the upper forewing, although the color, and that of the beading on the hindwing, varies from yellow to green. The band on the leading edge of the hindwing may vary in thickness between specimens. However, there is always a pronounced red band on the black forewing. A number of forms exist of this butterfly, which is found in dry scrubby areas of the Amazon basin.

HELICONIUS MELPOMENE AMARYLLIS
Postman

ZONE 2

3⅛in
84mm

This is one of several named subspecies of a very variable species. All the subspecies are similar to those of *H. erato*, although fresh specimens apparently smell of rice fields, while those of *H. erato* smell of witch hazel! The butterfly is found in all sorts of open and flowery habitats, and is known to breed on at least two species of *Passiflora*.

HELICONIUS METHARME

ZONE 2

3⅛in
80mm

Both surfaces of this butterfly are distinctive. The underside has radiating lines on the base of the hindwing, and the upper surface has two main yellow blobs on the black forewings, and a close-knit series of thin yellow lines around the margin of the hindwing which is repeated on the underside. The butterfly occurs in open areas within the rainforest.

GENUS
HESTINA

This is a small genus of "siren butterflies" found in Africa and Asia with indented forewings.

HESTINA NAMA
Circe

ZONE 5

4¼in
106mm

This is quite a large, dark brown-orange butterfly, with darker forewings than hindwings. White chevrons and lines are scattered over most of the forewings and base of the hindwings. On the hindwings, the pale lines never reach the margin. Subspecies exist. Butterflies frequent forested areas.

GENUS
HETERONYMPHA

A genus of browns from mainland Australia, which have size, color, and pattern similarities to the European genus *Lasiommata*. There is some sexual dimorphism, and females are generally larger than males. Found in grassy habitats, the butterflies breed on grasses.

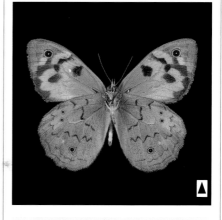

HETERONYMPHA MEROPE

ZONE 6

2½in
65mm

The sexes are completely different, the female being slightly larger with rounded wings and more strident patterns than the male. The female is mostly orange with yellow flashes on the dark forewing apex. The male has some similarity to the European *Lasiommata megera*, with an eye-spot on each wing and a long sex brand.

HETERONYMPHA MIRIFICA

ZONE 6

2³⁄₈in
60mm

The sexual differences are great, with the female being much bigger than the male. The male is rich orange with a few black marks on the wings and an irregular blackened forewing apex. The underside of the hindwing is mottled dark brown, the forewing orange with black spots. The female is brown with a black forewing apex and a broad yellow bar behind the apex. The female has two modest eye-spots on the trailing part of the hindwing.

GENUS
HIPPARCHIA

A large group of agile browns found in Europe and Asia. They range from light brown to dark brown in color, and their patterns tend to be very variable. Several species live in mountainous areas and have cryptic coloration to match the bleak, dry, light-colored terrain in which they move. They breed on grasses.

HIPPARCHIA ALCYONE
Rock Grayling

ZONE 3·4·5

2⁵⁄₈in
68mm

Like many of the graylings, this has brown uppers and a light band crossing both wings. The inner edge of the band is distinct, while the outer one is indistinct. On the forewing apex there is an eye-spot which shows through on the underside. There are also two smaller eye-spots on the uppers only. The underside of the hindwing is streaked gray-white with a central line marking the darker base. The butterfly flies in mountainous areas and breeds on tor-grass, *Brachypodium* species, among others.

HIPPARCHIA FAGI
Woodland Grayling

ZONE 3·5

3in
76mm

This is a large brown butterfly with lighter outers to its upper surfaces. The base of the wings is rich brown which contrasts with the very light area on the hindwing. The female is much larger, with two relatively large eye-spots on the forewing which are highlighted by yellow-white marks. The underside of the hindwing is mottled and waved in gray-brown. The butterfly flies in open woods, where it breeds on the grass called Yorkshire fog, *Holcus lanatus*.

HIPPARCHIA SEMELE
Grayling

ZONE
3·5

2in
50mm

The sexes are different. The female is the larger, with many more upperside markings than the male. There is a band of orange-brown on the wings, and within this are a pair of dark eye-spots on the forewing, and a single eye-spot on the trailing edge of the hindwing. The underside of the hindwing is mottled with gray to provide the butterfly with a camouflage. This is a very active little grayling, found in mountains and especially coastal grasslands and heaths. It breeds on various grasses, including the mountain-loving fescues, *Festuca* species.

GENUS
HYALIRIS

A genus of South and Central American butterflies which have characteristic "glassy-wings."

HYALIRIS IMAGUNCULA

ZONE
2

2⅞in
74mm

The wings are elongated and rounded, with transparent centers. A uniform black band is continuous around the forewings and thickens up around the hindwings. The antennae are not distinctly knobbed and are light orange at the tip. The abdomen is long.

GENUS
HYPNA

A South American genus whose single species has swallowtail-shaped wings and a tail.

HYPNA CLYTEMNESTRA

ZONE
2

3⅞in
98mm

The dark brown hindwing is scalloped and drawn out with a distinctive tail. The forewings are large and slightly hooked, with a bold pale yellow band. The butterfly is found in Surinam and Bolivia. It flies in lowland rainforest and breeds on *Croton* and *Codiaeum* species, both spurges.

GENUS
HYPOLIMNAS

A genus commonly called "diadem butterflies" because of the row of spots around the wings which look like a necklace. It includes one very widespread species in Asia and the Australian region, *H. misippus*. Sexual dimorphism is exhibited, and females sometimes mimic danaid butterflies. Found in open sunny areas, villages, glades, and forest edges, the adults are frequent nectar feeders.

HYPOLIMNAS ALIMENA
Blue-banded Eggfly

ZONE
5

2½in
65mm

The sexes are completely different, with the male possessing the blue bands across the wings to which its common name refers. The female is much paler with white or very pale gray at the margins of the wings. There are several subspecies recorded of this variable butterfly. It is found along waysides and in open areas, and breeds on *Pseuderanthemum variabale*, a member of the Acanthaceae.

HYPOLIMNAS ANTILOPE INTERSTINCTA

ZONE
5

3⅛in
80mm

Rather a plain brown butterfly unmarked on the uppers, at least in subspecies *mela*. The wings are rounded and generous, typical of *Hypolimnas* species, and there is a faint lightening toward the marginal areas. The margin itself is wavy and blackened, and it is slightly scalloped. Butterflies frequent open flowery areas. The caterpillar food plants are probably members of the purslane and nettle families, *Portulacaceae* and *Urticaceae*.

HYPOLIMNAS BOLINA
Common Eggfly, Great Eggfly

ZONE
5·6

4³/₈in
110mm

This is a variable species, with more variation among females than males. There are also regional differences. The smaller males are rich blue-black with a single mauve-white blotch in the center of each wing. The female has the same general pattern and colors as the male, though the white blobs are diffuse and there is a reddish patch near the outer edge of the forewing. The margins are scalloped in both the sexes. The butterfly is migratory and very widespread. It favors flowers and breeds on a wide variety of plants, especially those of the acanthus family.

HYPOLIMNAS MISIPPUS
Diadem Butterfly, Six-continent Butterfly, Danaid Eggfly

ZONE
1·2·4
5·6

2¹/₂in
65mm

This is one of the most widespread butterflies in the world, thanks in part to human activity. It is thought to have been introduced to the Americas in slave ships from Africa. The sexes are completely different, the male looking like a male *H. bolina*, but with white wing marks, the female having a number of forms which mimic various danaids such as *Danaus chrysippus*. Butterflies frequent open flowery places and woodland edges. They breed on members of the purslane family, *Portulacaceae*.

HYPOLIMNAS SALMACIS
Blue Diadem

ZONE
4

4in
100mm

This is a very pretty but variable butterfly which has a broad blue-violet necklace pattern around the wings, stronger on the hindwings than the forewings. The forewing tips are black with some white spots, and there are white spots around the margin of the hindwing. The female is slightly larger and may be tinged with yellow. Butterflies favor open flowery areas and probably breed on members of the purslane and nettle families, *Portulacaceae* and *Urticaceae*.

HYPOLIMNAS DIOMEA

ZONE
5·6

4¹/₂in
115mm

The difference between this and other similar species is the way in which the mauve-violet marks on the forewings are much expanded and divided by darker veins. In the female these marks are white. The inside of the margin of the hindwing carries a row of tiny white bead-like marks. The butterfly occurs on Sulawesi in Indonesia.

HYPOLIMNAS PANDARUS PANDORA

ZONE
5·6

4³/₄in
120mm

The sexes of this large butterfly are different. The male has black forewings and a violet patch on the hindwing in front of a rich orange suffusion. The female has brown forewings with white spots, yellow-brown on the hindwing instead of violet, and larger eye-spots. The butterfly occurs in Indonesia in open flowery areas and at the edges of woods.

GENUS
HYPONEPHELE

This genus of browns from Europe and Asia are dimorphic and breed on grasses.

HYPONEPHELE LYCAON
Dusky Meadow Brown

ZONE
3·5

1⁷/₈in
48mm

The dull brown male has a pronounced sex brand on the forewing. The female forewing has a yellow mark containing two eye-spots. The underside of the hindwing is drab; the forewing underside is orange toward the base. Butterflies occur in stony lowlands. Some populations are in decline.

GENUS
HYPOSCADA

A genus of eight South American rainforest species which live in deep shade.

HYPOSCADA KEZIA

2³/₈in 60mm	ZONE 2

This has a very typical heliconid shape and pattern. The white spots on the black forewing tip are regionally variable. The rest of the wing has thick red-orange bands against a black background. Very little is known about its life cycle.

GENUS
IDEA

A genus of large-winged, black and white speckled butterflies which inhabit the dense forests of Asia and the Australian region. The butterflies are easily recognized and have a characteristic weak flight.

IDEA BLANCHARDI

6¹/₄in 160mm	ZONE 6

This is a large butterfly with gently curved forewings and rounded hindwings. The ground color is somewhat translucent with black veins, and there are two or three black marks in the cell region of the forewing. At least six subspecies of this large and impressive butterfly are known; some are light, others brown. The forewings are long and slightly indented, with the dark veins very obvious over the light-colored wings. This species is found in the rainforests of Sulawesi.

IDEA D'URVILLEI

5³/₄in 144mm	ZONE 6

This New Guinean species differs from other ideas by the great irregular area of black across the forewings. Most of the hindwings and the remainder of the forewings are devoid of the speckled pattern typical of the genus, but the margins have white and black markings. It is a typical rainforest species, and caterpillars may feed on *Agonosma* species.

IDEA JASONIA

	ZONE 5
4⁷/₈in 124mm	

This Indian idea has particularly extended hindwings which appear lobed. The black spots are prolific over the off-white wings, and the dark brown veins are conspicuous. This butterfly flies in rainforest areas, clearings, and margins.

IDEA LYNCEUS
Tree Nymph

	ZONE 5
6¹/₂in 165mm	

The shape of the wings is most distinctive. The forewing is long and thin, and indented on its outer margin. The white wings are heavily endowed with black spots. The female is slightly larger with rounder wings. Three subspecies are known. It is a typical rainforest species which appears to float over the canopy.

IDEA LEUCONOË CLARA

	ZONE 5
6¹/₄in 160mm	

The large wings have a white ground peppered with various black spots, and a row of black-ringed white spots around the margins. There is a trace of yellow on the base of the forewings. It is a model for the swallowtail, *Graphium idaeoides*. At least 22 subspecies of this butterfly have been recorded from various islands and countries in southeast Asia. On Java, Indonesia, it may now be extinct, due to destruction of its mangrove-swamp habitat.

IDEA TAMBUSISIANA

	ZONE 6
7in 180mm	

Unlike other ideas, the wings are covered with heavy black spots, particularly toward the outside. The forewing apex is black. The white spots around the margin of the hindwing are organized into a row. Recently discovered on "Operation Drake," this stunning rainforest species is named after Mt. Tambusisiana in Sulawesi.

IDEOPSIS

A genus of seven species of the rainforests of Asia, often flying with *Idea*.

IDEOPSIS HEWITSONI

	ZONE 5
3⁷/₈in 98mm	

This is a large butterfly with rounded wings. The pattern is made up of dark brown bands around the margins of all wings and brown on all the veins.

INACHIS

This genus has a single species with "eyes" resembling those on a peacock's tail.

INACHIS IO
Peacock

	ZONE 3·5
2³/₈in 60mm	

Recognized by its unique coloration and shape, this butterfly gets its common name from the large round false eyes on the wings. The underside of the wings are black, which is useful during hibernation. The butterfly lives around farmyards and in valleys, and breeds on nettles.

GENUS
JUNONIA

A widespread genus of browns found in all regions. The false eyes prominent on the wings have given rise to the collective common name of "buckeyes." The precise number of species is unknown – but there are many which need classifying. At least six plant families are exploited as larval food plants.

JUNONIA ARCHESIA
Garden Inspector

	ZONE 4
2½in 65mm	

The sexes are similar in pattern, but the female is usually larger. There are seasonal forms, of which the dry-season form is the largest. The velvety brown wings have a row of bead-like spots around the edges; these are orangey in the wet-season form. There are also some diagnostic blue lines on the leading edge of the forewing. This butterfly visits gardens, as its common name suggests, but it is also common in open countryside, where it breeds on *Coleus* and *Plectranthus* species.

JUNONIA CERYNE
Marsh Commodore

	ZONE 4
2⅛in 55mm	

The key feature is the checkered margin around all the wings, to the inside of which is a band of orange, then an area of very pale orange. The base of the wings is very dark, and there is a thin band of blue around the inside of the checkered margins. The butterfly is common in damp areas and may be found throughout the year.

JUNONIA ALMANA
Peacock Pansy

	ZONE 5
2½in 65mm	

This is a variable species, which also has wet and dry seasonal forms so different that they were originally believed to be distinct species. Dry-season forms have, appropriately, a dried-leaf-like appearance with a tail. The tailless wet form has eye-spots on the underside. The butterfly visits all sorts of habitats from gardens to mountain clearings, and it occurs in India and Burma. It breeds on *Mimosa pudica*, the sensitive plant.

JUNONIA COENIA
Buckeye

ZONE 1·2

2³/₈in
63mm

This is a brightly colored and easily recognized butterfly. It has conspicuous eye-spots on both sets of wings; on the uppers the largest is on the hindwing, but on the underside the largest is on the forewing. There is a considerable amount of orange over the brown ground. The butterfly is common in many wayside habitats and in meadows and pastures. It is strongly migratory and breeds on various members of at least four plant families including *Scrophulariaceae* and *Verbenaceae*.

JUNONIA HIERTA
Yellow Pansy

ZONE 4·5

2¹/₈in
55mm

As its common name suggests, the butterfly has a lot of yellow on the wings in four main areas either as whole blobs of color, or divided. There is always a bright blue blob near the base of the hindwing. Otherwise, the ground color is black. There are a number of subspecies. This is a very widespread species, being found from Africa via Arabia to Asia. It may be seen in all sorts of habitats, from gardens to savanna and open scrub, where it breeds on members of the acanthus family such as *Asystasia*, *Justicia*, and *Ruellia* species.

JUNONIA OCTAVIA
Gaudy Commodore

ZONE 4

2⁵/₈in
70mm

Although the sexes are similar, they exhibit seasonal variation. Dry-season forms have more blue, compared to the pinkish red of wet-season forms. The size can vary, too. This butterfly occurs in savanna and light woodland, and breeds on a variety of plants including *Coleus* and *Plectranthus* species.

JUNONIA EVARETE ZONALIS
West Indian Buckeye, Florida Buckeye, Smoky Buckeye

ZONE 1·2

2¹/₂in
64mm

This differs from *J. coenia* in that it has much smaller eye-spots and lacks the blue-violet markings and prominent pale band on the forewing. The butterfly flies in open woodland-type habitats where it breeds on members of the figwort and acanthus families. It is a strong migrant.

JUNONIA NATALICA
Brown Commodore

ZONE 4

2³/₈in
60mm

The ground color is deep brown, and the outline of the wings is strongly curved. The hooked forewing has a small collection of white marks near the apex, and there are dull orange bands and spots over the wings. The butterfly is found in savanna and wooded areas, and breeds on *Asystasia*, a member of the acanthus family.

JUNONIA ORITHYA
MADAGASCARENSIS
Eyed Pansy, Blue Pansy

ZONE 4·5·6

2¹/₈in
55mm

This butterfly can be identified by the large amount of blue suffusion on the hindwing and the white flecks and small amount of blue on the black forewing. There is a pair of eye-spots on each of the wings. The sexes are essentially the same, but the female is slightly larger with larger eye-spots and a lighter shade of blue on the hindwing. The butterfly lives in open country and is on the wing throughout the year. It breeds on *Hygrophila*, a member of the acanthus family.

JUNONIA TEREA
Soldier Commodore

ZONE
4

2¹/₈in
54mm

This is a brown butterfly identifiable by a conspicuously broad and curved pale orange band on the forewing which continues on the hindwing. There are some very small white spots on the forewing tip, and some eye-spots on the hindwing. The female is larger than the male, with a larger band. The butterfly flies in wooded areas and breeds on *Asystasia*, a member of the acanthus family.

▲

GENUS
KALLIMA

A genus of "leaf butterflies" so named because of the cryptic leaf-like pattern of the undersides of the wings. When the butterflies settle with wings together, they become difficult for bird predators to see. The butterflies occur in Africa and Asia, and are typified by the Indian leaf butterfly, *K. paralekta*.

KALLIMA CYMODOCE
Western Leaf Butterfly

ZONE
4

2¹/₂in
65mm

In contrast to the leaf-like undersides, the uppersides are black with a bright blue base to the wings. The female is slightly larger than the male with a larger orange band on the forewing apex. The butterfly is on the wing throughout the year and lives in forested areas.

KALLIMA HORSFIELDI PHILARCHUS
Blue Oak Leaf Butterfly

ZONE
5

4³/₈in
110mm

This leaf butterfly is identified by the bright indigo blue on the forewing, the light green toward the base, and the dark margin. The undersides are typically leaf-like. The butterfly occurs in India and Sri Lanka, and breeds on *Strobilanthes*, a member of the acanthus family.

KALLIMA PARALEKTA
The Indian Leaf

ZONE 5

4in
100mm

This is the familiar leaf butterfly of Asia. On the uppers there is a blue sheen, and the forewings have an orange band inside the black tip. The shape of the wings is strongly curved, and the hindwing ends in a fine tail. There is a single tiny white spot on the forewing. The butterfly enjoys a wide distribution from India to China. It lives in heavily forested areas and breeds on *Strobilanthes* and *Pseuderanthemum* species which belong to the acanthus family.

KALLIMA RUMIA
African Leaf Butterfly

ZONE 4

3¹⁄₈in
80mm

In this species the sexes are different, but they share the same leaf-like underside and shape. Where the smaller male has a violet band across the forewing, the female has a broken band of white. The ground color of the male is dull russet brown, while that of the female is dull brown. This is a butterfly of the forests and may be found throughout the year.

KALLIMA SPIRIDIVA

ZONE 5

4in
100mm

This is very similar to male *K. rumia*. It differs in having black ground color to the forewings and dark brown to the hindwings. It probably flies in the same sort of forest habitat and breeds on members of the acanthus family.

GENUS
LASIOMMATA

A genus of European and Asian browns which are allied to members of the *Pararge* genus. They have brown or orange ground colors, sometimes of a speckled nature, but with false eyes on the wings. They live in open sunny sites and breed on grasses.

LASIOMMATA MAERA
Large Wall Brown

This is a larger version of *L. megera*, although it does not have the same intricate and strident patterns, especially in the male. The undersides are fairly similar with a beading of pupilled eye-spots running around the hindwing. Two subspecies are known. The butterfly occurs in grassy and rocky areas in forests, on mountains and along tracks, where it breeds on common grasses.

ZONE 3·5 — 2¹/₄in 56mm

LASIOMMATA PETROPOLITANA
Northern Wall Brown

This is the smallest of the wall browns. The male is dull brown on the uppers with a major eye-spot on the apex of the forewing, and a beading of tiny eye-spots around the margin of the hindwings. The eye-spots are a little more emphasized on the undersides. The female has much larger eye-spots in the same positions all set in an orange band. The butterfly enjoys woodland glades in lowland and upland, and breeds on common grasses such as the fescues, *Festuca* species.

ZONE 3·5 — 1⁵/₈in 42mm

LETHE APPALACHIA
Appalachian Brown, Woods Eyed Brown

The upper surface is brown with a row of black eye-spots inside the margin and some faint ones on the forewing. The undersides are more remarkable, with a series of beautiful ringed eye-spots on both wings. There are also fine lines crossing the wings and a lighter area to the outside. One of the subspecies from the Appalachians, *L. appalachia leeuwi*, has Federal status under Category 2. Butterflies live in wet grassy areas and breed on sedges, *Carex* species.

ZONE 1 — 2in 52mm

LASIOMMATA MEGERA
The Wall

The female is the larger with a more elaborate pattern on the wings. The male is distinguished by a dark sex brand on the forewing. Two subspecies are known. This is a widespread species which also occurs in North Africa. It is a familiar butterfly since it delights in basking on tracks only to be disturbed repeatedly by passing traffic. It breeds on various common grasses.

ZONE 3·5 — 2in 50mm

GENUS
LETHE

A genus of butterflies with representatives in the New World as well as Asia and the Australian region. They are browns with typical eye-spots and breed on members of the sedge (*Cyperaceae*) and grass family, *Gramineae*, including bamboos.

LETHE CONFUSA

This species can be distinguished from *L. europa*, which it resembles, by the more defined eye-spots on the underside of the hindwings and the broad pale cream band on the undersides of the forewings. Butterflies frequent grassy places.

ZONE 5 — 2³/₈in 62mm

171

LETHE DARENA SUMATRENSIS

	ZONE 5
3¹/₈in 80mm	

Females are slightly larger than the males, with rounded wings and a large cream bar across the forewings, repeated on the undersides. Both males and females have small black spots around the inside of the hindwing margin and a dark chocolate ground color, although males tend to be a little lighter toward the outside. Butterflies live in highland rainforest in Java, Sumatra, and Borneo.

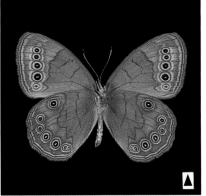

LETHE EURYDICE
Marsh Eyed Brown

	ZONE 1
2in 52mm	

The undersides have a rich brown glow not found in other species of this genus. The row of large eye-spots inside the margins of the hindwing undersides are well defined and ringed in yellow and pale brown. There are some faint lines crossing the wings. Two subspecies are known. The butterfly is widespread in north and northeastern America. It frequents damp habitats and breeds on a variety of sedges, *Carex* species.

LETHE PORTLANDIA
Southern Pearly Eye

	ZONE 1
2³/₄in 72mm	

The pearly nature of the underside is very evident, but this species is distinguished from others by a disjointed line of eye-spots on the underside of the hindwing and an orange club on the antennae. There are two subspecies known. The butterfly lives in wet areas where there are abundant stands of bamboo, its caterpillar food plant.

LETHE EUROPA
Bamboo Tree-brown

	ZONE 5
3in 75mm	

The sexes differ only in the distinctive white band across the female forewing; otherwise the ground color is a warm chocolate on the uppers. The undersides are a richer mottled chocolate with a series of diffuse eye-spots on the hindwing. There are at least three subspecies. The butterfly is named after its caterpillar food plants, bamboos, which occur both in villages and in the countryside.

LETHE MINERVA

	ZONE 5
2¹/₂in 64mm	

This butterfly has brown uppers which are uniform in the male, but lighter and crossed with a broken white band in the female. There are small black spots inside the margin of the hindwing. The underside is a pearly silver with pale yellow ringed eye-spots around the hindwing margin. There are at least two subspecies. The butterfly occurs in Malaya, Java, Sumatra and Borneo, up to 4,000ft (1,200m).

G E N U S
LEXIAS

This is a genus of butterflies typical of the Australian region. Venation can be helpful in identification, but is, at the same time, variable.

LEXIAS AEROPA

The undersides are the key feature in this species. They are orange-yellow with a row of black marks running across the wings, and a particularly distinctive large mauve eye-spot near the base of the forewing. There is a thick pale yellow band which crosses the uppers. Butterflies live in lowland and open forest. They probably breed on plants belonging to the *Guttiferae*.

LEXIAS DIRTEA

The sexes are different. The smaller male has a black ground and a prominent blue band on the hindwing, at least in the *merguia* race from Malaya. The female has no blue and is completely speckled in yellowish green spots against a dark brown ground. The butterfly lives in upland areas and may be abundant. It has been found breeding on *Garcinia laterifolia*, a gutteriferaceous plant. The butterfly occurs from northern India to the Philippines.

LEXIAS SATRAPES ORNATA

The forewings are black with a multitude of white spots. The hindwing is black to deep brown with a chain of marginal white spots and a broad violet band to the inside. The margins of all wings are gently scalloped.

LEXIAS CYANIPARDUS

Big, blue and speckled, this is a giant among the lexias butterflies. The ground color is black with a pleasant blue suffusion over the trailing edge of the hindwings. In the male the ground color is unbroken, but the female is speckled. Another important identification feature is the green hue on the undersides. This has at least five subspecies, many of them much smaller. In *L. cyanipardus albopunctata*, the wings are almost black with just two unequal-sized spots on the apex of the forewing. Butterflies inhabit lowlands.

GENUS
LIBYTHEA

This is a group of snouts which have protruding palps like those of the *Libytheana*. Members of this genus occur in both the New and Old Worlds, and have smooth green caterpillars, unlike the hairy ones generally associated with the *Nymphalidae*. Male butterflies have four functional legs, females have only three.

▲

LIBYTHEA GEOFFROYI MAENIA

 ZONE 5·6 2¼in 58mm

This is a remarkably colorful species. It has the shape of an *Appias* with curved forewings, quite unlike a snout butterfly. The color is exceptional, due to a blue-violet suffusion over the forewings and the base of the hindwings. The sexes are often dissimilar. There are many forms so far recorded. The butterfly occurs in open woody habitats from Burma through to Sulawesi.

LIBYTHEA CELTIS
Nettle-tree Butterfly

 ZONE 3·5 1¾in 44mm

This species is recognized by the hooked forewings and the orange blobs over the warm brown wings. The undersides are relatively cryptic. This is the only snout butterfly in Europe. It also occurs in North Africa and has a wide distribution through to Japan. It lives in wooded areas, especially in valleys, and takes its name from its caterpillar food plant, *Celtis australis*, the nettle tree. The butterfly hibernates and feeds on exudates from tree buds in the spring.

LIBYTHEA LABDACA
African Snout

 ZONE 4 2in 50mm

This butterfly has very dull colors, which follow the usual snout pattern of orange marks over the dark wings, and about three white marks on the apex of the forewing. The wings have a sculptured appearance, and the palps are exceptionally long. This butterfly is strongly migratory and is the only snout found throughout Africa. It prefers forested areas.

GENUS
LIBYTHEANA

This is a genus of snout butterflies. They have long palps which protrude under the head like a snout. There are about ten species which occur in South and Central America, and they breed on members of *Celtis* which belong to the elm family, *Ulmaceae*.

LIBYTHEANA CARINENTA
Southern Snout

ZONE 1·2	1⁷⁄₈in 48mm

The markings on this butterfly are very diffuse, which distinguishes it from *L. bachmanii*. The undersides of the hindwing are lighter, even silvery purple, while the forewing base is orange. A number of subspecies exist. Although the caterpillar food plants have yet to be determined, they are probably hackberry trees. The butterfly is a strong migrant.

LIBYTHEANA BACHMANII
Snout Butterfly

ZONE 1·2	1⁷⁄₈in 48mm

This snout has relatively well-defined markings, with white-cream forewing spots and flashes of orange on both forewings and hindwings. The forewing markings are repeated on the underside, but the hindwing is drab overall. The butterfly is a strong migrant and moves out of the woodlands where it breeds on hackberries, *Celtis* species.

LIMENITIS LYMIRE

ZONE 6	3¹⁄₂in 86mm

This is the most stunning of the Asian limenitids with the blue-gray-black ground richly embellished with wavy gray marks. A white flash at the base of the hindwings has a touch of orange. The undersides are equally amazing and very different. They are overall silvery white with a band of blue-white open spots around the wings, and there is a distinct band of orange. At the base of the wings, the scales have a greenish hue. Butterflies fly along woodland edges.

GENUS
LIMENITIS

A genus of white-marked admiral butterflies which are allied to members of the *Ladoga* genus. Species are found in North America as well as Europe, Asia and the Australian region. Their young larvae hibernate in a rolled-up leaf.

LIMENITIS POPULI
Poplar Admiral

ZONE 3·5	3¹⁄₈in 80mm

This is the largest of the admirals, or "admirables" as the Victorians would say. Female admirals are unusually large, but they share the same basic pattern of the male, a dark ground color with white marks. In this species there is also a series of orange chevrons which run around the inside of the margins. The butterfly lives in woodland areas and breeds on aspens and poplars, hence its name.

LIMENITIS REDUCTA
South White Admiral

ZONE
3

2¹⁄₈in
54mm

This pretty white admiral is brighter than *L. camilla* and has a purple-blue sheen in strong light. The undersides are also very different, with bright orange, white and brown. There is a single row of black spots around the margin of the hindwing underside. The white band is very distinctive across the hindwing. Like *L. camilla*, it breeds on honeysuckle, *Lonicera* species. It is confined to southern Europe.

GENUS
LYCOREA

This is a group of heliconid mimics which have long wings, long bodies, and share similar patterns.

LYCOREA CLEOBAEA ATERGATIS

ZONE
2

4in
102mm

These butterflies are much larger than the true heliconids and, in addition, the male has hair pencils protruding from the abdomen. A number of subspecies are known, and the butterfly occurs in wood and scrub habitats breeding on *Carica*, *Ficus*, and *Asclepias*.

GENUS
MARPESIA

A genus of mostly Central and South American butterflies which also occurs in Africa. They are called "dagger wings" after the long tail on each hindwing. Butterflies, some of which are dimorphic, engage in mud-puddling. One species, M. *berania* (not described), has communal roosts and lives for up to five months. Caterpillar food plants are found among the mulberry family, *Moraceae*.

MARPESIA ELEUCHEA
Antillean dagger wing, Cuban dagger wing

ZONE
2

3in
76mm

The key difference between this and M. *petreus*, which it resembles, is the bent lines crossing the wings; in M. *petreus* they are straight. At least three subspecies are known. This is a species of the West Indies, most common in the Greater Antilles. It breeds on *Ficus* species and strays occasionally into southern Florida.

GENUS
LOPINGA

A genus of browns which has a series of prominent eye-spots.

LOPINGA ACHINE
Woodland Brown

ZONE
3·5

2¹⁄₄in
56mm

This is a very distinctive butterfly, with a series of prominent eye-spots, ringed with dull orange, around the margins of the wings, repeated on the underside. The ground color is dirty brown. Females are slightly larger than males. Butterflies live in open woody areas and breed on common grasses.

GENUS
MANIOLA

A genus of satyrid browns which has members in Europe, Asia, and South America.

MANIOLA JURTINA
Meadow Brown

ZONE
3·5

2in
50mm

The female is larger and brighter than the somber-colored male. A number of subspecies exist. This is a very successful butterfly over the whole of its range, since it breeds on common grasses and produces two or three generations each year.

MARPESIA PETREUS
Ruddy Dagger Wing, Red Dagger Wing,
Southern Dagger Tail

ZONE 1·2

3 ¹/₈in
82mm

The "dagger" refers to the long tails which helps to distinguish this from *Dryas iulia*. On the upper surface, the orange ground is crossed by three straight dark lines, and the tails are also dark. The undersides have a slight bloom of purple-brown. The butterfly is found in open swampy areas and breeds on *Ficus* and *Anacardium* species. It is a strong migrant and may be seen visiting flowers or mud-puddling.

GENUS
MEGISTO

This is a North American genus of browns. The two species have a dark brown to reddish ground color and false eyes. They live in grassy habitats and probably both breed on grasses.

MEGISTO CYMELA
Little Wood Satyr

ZONE 1

1 ⁷/₈in
48mm

This butterfly with rounded wings has a uniform brown ground color on the uppers, marked on the forewing by a pair of yellow-ringed eye-spots. These are repeated, but much more strongly emphasized on the undersurface which is also crossed by two black lines. The butterfly lives in many grassy places, from open meadows to forest clearings. It breeds on grasses and sedges.

MEGISTO RUBRICATA
Red Satyr

ZONE 1·2

1 ⁷/₈in
48mm

This satyrid has a red suffusion over the uppers, but still maintains one prominent yellow-ringed eye-spot on the forewing and two on the hindwing. These are repeated on the undersides, where they fall within a lighter area to the outside of the wing. Although their food plants are unknown in the wild, the caterpillars have been reared in captivity on grasses.

GENUS
MELANARGIA

This is a large genus of satyrid browns known as marbled whites.

MELANARGIA GALATHEA
Marbled White

	ZONE 3
2 in 52mm	

This is one of the most common marbled whites in western Europe. The black spotting on the white wing is very variable. In the south and east of its range, it is replaced by other species of this widespread group. It breeds on grasses.

GENUS
MELANITIS

A genus of browns which occur in Africa, Asia, and the Australian region. The forewing is curved, hooked, and indented, a characteristic feature of the genus. The wing shape of the female butterflies is more pronounced. Seasonal forms occur, and these differ in shape and color.

MELANITIS AMABILIS

	ZONE 6
3⅛in 80mm	

Overall, this is a brown butterfly with a band of ocher across the forewing repeated on the underside. There are two very faint bands to the inside of the ocher band on the underside. On the somber hindwing underside, there is a large, yellow-ringed, pupilled eye-spot and a series of three smaller eye-spots on the trailing edge. Butterflies frequent open grassy areas and breed on various grasses.

MELANITIS LEDA
Evening Brown, Common Evening Brown

	ZONE 4·5·6
3⅛in 84mm	

The wing shape is a useful guide to identification, since the forewing is hooked, and the hindwing is strongly angled with a stubby "tail." There is a conspicuous orange-brown eye-spot on the forewing. This is one of the most widespread of browns worldwide. The butterfly flies at dusk in various habitats: in woodland, bush and scrub. It breeds on various common grasses, and caterpillars also feed on rice (a grass).

MELANITIS ZITENIUS SUMATRANUS

ZONE 5
3½in 90mm

This is slightly larger than M. *leda*, and it has a much more definite eye-spot and a smudge on the forewing, at least in the normal form. There are subspecies and seasonal forms which are more uniform brown all over. The wing profiles are strongly sculptured. The butterfly flies in thickets, between 1,800 and 3,300ft (550-1,000m) and occurs in Sikkim, Malaya, and from Assam to Burma. The caterpillars may feed on bamboo.

GENUS
MELINAEA

These are Central and South American butterflies similar in appearance to *Heliconius*. However, they have smaller compound eyes, and androconial hairs are present between their wings. There are three species known from Central America. Butterflies are found in many forested habitats up to 5,000ft (1,500m) and breed on members of the *Solanaceae*.

MELINAEA LILIS FLAVICANS

ZONE 2
3in 76mm

With long wings and colors typical of heliconids, this species is deeply involved with mimicry, in which many other species of butterfly and moth are also associated. The ground color is rich orange and may be unmarked or filled with black lines. There are different subspecies, some with white spots on the black forewing tips, others (see M. *lilis messatis*) with pale yellow on the forewing tip. The butterfly lives in open flowery areas where it sips nectar.

MELINAEA LILIS MESSATIS

ZONE 2
3in 76mm

Both fore- and hindwings are elongated, the forewing tip is black and contains two broken bands of yellow. The overall ground color is rich orange with four bands of dark brown to give a striped effect. The body is long and thin which, along with the coloration, further mimics the heliconids. The butterfly lives in open flowery areas and visits flowers for nectar with other mimics and models associated with this subspecies.

MELINAEA ZANEKA

ZONE 2

3⅞in
98mm

Heliconid-like in shape, color and pattern, the wings are elongated, orange, and with a black apex to the forewing. There is an orange band across the forewing and a series of black dots. The abdomen is very long, another characteristic of heliconids, with which it probably has a mimetic relationship.

♀

GENUS
MELITAEA

A genus of 40 species of fritillaries which are found in Europe, Asia, and North America. They are medium-sized and allied to the *Argynnis* genus. Spotting on the wings is very variable, and typical of many fritillary genera.

MELITAEA CINXIA
Glanville Fritillary

ZONE 3·5

1½in
40mm

This is a fairly dark-colored fritillary which has rows of continuous black marks running across the wings. It lives in grassy areas and breeds on plantains and knapweed. This is quite a common butterfly in Europe, though it is restricted in Britain. It also occurs in North Africa.

MELITAEA DIAMINA
False Heath Fritillary

ZONE 3·5

1⅝in
42mm

Appropriate for its mountainous habitat, this butterfly is very heavily marked in black which almost obscures the orange ground. The female is slightly larger and less dark. In contrast to the uppers, the underside markings are very light with a prominent white band, edged in black, crossing the hindwing. There are a number of subspecies. The butterfly flies in grassy and flowery meadows and breeds on cow-wheat, *Melampyrum*, and plantain, *Plantago*.

MELITAEA DIDYMA
Spotted Fritillary

ZONE
3·5

1³/₄in
44mm

This butterfly varies widely in the amount of spotting and the shade of its brown-black ground color. Females tend to be paler than males and sometimes have two-toned wings, the forewings being duller than the hindwings. The undersides are lighter and much speckled. There are a number of subspecies, some of which are much darker than the species. Butterflies frequent flowery meadows and breed on plantain, *Plantago*, and toadflax, *Linaria*.

MELLICTA AURELIA
Nickerl's Fritillary

ZONE
3·5

1¹/₄in
32mm

This can be a very difficult butterfly to identify, since it has the characteristic dark spotting typical of most fritillaries. The markings on the upper surface are more uniform and appear checkered, with orange and black spots. The reddish band of lunules on the underside of the hindwings is distinctive. The butterfly flies in flowery meadows and breeds on a wide variety of plants such as *Plantago*, *Melampyrum,* and *Veronica* species.

GENUS
MEMPHIS

A genus of about 100 species which occur in Central America. They resemble butterflies of the genus *Anaea*, to which they are related. All species have cryptic undersides which are leaf-like. Species may be tailed or tailless, dimorphic or similar. They live in the rainforest and are powerful fliers. The principal caterpillar food plants are in the *Piperaceae*, *Euphorbiaceae*, and *Lauraceae* families.

GENUS
MELLICTA

A genus of about a dozen species which are found in Europe and Asia. They are considerably spotted, very variable, and good fliers.

MELLICTA BRITOMARTIS
Assmann's Fritillary

ZONE
3·5

1³/₈in
36mm

The markings on the upperside are very dark, with rows of black marks crossing the deep orange ground. The orange on the undersides is also rich and in strong contrast to the yellow bands which cross the wing. This butterfly of eastern Europe is found through the Commonwealth of Independent States (formerly USSR) to Korea. It lives in lowland meadows and breeds on *Plantago* and *Veronica* species.

MEMPHIS AUREOLA

ZONE
2

2⁵/₈in
68mm

The female is the larger sex, with tails and a definite pale green band across the forewing which is turquoise to the inside. The male has a diffuse greenish hue around the outer parts of the wings. In both sexes the forewing tip is black, and the undersides resemble a dead leaf, though in the male these are speckled with a little pale orange. This is a species of the rainforest canopy which occasionally comes to the ground. Its caterpillar food plants are unknown.

MEMPHIS PROSERPINA

	ZONE 2
2⁷/₈in 74mm	

The female is larger than the male, with tails and much more metallic green-blue on the uppers. The female hindwing is much more angular than that of the male. The undersides of both sexes are very much the same, and their hatchet-shaped forewing is characteristic. The butterfly occurs from Mexico to Costa Rica and flies in open forested areas up to about 1,600ft (485m). Its caterpillar food plants have not been found.

GENUS
MINOIS

This is a genus of medium-sized butterflies which are related to the satyrids.

MINOIS DRYAS
The Dryad

	ZONE 3·5
2⁵/₈in 70mm	

The dark males are easy to see in their mountainous habit, and the slightly larger, but lighter females are usually close by. On the forewings are a pair of bluish eye-spots, repeated on the undersides. A number of subspecies occur. The butterfly breeds on various grasses.

GENUS
MORPHO

A genus of six Central and South American species which has always attracted a lot of attention, since the males are a very bright metallic blue. The female is very drab in comparison. The butterflies live in the rainforest, especially on the rainforest canopy. The larval food plants, where known, are mostly members of the pea and bean family, *Leguminosae*. Males are collected by the million each year for the jewelry trade.

MORPHO AEGA
Morpho

	ZONE 2
3¹/₂in 90mm	

The sexes are completely different. The male has the flashy blues on the uppers, the female is yellow-brown with a brown margin. This is a species mainly found in Brazil, where it is much collected for jewelry and curios. About six million specimens are taken annually, but this does not appear to have affected population levels. The butterflies breed on bamboo, which is widespread.

MORPHO CYPRIS
Morpho

	ZONE 2
5¹/₄in 136mm	

The sexes are completely different. The male is the most often seen, brilliant metallic blue with a white band across the wings and a series of white spots around the wing. The larger female rarely ventures from the rainforest canopy and is rich orange-yellow with a brown margin. The undersides of both sexes are brown and white. Little is known about the biology of this species, although it breeds on *Inga marginata*, a member of the pea family. The male has been exploited by the jewelry trade for its colorful wings.

MORPHO DIDIUS
Morpho

	ZONE 2
2²/₃in 67mm	

The sexes are completely different. The male is a flashy blue, while the female has a rich orange-brown ground with a thick dark, rather speckled, margin to the wings. The butterflies frequent the rainforest canopy and clearings.

MORPHO GRANADENSIS
Morpho

 ZONE 2 — 5⅞in 148mm

This morpho is distinguished from its subspecies by having most of the uppers light metallic blue with a dark margin in both sexes. The undersides are very dark, but with a series of large eye-spots and a marginal yellow-green band. The wings are scalloped. The butterfly flies in rainforests and breeds on *Macharium seemani*, a member of the pea family.

MORPHO PELEIDES CORYDON
Morpho

 ZONE 2 — 6⅛in 156mm

Both sexes have metallic blue on the wings, more so in the larger female. Males may have the blue area reduced to just the forewing, and there are also all-brown forms. There is always a dark margin on the uppers. The undersides are dark with rows of eye-spots and a light wavy margin. A number of subspecies exist. The butterfly lives in rainforest, and it is the most common morphos in Central America. There are a number of plants belonging to the pea family on which the caterpillars feed.

MORPHO RHETENOR
Blue morpho

 ZONE 2 — 5½in 140mm

Males have metallic blue uppers with a suspicion of black at the tip and along the leading edge of the forewing. The strongly curved forewing has an indented edge. Females are orange, yellow and brown. The butterflies live in the rainforest and breed on grasses including bamboo. The males are often collected.

MORPHO MENELAUS
Blue Morpho

 ZONE 2 — 5½in 140mm

The sexes are completely different. The male is a flashy blue with thin black tips to the forewing containing a small white flash. The female is mainly white and brown with black margins. Despite being one of the most widespread morphos, its life cycle is unknown. Males are attracted to anything bright blue, such as a piece of cloth waved about. It is a butterfly of the rainforest canopy and clearing.

GENUS
MYCALESIS

This is a genus from Africa, Asia, and the Australian region. Species have characteristic curved forewings and generally drab colors. There are seasonal forms which also display sexual dimorphism. Butterflies live in the shade of dense rainforest and breed on grasses, including bamboo.

MYCALESIS LORNA

ZONE 6
2¼in 56mm

This has a very typical satyrid shape. The female has rounded wings with more accentuated, but less bright markings than the male. The hindwing margin is slightly scalloped, and the ground color is brown, lighter to the outside. There is a prominent eye-spot on the forewing and a row of bead-like spots running around the inside of the hindwing. The butterfly comes from New Guinea.

GENUS
MYNES

A genus of butterflies found in the Australian region and exhibiting variation.

MYNES GEOFFROYI
White Nymph

ZONE 6
2¾in 72mm

The uppers are lemon-yellow with a black apex on the forewings and white on the hindwings. The undersides are mottled white, brown, yellow and red, with white being the dominant color on the forewings. The butterfly occurs in New Guinea and along the northeastern Australian coast.

GENUS
NEOMINOIS

This genus of satyrid browns resemble *Hipparchia semele* in appearance.

NEOMINOIS RIDINGSII
Riding's Satyr

ZONE 1
1⅞in 48mm

The washed-out appearance of this satyr is very distinctive. The underside is very pale, to camouflage it very well. The eye-spots on the forewing are repeated on the underside. The butterfly flies in open grassy areas and breeds on various species of grass.

MYCALESIS DUPONCHELI

ZONE 6
2⅜in 62mm

The most noticeable feature is the generous amount of reddish orange on the trailing edge of the hindwing. There are two or three unequal-sized dots within the colorful band, and two pupilled eye-spots within the dark forewings. The butterfly comes from New Guinea.

MYCALESIS MESSENE

ZONE 6
2in 50mm

The key feature of this species is the bronze-orange color of most of the wings. The apex of the forewing is black, and there is a black margin around the hindwing which contains one large and a few unpupilled eye-spots. The butterfly occurs in the Moluccas.

GENUS
NEONYMPHA

A genus of dark browns from North America with eye-spots on the underside of the hindwing.

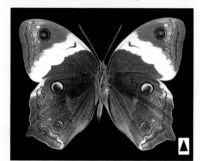

NEONYMPHA PATRIA

The undersides are most distinctive. There is a broad cream band crossing the forewing which has a large black eye-spot in the dark apex. The hindwing is scalloped and dark, with two eye-spots.

ZONE 1 — 4³/₈ in 110mm

GENUS
NEOPE

A genus of Southeast Asian satyrids which have large speckled wings and partial tails on the hindwing. The undersides are a pattern of lines, spots, and bars.

NEOPE BHADRA

Like a giant European *Pararge aegeria*, this butterfly has scalloped margins, accentuated to form a short tail on the hindwing. The forewings are dark brown with a variety of yellowish spots on the wings, the hindwings are mostly orange over what is left of a dark ground color. There are two or three dull black spots inside the margin of the hindwings. The butterfly occurs from Sikkim to Burma.

ZONE 5 — 3¹/₂in 90mm

NEOPE PULAHA

The speckled markings of the butterfly and its wing shape are characteristic. The ground color is black, but scattered with many orange flecks and spots, and orange running along the forewing veins. The mildly scalloped hindwing is formed into a suggestion of a tail. The butterfly is found in lowland and breeds on grasses including bamboo.

ZONE 5 — 2⁵/₈in 70mm

GENUS
NEORINA

A genus of rainforest butterflies found from Sikkim to Java, including Malaya. Their antennae are longer than those of most butterflies, being about half the length of the forewing. Their palps have long setae (sensory hairs) on the topside. The caterpillar food plants are as yet unknown.

NEORINA HILDA

This is a large black butterfly with a conspicuous yellow band which crosses the forewing and clips the hindwing outer margin. There are two dots in the black forewing apex. Although the forewing is curved, the hindwing is slightly scalloped with a modest tail. There are a number of subspecies known. The butterfly occurs from India through to western China.

ZONE 5 — 3¹/₃in 86mm

NEORINA KRISHNA

ZONE 5

3¹/₂in
93mm

This is a big butterfly with bold features. The ground color is a warm brown, and the hindwing is extended into a proper tail. The forewing has a distinctive yellow band which cuts right across the wing, and there is a large unpupilled eye-spot in the apex. The butterfly is found on the heavily populated Indonesian island of Java.

NEORINA LOWII
Malayan Owl

ZONE 5

4¹/₄in
106mm

Although this is also a large black butterfly with roughly the same shape as *N. hilda*, it differs in having more of the yellow band on the hindwing, a more pronounced tail and more white dots on the forewing. The forewing is strongly curved and indented on its outer edge and lacks the large yellow band of *N. krishna*. The butterfly is found in Malaya and Sumatra. It lives in dense forest, but its life cycle is unknown.

GENUS
NEPTIS

A large genus of 40 small-sized species which occur in Africa, Europe, Asia, and in the Australian region. They are commonly called "gliders" or "sailors" because of the way in which they glide through the air. Their colors are highly characteristic, with a black ground color beneath white lines and spots.

NEPTIS MAHENDRA

ZONE 5

2³/₈in
62mm

This has the very typical and familiar color and pattern of several *Neptis* species, with two white bands across the hindwings and two on the forewing. There is a marginal bead of white spots on the forewing and a bold white line broken by a dark vein. The butterfly is quite large compared with many other *Neptis* species. It is found in open, flowery places in India.

NEPTIS SACLAVA
Small Spotted Sailor

	ZONE 4

This is quite a small *Neptis* species with unequal-sized white spots on the forewing apex, and a row of white marks across the hindwing. The hindwing has a row of brown spots and a row of white spots. The butterfly flies in open savanna, bush country, and forest margins. It breeds on *Acalpha* and *Combretum* species, which are members of the *Euphorbiaceae*, spurge family, and *Combretaceae* respectively.

1³⁄₄in
45mm

NEPTIS ZAIDA MANIPURENSIS

	ZONE 5

2⁵⁄₈in
68mm

The basic *Neptis* pattern is retained in this modest-sized species, but the light bands are pale yellow-orange rather than white. There are several subspecies known. The butterfly may be found from the Himalayas, via Burma to China.

GENUS
NYMPHALIS

A small genus of butterflies which occur in Europe, Asia, and North America. They are generally powerful butterflies and are allied to the *Vanessa* genus. Some species are migratory and hibernate as adults.

NEPTIS SHEPHERDI
Common Aeroplane, Common Sailor

	ZONE 6

2³⁄₄in
72mm

The basic pattern of the *Neptis* is retained, but the white marks on the forewing are well dispersed and not arranged in a band, as in *N. shepherdi latifasciata*. There is a broad white band across the hindwing. There are a number of subspecies.

GENUS
NEUROSIGMA

A genus of butterflies which have speckled wings, thin bodies, and long antennae.

NEUROSIGMA DOUBLEDAYI

	ZONE 5

2⁵⁄₈in
70mm

The butterfly resembles a moth with its dull black and weak orange marks. The ground color is basically white, but it is spotted and heavily marked on the veins and margins with brown-black. The base of the forewings have a distinctive rich yellow hue.

NYMPHALIS ANTIOPA
Mourning Cloak, Camberwell Beauty

	ZONE 1·2 3·5

2¹⁄₂in
65mm

This is a spectacular butterfly on the wing with its velvety purple ground color and dramatic cream borders so distinctive in flight. A fine line of blue spots separate these contrasting blocks of color. The undersides are very dark and help to camouflage the butterfly during its hibernation. It is a migrant often found in pine woodlands and along forest rides and glades, where it breeds on willows, beeches, and elms. Its English name comes from the village south of London, now completely built up, where it was originally found.

NYMPHALIS POLYCHLOROS
Large Tortoiseshell

	ZONE 3·4·5
2½in 64mm	

This differs from the Small Tortoiseshell, *Aglais urticae*, in having muted colors over a very similar pattern. The undersides of both species are dull, since they both hibernate. There is rather more orange on the hindwing than in the Small Tortoiseshell and more of a scalloped forewing. The butterfly lives around farms in wooded countryside, where it breeds on elm, poplar and willow. In North Africa it may be found up to 6,000ft (1,800m).

NYMPHALIS XANTHOMELAS
Yellow-legged Tortoiseshell

	ZONE 3·5
2½in 64mm	

Named after its diagnostic feature, the yellow legs are conspicuous. The uppersides are very similar to *N. polychloros*. The hindwing has more orange than other close relatives. The butterfly lives in lowland valleys where it breeds on willows. Its caterpillars are gregarious and live in silken webs. The butterfly is a migrant which hibernates.

OENEIS ALBERTA
Eskimo Arctic

	ZONE 1·5
2⅛in 55mm	

This is a very drab butterfly, which has diffuse gray-brown wings and a suspicion of dots on the margin of the hindwing. The butterfly occurs in the high arctic and, because of the cold conditions in which it lives, takes two years to go through its life cycle. It probably breeds on grasses and sedges.

NYMPHALIS VAU-ALBUM
Comma Tortoiseshell, False Comma

	ZONE 1·3·5
2½in 66mm	

Rather grander with more pronounced markings than *N. polychloros*, this species is very black around the margins and the apex of the forewing. It has white marks on the apex and also on the leading edge of the hindwing. The butterfly occurs in forested areas, especially valleys, where it breeds on willows. The adult hibernates. It is an occasional vagrant in Europe and an occasional migrant in North America.

GENUS
OENEIS

A genus of browns found in North America, eastern Europe, and Asia. The leading edge of the forewing is thickened, marking the *Oeneis* out from other genera. Generally they have muted light brown colors with no pronounced false eyes. They breed on grasses.

OENEIS BORE UCKLINLEYENSIS
Arctic Grayling

	ZONE 1·3·5
2in 50mm	

The uppersides are pale fawn and very pallid with a suggestion of some darker marks around the margin. The underside of the hindwing is much darker and mottled in bands of black and gray. The butterfly occurs in the arctic region and in alpine areas, where it breeds on various grasses.

OENEIS CHRYXUS
Chryxus Arctic, Brown Arctic

2in
51mm
ZONE 1

The forewings of this species are strikingly pointed, and in the male there is a prominent sex brand. The female has more rounded wings, and the eye-spots on the forewing are more prominent. The ground is a very pale straw color, a little more exciting in the female. The butterfly flies in wild grassy habitats where it breeds on various grasses.

OENEIS MACOUNII
Canada Arctic, Macoun's Arctic

2¼in
57mm
ZONE 1

This is similar to O. nevadensis, but slightly smaller and less bright. It does have the two spots on the forewing and a single one on the hindwing. The butterfly lives in pine-forest clearings and takes two years to develop as a caterpillar. It breeds on grasses.

OENEIS NEVADENSIS
Great Arctic, Nevada Arctic, Pacific Arctic

2½in
63mm
ZONE 1

For a butterfly of the cold north, this species is surprisingly bright with its rich straw-colored ground and dark margins. It is also relatively large. The orange is carried below on the forewings, but in line with others of this family, the underside hindwing is dull and mottled and suitable for camouflage. There are two black eye-spots on the forewing. The butterfly flies in clearings, meadows and waysides. It takes two years to develop and breeds on grasses.

OENEIS JUTTA
Forest Arctic, Baltic Grayling

2¼in
56mm
ZONE 1·3

The male has pointed wings compared to the rounded ones of the female. Both sexes have light fawn patches on each wing. These patches contain black spots which are much larger in the female. The underside of the hindwing is mottled gray in a variable wavy pattern. Like several other species that live in cold conditions, the caterpillars take two years to reach maturity. The butterfly is found in bogs, moors and tundra, and probably breeds on sedges and rushes.

OENEIS MELISSA SEMPLEI
Melissa Arctic, White Mountain Arctic, Mottled Arctic

1⅞in
48mm
ZONE 1·5

This is a very somber-looking butterfly with a very cryptic hindwing underside covered in black-gray speckles. The uppers are dark brown, with a smudging of orange in the female. The butterfly lives in grassy areas of tundra as well as meadows and breeds on the abundant sedges.

OENEIS POLIXENES KATAHDIN
Polixenes Arctic, Katahdin Arctic, Banded Arctic

1¾in
44mm
ZONE 1

This is another somber-looking butterfly. The key feature is the translucent nature of the wings, which are the palest gray-brown. The underside of the hindwing is dark; the underside of the forewing is slightly red-orange toward the base. It is variable across its range from Alaska to Maine since it has three subspecies. The butterfly lives in tundra and on alpine wastes. It takes two years to develop and breeds on grasses. The species is protected within the Baxter State Park wilderness.

OENEIS TAYGETE
White-veined Arctic, Labrador Arctic

ZONE 1·5	
1⁷/₈in 48mm	

The "white-veins" are on the underside of the hindwing, where they mark each side of the dark band which crosses the wing. The ground color is very dark on both surfaces. The butterfly flies in tundra regions and on stony summits, but its caterpillar food plants have yet to be identified.

OENEIS UHLERI
Uhler's Arctic, Rocky Mountain Arctic

ZONE 1	
1⁷/₈in 48mm	

This is a pale, straw-colored butterfly with relatively pointed forewings. The undersides are covered with a very attractive gray-white wave-like pattern. The forewing underside is orange toward the base, with a single eye-spot which is repeated on the upperside. There may be up to five spots by the hindwing margin. Butterflies are to be found in the foothills of the Rocky Mountains, forest glades, and areas of tundra.

GENUS
OLYRAS

A genus of three species found in Central and South America. Two of these species occur in Costa Rica.

OLYRAS PRAESTANS

ZONE 2	
3¹/₂in 93mm	

The transparent patches on the forewing are more numerous than in *O. montagui* (not described), and there is a complete lack of the bright bronze color present in that species. The hindwings have much black on the margins, and this is continuous with the black veining and marking on the forewings.

GENUS
OPSIPHANES

The 13 species all have stout bodies, thick scaled wings, and large heads.

OPSIPHANES BATEA

ZONE 2	
3¹/₂in 90mm	

This substantial butterfly is black with a brown-bronze base to the wings. There may be some small brown marks in the black forewing. The butterfly flies in the evening and feeds on rotting fruit, which it pierces with its powerful tongue. It probably breeds on palms.

GENUS
OREIXENICA

A genus of relatively small, speckled brown butterflies typical of the Australian region.

OREIXENICA KERSHAWI
Kershaw's Brown

ZONE 6	
1¹/₂in 40mm	

This species has yellow spots, a prominent eye-spot on the trailing hindwing edge, and a black spot near the forewing apex. The hindwing underside has dull pearl and brown lines, a checkered margin and accentuated eye-spot. From mainland Australia, the butterfly breeds on grasses.

GENUS
PANTOPORIA

A genus of Asian and Australian butterflies which is found from Sri Lanka to China. They fly in forest clearings and along forest edges in sunny situations.

PANTOPORIA ASURA

ZONE 5

3¹/₈in
80mm

This is a variable species resembling a *Neptis*. It is dark brown, almost black all over. There is a cream band which neatly crosses both wings and a variety of cream marks on the forewing. The hindwing has a key recognition feature in a series of rectangular cream marks – like a diadem – each of which contains a black dot. At least seven subspecies are known.

PANTOPORIA EULIMENE BADOURA

ZONE 6

3¹/₃in
86mm

This is quite a large and brightly colored species compared to other *Pantoporia*. The rich brown ground color is crossed by three bright orange-brown lines which end in the dark forewing. One of the lines crosses the abdomen, giving it an orange stripe. The forewing also contains a collection of other orange-brown marks.

GENUS
PARANTICA

A genus of butterflies from the Asian and Australian regions. They are often brown or chocolate-colored, sometimes pale yellow, and may be sexually dimorphic.

PARANTICA SCHENKI

ZONE 6

2⁵/₈in
70mm

The sexes are different. The male has a pale yellow ground with black markings; the female has a white ground with very pale yellow toward the base of the wings. The borders are dark, and there is a beading of small white marks around the inside of the wing margins. Butterflies are found in open areas and forest margins. They probably breed on members of the *Asclepiadaceae*.

PARANTICA VITRINA

ZONE 5

3¹/₈in
80mm

The sexes are fairly similar, although the female is much bigger and darker than the male. The male has a dark brown ground, but much of its wing surface is covered with white radiating from the base and divided by the darker veins. The female ground color is black, and the series of white spots around the margin of the forewing are more pronounced than in the male. There are at least two subspecies known.

GENUS
PARARGE

This genus of shade and woodland-loving satyrids is well represented in Europe and Asia.

PARARGE AEGERIA TIRCIS
Speckled Wood

ZONE 3·5

1³/₄in
44mm

There are two color forms: the typical orange-colored form occurs in southern Europe, the darker one in the north. The butterfly occurs in valleys, waysides and woodland margins, and breeds on couch grass, *Agropyron*. The butterfly is territorial in woodlands.

GENUS
PARASARPA

These are powerful butterflies which are similar to European apaturas.

PARASARPA DUDU

ZONE
5·6

4¼ in
108mm

The distinctive underside has a violet-purple sheen and tiny brown edging marks. The uppers are brown with mottled orange. On both sides a thick white band dominates the pattern. There are at least four subspecies of this butterfly, which occurs from Sikkim to Taiwan. Butterflies enjoy open forest.

GENUS
PAREBA

This genus of delicate-looking butterflies have elongated forewings.

PAREBA VESTA

ZONE
5·6

2⅜ in
60mm

The elongated wings are the main identification feature, although the rich straw ground color is distinctive. There are few wing markings, but there is an attractive border of little orange marks within a thin dark margin. This species occurs from India to China.

GENUS
PARTHENOS

This genus of butterflies are found widely in Asian and Australian regions.

PARTHENOS SYLVIA LILACINUS

ZONE
6

3⅜ in
88mm

The forewings are typically pointed, the hindwings well rounded and scalloped. The dominant feature on this butterfly is the white band which runs from near the apex of the forewing to the hindwing, where it changes into a blue suffusion. The base of the wings is metallic green. The hindwing has a zigzag pattern.

GENUS
PEDALIODES

A genus of over 100 species, these are the South American equivalent of the Old World genus *Erebia*. These two genera are similar in size and appearance, and occupy many habitats, including mountains. The life histories of the *Pedaliodes* have yet to be fully ascertained, but it appears that the principal caterpillar food plant is within the bamboos, possibly *Chusquea* species.

PEDALIODES PEUCESTAS

ZONE
2

2¼ in
56mm

This species is particularly black, as are the many arctic-living erebias, but there is a distinctive white band across the forewing. The hindwings are scalloped. The butterfly lives in open lowland areas and along streams and rivers.

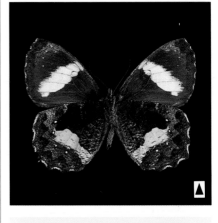

PEDALIODES PHAEDRA

ZONE
2

2⅜ in
60mm

The butterflies are brown with distinct scalloped hindwing margins. There is a yellow or white band across the forewing, and a yellow or white patch in the middle of the hindwing, depending on the forms. The butterflies live in forested areas and possibly breed on bamboos of the *Chusquea* genus.

GENUS
PENROSADA

A South American genus of brown butterflies of fairly similar appearances.

PENROSADA LEAENA

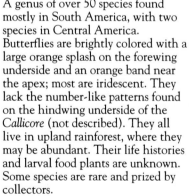

ZONE 2
1½ in 40mm

The underside has the characteristic feature, a uniform white band which contrasts strongly with the warm-brown ground color found throughout the rest of the wings. The butterfly occurs in Ecuador.

GENUS
PERISAMA

A genus of over 50 species found mostly in South America, with two species in Central America. Butterflies are brightly colored with a large orange splash on the forewing underside and an orange band near the apex; most are iridescent. They lack the number-like patterns found on the hindwing underside of the *Callicore* (not described). They all live in upland rainforest, where they may be abundant. Their life histories and larval food plants are unknown. Some species are rare and prized by collectors.

PERISAMA CHASEBA SAUSSUREI

ZONE 2
1¾ in 44mm

The blue uppers are distinctive in this species, and there is a definite black apex to the forewing and over much of the hindwing. The undersides are rich orange on the hindwing and dark brown on the forewings with orange tips. Little is known about the biology of this butterfly.

PERISAMA VANINKA

ZONE 2
2in 50mm

This chubby-shaped species has a rich green band across the forewing which continues around the margins of the hindwing. The ground color is black. The undersides are startling with white on the hindwing, and red, blue, white, and black on the forewing. Males engage in mud-puddling; otherwise, little is known about the biology of this species.

GENUS
PHAEDINA

This genus has close similarities with *Neptis*, under which it was formerly classed.

PHAEDINA SATINA

ZONE 6

2⅝in 68mm

The thick white bar which crosses both wings is characteristic and in striking contrast to the black ground color. Toward the apex of the forewing and around the edges are a number of irregular-sized white marks.

GENUS
PHALANTA

These orange-brown butterflies occur in Africa, Asia, and the Australian region.

PHALANTA PHALANTHA
Common Leopard

ZONE 4·5·6

2⅜in 60mm

The butterfly is orange overall with a rounded hindwing, the feature which separates it from other similar species. The wings are scattered with small black spots. The butterfly lives in woods, savanna and bush, and breeds on *Aberia* and *Dovyalis* species.

GENUS
PHILAETHRIA

A genus of three South and Central American species which breed on *Passiflora*.

PHILAETHRIA DIDO
Scarce Bamboo Page

ZONE 2

4¼in 108mm

The underside of this heliconid is green divided by a chocolate band. The upperside is a more vivid green, with green bars on all wings and green spots around the hindwing. Butterflies mostly remain in the rainforest canopy; females occasionally descend to lay eggs.

GENUS
PHYCIODES

A genus of North and South American butterflies which often have a speckled and very variable pattern. Some species are sexually dimorphic. They live in open sunny meadows and pastures, and visit flowers regularly for nectar. A few species are migratory, but most are not. Where known, the caterpillars feed on members of the acanthus, daisy and nettle families: *Acanthaceae*, *Compositae* and *Urticaceae*.

▲

PHYCIODES CASTILLA

ZONE 2

1¾in 46mm

The male is more colorful than the female. Both sexes have a black background, though in the female it covers a larger area. There is a band across the forewings, yellow in the male and red in the female. While the female hindwings are black, the male has red lines radiating from the base of the wings.

PHYCIODES MYLITTA
Thistle Crescent, Mylitta Crescentspot

ZONE 1

1⅜in 35mm

The overall appearance is of a mottled rich orange and black butterfly. The undersides are much more subdued than the uppers and have a different pattern. The female has larger and more rounded wings than the male. There are two subspecies of this butterfly widespread in western USA. It may also move south into Mexico. Butterflies occur in most habitats with thistles, as these plants are favored for their nectar as well as used for breeding purposes.

PHYCIODES PHAON
Cayman Crescentspot, Phaon Crescentspot,
Mat-plant Crescent

| | ZONE 1·2 |
| 2½in 64mm | |

Although similar to *P. frisia*, this species can be identified by the unbroken bars on the forewing and more pronounced markings. The undersides are light on the hindwing and orange-black and white on the forewing. The butterfly is an occasional migrant and moves north into most of the southern US. It lives in damp habitats, along creeks, valleys and riversides, where it breeds on *Lippia lanceolata* belonging to the *Verbenaceae*.

PHYCIODES TEXANA
Texas Crescent

| | ZONE 1·2 |
| 1½in 40mm | |

This is a dark-looking but speckled butterfly. The ground color is mostly black, broken by a white band across the hindwing and a scattering of white spots on the forewing. The undersides are remarkably light, especially on the hindwing, and the base of the forewing is orange. It has at least two subspecies. The butterfly lives in open desert areas and breeds on various members of the acanthus family, *Acanthaceae*.

GENUS
PHYSCOPEDALIODES

This genus is closely related to *Pedaliodes*, in which it is sometimes included.

PHYSCOPEDALIODES PHYSCOA

| | ZONE 2 |
| 2⅝in 70mm | |

Mostly a uniform brown butterfly, it has a distinctive orange blob toward the outer edge of the forewing visible on both surfaces. The hindwing is rounded and gently scalloped. The sexes are similar.

GENUS
PIERELLA

A genus of 12 to 15 species from Central and South America, the greatest diversity is found in the Amazon basin. Species live from sea level up to about 6,000ft (1,500m) in cloud forest and breed on members of the *Heliconiaceae* and *Marantaceae*.

PIERELLA HORTONA
MICROMACULATA

| | ZONE 2 |
| 2⅜in 62mm | |

A beautiful butterfly with blobs of pale blue set in its brown wings. There is a little orange around the anal area of the hindwing in the male. The wing shape is unusual, the forewing being modestly lobed. The butterfly flies in the Amazon rainforest in Ecuador and probably breeds on plants of the heliconia family.

PIERELLA RHEA

| | ZONE 2 |
| 2⅞in 74mm | |

The wing shape is a key identification feature, as the forewings are elongated in contrast to the hindwings. There is also a basic color difference between the wings: the forewing has a brown ground color, while that of the hindwing is purple-black. There is a row of black-ringed white-pupilled eye-spots around the wing margins. The butterfly flies in various countries within the Amazon rainforest and probably breeds on plants of the heliconia family.

GENUS
POLYGONIA

A genus known as "comma" butterflies in Europe or "question mark" or "anglewing" butterflies in the USA, they occur also in Asia. They have dark brown, orange, and black wings with ragged edges and an underside which is usually cryptic. The butterflies are strong fliers and hibernate. They often breed on nettles, *Urtica* species.

POLYGONIA FAUNUS
Green Comma, Faunus Anglewing

	ZONE 1
2in 51mm	

The distinguishing features of this comma are the green hue over the wings when it is fresh, the little orange marks on the margin of the wings, and the deep russet colors of the uppers. The ragged outline is typical of so many comma species. This one may be found in clearings and waysides where it breeds on alder, birch, and willow.

POLYGONIA C-ALBUM
Comma

	ZONE 3·5
1⁷/₈in 48mm	

The white mark on the underside of the hindwing is the feature after which this species is named. There are seasonal variations, the first generation being lighter than the second generation. The butterfly is territorial, but not migratory. It breeds on nettle, *Urtica*, and hops, *Humulus*. This specimen is from Japan.

POLYGONIA INTERROGATIONIS
Question Mark

	ZONE 1
2³/₈in 62mm	

The key feature is the darkened hindwing which is squared off and has a distinct tail. The forewing is a little curved, but it has the usual range of black spots. The butterfly lives in open sunny places, in clearings, along wood edges, and in waysides; and it breeds on elms, hops, and nettles. In Canada, there is some evidence that it might migrate.

POLYGONIA PROGNE
Gray Comma, Dark-gray Comma, Dark-gray Anglewing

	ZONE 1
1⁷/₈in 48mm	

This butterfly can be recognized by the dark margins on all wings which contain a few orange flecks, and the sparsity of black spots over the wings in comparison with other commas. The trailing part of the hindwing can be considerably darkened. There are a number of subspecies of the butterfly, which has a wide distribution through much of North America. The butterfly lives in clearings, waysides, and in urban areas where, particularly, it breeds on *Ribes*, especially gooseberries.

GENUS
POLYGRAPHA

A genus of South American butterflies whose wing shape is similar to that of *Charaxes*.

POLYGRAPHA CYANEA

	ZONE 2
3¹/₈in 83mm	

This is a stunning butterfly, with curved forewings and a tailed hindwing. The black ground has a bright pale blue band crossing both wings, and toward the base of the wings a bright dark blue to violet suffusion – hence *cyanea*.

GENUS
POLYURA

A genus of powerful butterflies which belong to the *Charaxinae* subfamily, found in Asia and the Australian region. The larvae all have two unequal pairs of horns projecting from the top of the head and feed on a wide variety of food plants.

▲

POLYURA EUDAMIPPUS
Great Nawab

	ZONE 5·6
4in 102mm	

This is an extremely attractive butterfly on both surfaces. The uppers are lemon-cream to white with a speckled black apex to the forewing containing a few yellowish dots. The hindwing has a row of black spots with white centers and two silver-blue tails. The undersides are silvery white with yellow tracery around the margins and two thin bands across the wings. It has at least seven subspecies. This is a lowland species with a widespread distribution from India to China and Taiwan.

POLYURA ATHAMUS
Common Nawab

	ZONE 5·6
3⅛in 80mm	

This attractive double-tailed butterfly has indentations on the outer edge of the forewing. The uppersides are dark brown with a very generous band of lemon-yellow crossing both wings. There is a single yellow dot well in from the forewing tip. The undersides repeat the pattern on the uppers, but in completely different colors, being silver-gray with a band of ice blue. At least seven subspecies are known. The caterpillar feeds at night on many members of the pea family, *Leguminosae*.

POLYURA GALAXIA

	ZONE 5·6
5in 130mm	

This species shares the same body shape as *P. eudamippus*. The uppers are black at the extremities and very pale lemon toward the base of the wings. There is a distinctive row of pale yellow marks around the inside of the margins of all wings, and yellow spots in the black apex. The undersides are mustard to rusty yellow-brown with a bloom of pale blue toward the margins. There is a row of three red lunules. There are a number of subspecies of this butterfly, which occurs across two regions and frequents open areas close to forests.

GENUS
PREPONA

A genus of South and Central American butterflies of which the total number of species is unclear since there are so many confusing forms. They have bright blue-green bands on the upperside and, often, large false eyes on the underside. These are butterflies of the rainforest canopy and infrequently come down to ground level. Caterpillars feed on members of the *Leguminosae*.

PREPONA PHERIDAMAS

ZONE 2 · 3½in 93mm

This species is very similar to *P. demophon*, but can be differentiated by the broken nature of the metallic green band on the leading edge of the forewing. It is also slightly smaller. The butterfly occurs over a wide area of the Amazon rainforest.

PREPONA DEMOPHON
Silver King Shoemaker

ZONE 2 · 5½in 140mm

Of the 30 or so species of *Prepona* in South America, this is one of the most common. It has a distinctive metallic green band across the dark brown wings. The forewings are curved, pointed, and indented on the outer edge. The undersides are completely different, being fawny white with various interlacing lines. The butterfly lives in the rainforest canopy and smells of vanilla.

PREPONA PRAENESTE BUCKLEYANA

ZONE 2 · 4in 102mm

This butterfly has the same wing shape and sturdy body of *P. pheridamas*, though it differs considerably in other respects. There are bands of red which traverse the forewings, and a thick red band which runs around the inside of the margin of the hindwing. To the inside of the hindwing is a purple hue to this butterfly, which otherwise has a dark brown ground. It occurs widely in Amazonian rainforest.

GENUS
PRONOPHILA

A genus of about 50 species found mostly in South America, with a single species in Central America. They are medium-sized butterflies with rounded wings and a yellow or white band on the forewing. They are found in areas of bamboo thickets in upland rainforest. Nothing is known about their life cycle or larval food plants.

PRONOPHILA CORDILLERA

ZONE 2 · 3⅛in 83mm

This is one of the smaller species of the 50 or so *Pronophila* found in South America. It is identified by the curious white forewings, which have a distinct brown border. The hindwings are entirely brown, unmarked, and rounded. The underside of the forewings are reddish with white spots. Very little is known about the caterpillar food plants, but bamboo is a possibility. The butterfly inhabits the upland woods and thickets of Bolivia where bamboo is found.

PRONOPHILA THELEBE

	ZONE 2
2⁷/₈ in 74mm	

This is one of the largest species of *Pronophila*. It is black over most of its wings, and it has a distinguishing white mark on the apex of the forewing visible on the undersides. The hindwing is rounded and gently scalloped. In comparison with the large wings, the body seems very small. The butterfly is widespread in the Amazon rainforest.

GENUS
PSEUDACRAEA

An African genus of *Acraea* mimics which have an open cell on the hindwing.

PSEUDACRAEA BOISDUVALI
Trimen's False Acraea

	ZONE 4
4 in 100mm	

The bright red on the base of the wings is diagnostic, and within this area there is a flurry of uniform black dots. The margin of the hindwing has a thick black band containing a series of red spots. The outer part of the forewing is dark with a greenish tinge. The female has the same coloration, but is larger.

GENUS
PTYCHANDRA

A genus of similar-looking browns in which the sexes are dimorphic.

PTYCHANDRA LORQUINI

	ZONE 5
2¹/₈ in 54mm	

The male has deep blue uppers with a cobwebbed outer margin to the forewing and somber brown and spotted undersides. The light brown female has two white areas on the forewing. The female's tailed hindwing has marginal eye-spots and a big dark spot on the leading edge.

GENUS
PROTHOE

A genus of three powerful species, one in Asia, the others in the Australian region.

PROTHOE CALYDONIA
The Glorious Begum

	ZONE 5
4³/₄ in 120mm	

The forewings have a black apex and yellow base. The hindwing is blue to the inside of the thick black margin and drawn out to form a blunt tail. The underside is speckled brown, yellow, black, and white. Butterflies live in rainforest and have a fondness for dung moisture.

GENUS
PYRONIA

A large genus of browns from Europe and Asia which have brown to russet colors with false eyes. They live in sunny areas, along the edges of woods and forests, in woodland glades, and in the open. Individual variation and subspeciation has occurred widely. Species generally breed on grasses.

PYRONIA TITHONUS
Gatekeeper, Hedge Brown

	ZONE 3·5
1½in 38mm	

The male has a characteristic sex brand on the forewing, and the female has more rounded wings and less intense orange on her wings than the male. The underside of the hindwing has a wiggly orange line dividing the dark base from the lighter outside, and some little eye-spots are present. Unlike *P. cecilia*, this species does not occur in North Africa. It is a familiar and widespread butterfly which may be seen along waysides and in hedges. The butterfly breeds on various common grasses, such as *Poa* and *Milium*.

PYRONIA CECILIA
Southern Gatekeeper

	ZONE 3·4·5
1¼in 32mm	

Very similar to *P. tithonus*, but lacks eye-spots on the underside of the hindwing. The uppers are orange with a single large pupilled eye-spot on the apex of the forewing, and, in the male, there is a rectangular brown sex brand. The underside of the hindwing is mottled and provides useful camouflage in the hot, dry habitats in which it flies and has to take refuge. The butterfly breeds on the grass, *Deschampsia*.

GENUS
RHAPHICERA

A small Asian genus which resemble *Pararge aegeria*, the European Speckled Wood.

RHAPHICERA MOOREI

	ZONE 5
2½in 64mm	

The butterfly has an orange-speckled, brown upperside and lighter underside which has a few eye-spots on the hindwing. The female has a rounded hindwing and is duller overall than the male. The butterfly is found in Sikkim and Bhutan.

GENUS
RHINOPALPA

A small genus of woodland butterflies found from Burma to Sulawesi. They feed on nettles.

RHINOPALPA POLYNICE EUDOXIA
The Wizard

	ZONE 5·6
3⅛in 80mm	

A variable species in which males are darker than females. Males may be entirely dark or have thick black outers with orange-brown to the inside and base. The dark undersides, mottled with wavy lines, have a series of marginal eye-spots. About ten subspecies occur.

GENUS
SALAMIS

A genus of butterflies which is found in Africa to India via Saudi Arabia. They are related to *Hypolimnas* and are characterized by their large hooked forewings, with tails or lobes on hindwings. The caterpillars, like those of *Hypolimnas*, have pairs of spines along the body.

SALAMIS ANACARDII
Clouded Mother of Pearl

ZONE 4

3¼in
85mm

In this Mother of Pearl, the markings are creamy white and rather modest. The outer parts of the wings are dark, and may contain small cream dots and two unequal-sized red-pupilled eye-spots on the hindwing. The butterfly lives along rivers, in forests and glades, and in coastal bush, and may sometimes be gregarious.

SALAMIS PARHASSUS
Mother of Pearl

ZONE 4

3½in
90mm

This species is very attractive with its green pearly livery and contrasting black hooked tip to the forewing. There is a series of dark spots on both sets of wings, as well as a loose series of black dots around the margins. The undersides are pearly with eight distinct red dots. The butterfly is larger than *S. anacardii*, and lives in forests, woodland, and scrub throughout most of Africa. It breeds on *Asystasia*, a member of the acanthus family.

GENUS
SALLYA

This is a genus of African butterflies commonly called tree-nymphs. (Other related species, such as *Eunica occidentalium* – not described – are still called tree-nymphs although they have been reclassified into different genera.) As the common name suggests, these butterflies prefer woodland habitats, scrub and secondary forest which has developed where primary forest has been cleared. There the butterflies perch and flit among the trees, now and then resting on tree trunks. They are often migratory.

SALLYA AMULIA ROSA
Lilac Tree-nymph, Lilac Nymph

ZONE 4

2in
50mm

The color combinations are very unusual, but very attractive. The uppers are a rich violet-blue, and the undersides are rich orange on the forewing and slate blue with orange bands, rather like an accentuated fritillary pattern. There is a series of small black dots on the hindwing and a small black spot near the forewing tip, all of which are repeated on the underside. This butterfly is one of a number of migratory subspecies. It lives in forests and clearings.

SALLYA BOISDUVALI
Brown Tree-nymph

ZONE
4

2¹/₈in
55mm

The uppers are soft brown with a dark margin around the hindwing. To the inside is a row of small black dots. On the leading edge of the forewing there are two black bands. The sexes are similar, but the female has darker markings. The butterfly may occur in very large numbers in forested areas within the Ethiopian region, where it breeds on *Excoecaria*.

GENUS
SIPROETA

A genus of butterflies found in Central and South America, and the southern USA.

SIPROETA STELENES
BIPLAGIATA
Malachite

ZONE
1·2

3in
76mm

This beautiful butterfly has bright green on the uppers set against a dark brown ground, and pale green on the underside set against a pale brown ground. The hindwing is slightly scalloped with a definite tail. It frequents open habitats, breeding on plants of the acanthus family.

SPEYERIA ATLANTIS
Atlantis Fritillary

ZONE
1

2⁵/₈in
67mm

This is one of the larger and more common fritillaries. The ground color is typically rich orange speckled with a generous amount of black. There are some distinctive bars on the leading edge of the forewing in the male. The underside of the hindwing has silvery spots set in a background of russet-brown. It is very variable, and a number of subspecies exist. The butterfly lives in open areas and breeds on several species of violet.

GENUS
SIDERONE

These butterflies have red flashes on their elliptical forewings and leaf-like undersides.

SIDERONE NEMESIS

ZONE
2

2³/₄in
72mm

The wing shape is characteristic, especially the hindwing with its drawn-out and stubby tails. Two red bands take up most of the forewing. The butterfly frequents all sorts of habitats, occasionally the rainforests, and probably breeds on members of the *Flacourtiaceae*.

GENUS
SPEYERIA

A genus of North American fritillaries, which are related to members of the *Argynnis*. They are very variable butterflies and have produced plenty of subspecies and forms. Species live in open sunny habitats such as meadows, pastures and forest edges, and breed on violets.

SPEYERIA DIANA
Diana

ZONE
1

3⁷/₈in
98mm

This species can still be recognized as a fritillary though it has departed somewhat from the norm. The male has bright orange on the outer third of its wings, the inside being black. The underside is mainly orange, with few of the typical fritillary marks. The female is mostly black and blue on the upperside. The butterfly lives in open glades and forest edges and breeds on violets. It has died out in some of its former haunts in the Appalachians due to habitat loss.

SPEYERIA NOKOMIS
Nokomis Fritillary, Western Seep Fritillary

ZONE 1·2

3in
76mm

This is another large fritillary. The male is bright orange on the uppers, but it does not have the extensive black spotting found on other fritillaries. The undersides are yellow-green between muted spots. The female is yellowish white on the uppers. The butterfly lives in meadows and along riversides, and it breeds on *Viola nephrophylla*. There are populations in the southwestern US and in Mexico, but a blue form from Arizona has become extinct. Like *S. diana*, it is highly prized by collectors.

GENUS
STIBOCHIONA

A genus of butterflies from Asia, including Malaya, Indonesia, and Borneo. At present no more than six species are known. They live in rainforest habitats. Details of larval food plants and life cycle are, as yet, unknown.

STIBOCHIONA CORESIA

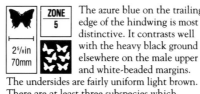

ZONE 5

2⁵⁄₈in
70mm

The azure blue on the trailing edge of the hindwing is most distinctive. It contrasts well with the heavy black ground elsewhere on the male upper and white-beaded margins. The undersides are fairly uniform light brown. There are at least three subspecies which display spectacular differences, some with violet instead of azure and one all black. The butterfly lives deep in rainforest and occurs in Malaya, Java, and Sumatra.

STIBOCHIONA NICEA

ZONE 5

2⁵⁄₈in
70mm

In this species the male is black with a white-speckled margin. The trailing edge of the hindwing is whitish, but may be blue or green in the various subspecies. The female tends to be slightly larger and browner. As for fine detail, the compound eyes of the species are hairy, those of *S. coresia* hairy only on the lower half. This is a variable species, with seasonal forms and subspecies. The butterfly occurs in rainforest at moderate elevations.

GENUS
STICHOPTHALAMA

This is a genus of large Asian butterflies from India to Burma. The antennae have a useful identification feature in that they broaden toward the tip, rather than having a definite club. Species live in rainforest, and probably all of them will be found to breed on grasses, including bamboo.

STICHOPTHALAMA CAMADEVA
Northern Jungle Queen

ZONE 5

6in
150mm

This huge butterfly is pale blue on the uppers and green on the undersides. It can hardly be mistaken for anything else as it flies through the jungle at ground level, sometimes pausing to feed on dung, fruit, or sap. There are at least three subspecies known. The butterfly, which occurs from Sikkim to Burma, probably breeds on bamboo or palms.

STICHOPTHALAMA LOUISA

ZONE 5

5¹/₂in 140mm

This species is unmistakable with its orange suffusion to the inner two-thirds of the uppers and the band of black arrow marks around the margin of the wings. The undersides are very pale with the inner parts very slightly darker and marked in thin lines. There are two eye-spots on each of the hindwings.

GENUS
TAENARIS

A genus of relatively large brown-colored butterflies from the Australian region.

TAENARIS DOMITILLA

ZONE 6

4in 100mm

The hindwings are disproportionately large and rounded with a pair of black-ringed eye-spots close together and enclosed by an orange-red band. The trailing edge of the hindwing is black, the rest of the wings pale brown. The butterfly is found in the Moluccas.

TAENARIS PHORCAS URANUS

ZONE 6

4¹/₂in 115mm

This is a large brown butterfly with distinctive cream-white patches on each wing. The patch on the forewing is whiter and unmarked compared with that on the hindwing which is creamier and contains a single black eye-spot surrounded by a thick orange-yellow band. All the wings are very rounded. The butterfly occurs on the Solomon Islands and in the Bismarck archipelago.

GENUS
TANAECIA

A large genus of Asian butterflies found from the rainforests of India to the Philippines. They are similar to the *Euthalia* and have some aristocratic-sounding common names such as Baron, Count and Viscount.

TANAECIA CLATHRATA

ZONE 5

2¹/₂in 64mm

The hindwings are rounded with a thick violet band on the trailing edge. The violet also extends onto the forewing, which in this species is not hooked. The ground color is a rich brown. There is a trace of violet suffusion on the undersides of the hindwing, and the ground color of the underside is pale brown with several fine lines.

TANAECIA LEPIDEA
Grey Count

ZONE 5

2⅝in
70mm

A variable species, it is recognized by its two-tone uppers, mostly dark brown, but the trailing edge of the hindwing is a pale fawn to cream. The forewing shape is curved and hooked. The undersides are a much lighter brown compared to the uppers. At least six subspecies exist. The butterfly occurs in hilly country from about 2,500ft (760m) and breeds on *Melastoma malbathricum* and *Careya arborea*.

G E N U S
TAYGETIS

This is a genus of about 27 species of browns from Central and South America. They are medium- to large-sized butterflies which have brown or gray uppers with false eyes on the underside. They mostly prefer the shaded rainforest understory. Their caterpillar food plants in the wild have yet to be ascertained, but it is likely that some feed on grasses.

TAYGETIS ALBINOTATA

ZONE 2

3⅛in
83mm

True to form, this species is large and brown with a neat series of large white spots on the hindwing. The cream and brown markings on the margin give a scalloped effect. The scalloped undersides are light and dark brown with two cream bands crossing the wings.

TAYGETIS CHRYSOGONE

ZONE 2

4in
100mm

Chryso is from the Greek for gold and refers to the thick orange-gold jagged border on the trailing edge of the hindwing. The ground color is a warm brown. The wings are noteworthy, since the forewing is pointed and elliptical and the hindwing strongly scalloped with a modest tail.

G E N U S
TELLERVO

This genus of black-and-white butterflies with long forewings occurs in the Australian region.

TELLERVO ZOILUS
Hamadryad

ZONE 6

1½in
38mm

This small mimic of *Neptis* butterflies has a yellow eye-spot when fresh. The black ground and hindwing is taken up mostly with a white patch, repeated on the underside. White spots run around the underside hindwing margin. Subspecies occur, and butterflies live in dense rainforest.

G E N U S
THAUMANTIS

Species have blue or purple iridescence, and a camouflaged pattern on the undersides.

THAUMANTIS DIORES
Jungle Glory

ZONE 5

1⅞in
48mm

The wings are fairly rounded with a dark brown to black ground color. In the center of each wing is a blue-violet iridescent patch. The butterfly is on the wing at dusk in the rainforest. It occurs from India to China.

GENUS
TIRUMALA

A genus of butterflies found from Africa, via Asia, to the Australian region. They have close affinities with members of the *Danaus* genus both in color and venation. Males have a large sex brand on the hindwing.

TIRUMALA SEPTENTRIONALIS

ZONE 5 · 4¼in 106mm

This has the same general shape and pattern as *T. limniace*, but the spotting is of pale greenish blue. Areas between the veins at the base of the wing are colored to form long stripes, and toward the margins of the wings there is a loose string of small spots. There are a number of subspecies of this butterfly which occurs from India to Taiwan. It is found in lowland and upland forest and breeds on members of the milkweed family, *Asclepiadaceae*.

TISIPHONE ABEONA
Sword Grass Brown

ZONE 6 · 2⅝in 70mm

This species is confined to Australia where it exists in several races and forms. Essentially the uppers are dark with various unequal-sized eye-spots, one large one with a bluish center being on the forewing. The margin of the hindwing is slightly scalloped. The female is much larger than the male. The butterfly lives along swamps and stream banks, and is named after its caterpillar food plant, sword grass.

TIRUMALA FORMOSA
Forest Monarch, Beautiful Monarch

ZONE 4 · 3½in 90mm

The beauty of this forest butterfly is in the juxtaposition of the cream speckles on the dark wings and the deep suffusion of rich brown-bronze at the base of the forewing and over much of the hindwings. The cream spots are rather like irregular-sized snowflakes. This species is used as a model by *Papilio rex*. Butterflies may be found in gardens as well as woods and forests, in fact, anywhere they can breed on members of the milkweed family, *Asclepiadaceae*.

GENUS
TISIPHONE

This is a genus of brown butterflies from the Australian mainland which have a typical brown or black ground color and a variety of false eyes. They appear to exploit the grass family as larval food plants.

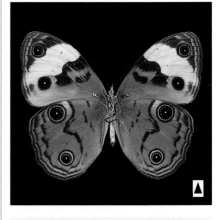

TISIPHONE HELENA
Helene Brown

ZONE 6 · 2⅝in 70mm

The forewings are very rounded, and the female butterfly is much larger than the male. The underside of the hindwing has two large eye-spots which have yellow rings and a white pupil. The forewing uppers are mostly suffused with weak orange and contain a single eye-spot. The rest of the uppers are a muted brown.

GENUS
TITHOREA

A South American genus of about 15 species which belong to the *Ithomiinae* subfamily.

TITHOREA TARRICINA PINTHIAS

ZONE 2

3³/₈in
88mm

The pointed forewings are black speckled with yellowish marks, and the hindwings are red with a black margin. Unusually for a butterfly, this species has tough wings which can resist some attacks by birds and lizards. The butterfly flies in forested areas and breeds on *Prestonia portabellensis*.

GENUS
VANESSA

A widespread genus of strong fliers, sometimes migratory, in bright oranges and reds.

VANESSA ATALANTA
Red Admiral

ZONE 1·2·3 5·6

2¹/₂in
63mm

The intricate pattern on the hindwing underside is unique, and overall the colors and patterns of this butterfly are very constant. Its migratory powers plus artificial introductions have helped in its success. Butterflies occur in many open habitats and breed on the ubiquitous nettle. This specimen is from Mexico.

GENUS
VINDULA

Members of this genus are large powerful butterflies found in Asia and in the Australian region, including Australia. Colors are often rich orange. Males are partial to mud-puddling and sap-sucking.

VINDULA ARSINOE ANDEA
Cruiser

ZONE 5·6

4in
100mm

The male is rich orange with rows of black bead-like spots around the wing margins. The elusive female is slightly larger than the male, with a much less strident orange over her uppers. The hindwing margins of both sexes are slightly scalloped with a faint trace of a tail, and there are small black markings around the margins. This is a fairly common butterfly of rainforest clearings, riverbanks, and tracks, where the male can be seen, often mud-puddling.

VINDULA EROTA
Cruiser

ZONE 5

3³/₄in
95mm

This is a very variable butterfly. The male is the brighter of the sexes with golden orange uppers with some black marks to the margins. The female is larger than the male, with a greenish blue suffusion and a pair of brown-ringed eye-spots on the hindwing. The tail is much more pronounced in this species compared to *V. arsinoe*. Butterflies occur in hilly country where they breed on *Adenia palmata*, a member of the passion flower family.

GENUS
XANTHOTAENIA

A genus of a single species which occurs from Burma to Malaya.

XANTHOTAENIA BUSIRIS

ZONE 5

2⁷/₈in
74mm

Named after the yellow forewing band – *xantho* meaning yellow – the butterfly has black tips and brown bases to the forewings. The hindwing is brown. A number of subspecies exist. The butterfly lives in open forests in lowlands and mountains, flying close to the ground. It probably breeds on the passion flower family.

GENUS
YOMA

This genus is represented by a single species found from Burma to Australia.

YOMA SABINA VASILIA
Australian Lurcher

	ZONE 5·6
3⅛in 80mm	

The hooked forewing and the strongly scalloped hindwing with a tail are key features. The overall color is brown, and there is a distinctive thick cream to violet-red-brown band which runs across the wings. The butterfly breeds on *Ruellia ripens*, a member of the *Acanthaceae* family.

GENUS
YPTHIMA

A genus of brown butterflies found in Africa, Asia, and the Australian region. They have brown and drab colors with pronounced eye-spots. Species live in grassy habitats, such as savanna, and breed on various grasses.

YPTHIMA CONJUNCTA

	ZONE 5
2⅜in 60mm	

This is a drab butterfly. On the forewing there is a single eye-spot near the apex of the wing, and on the hindwing there are a pair of eye-spots and a smaller one. The undersides are lighter and mottled with masses of peppery lines. There are at least two subspecies of this butterfly, which occurs in China and Taiwan.

YPTHIMA NAREDA

	ZONE 5
1¾in 44mm	

This is a brown butterfly with proportionally large and bright eye-spots. Generally there is a double-pupilled eye-spot on the forewing and one on the hindwing. There are three eye-spots on the underside of the hindwing and one on the underside of the forewing, all very pronounced. At least four subspecies exist. This is a widespread species occurring from the Himalayas to China.

GENUS
ZETHERA

A genus of large butterflies found in the Asian and Australian regions. There is sometimes strong sexual dimorphism. The butterflies have a very speckled pattern and live in the rainforest.

ZETHERA INCERTA

	ZONE 5·6
5⅛in 132mm	

The female is about ¾in (20mm) larger than the male, but they share the same colors and patterns, with gray-brown on the forewing and a lighter center. The hindwings have a distinctive zigzag line around the margin and a pale yellow tinge over most of the wings. A notable feature is the networking of the veins in brown. There is also a series of modest eye-spots around the wings on both surfaces. This species occurs in Sulawesi and mimics *Ideopsis*.

ZETHERA MUSA

3¹/₂in 90mm	ZONE 5

The male is black with a lemon flash on the hindwing which links up with a series of dots on the forewing and hindwing. There is also a uniform series of tiny lemon dots around the margin of the hindwing. The females are very different and have a number of forms. Some are all brown; others have a brown-white appearance with the veins emphasized in brown.

GENUS
ZEUXIDIA

A genus of Asian butterflies which are found from Burma through Malaya to the Philippines. Species display strong sexual dimorphism, and males have tufts of hairs and scales on the uppersides of their hindwings.

ZEUXIDIA AURELIUS

6¹/₂in 164mm	ZONE 5

The female is brown with a diffuse white patch on the forewing tip, and at least ¹/₈in (3mm) larger in wingspan than the male. The male has a huge splash of iridescent blue on the forewing and a splattering of blue on the trailing edge of the hindwing. The ground color is otherwise brown. The shape of the hindwing is drawn out into a partial stubby tail.

ZEUXIDIA AMETHYSTUS
Saturn

4¹/₄in 106mm	ZONE 5

Stunning in its colors, the male butterfly has shocks of blue across the forewing tip and on the trailing edge of the hindwing; otherwise, the ground color is a deep brown. The female is brown. The shape of the forewing is somewhat curved and pointed, and the hindwing is drawn out as a short stumpy tail. At least four subspecies are known. The butterfly occurs in Malaya, the Philippines and Sumatra, and flies near water in dense rainforest. This male is from Malaya and shows tufts of hairs on the hindwing.

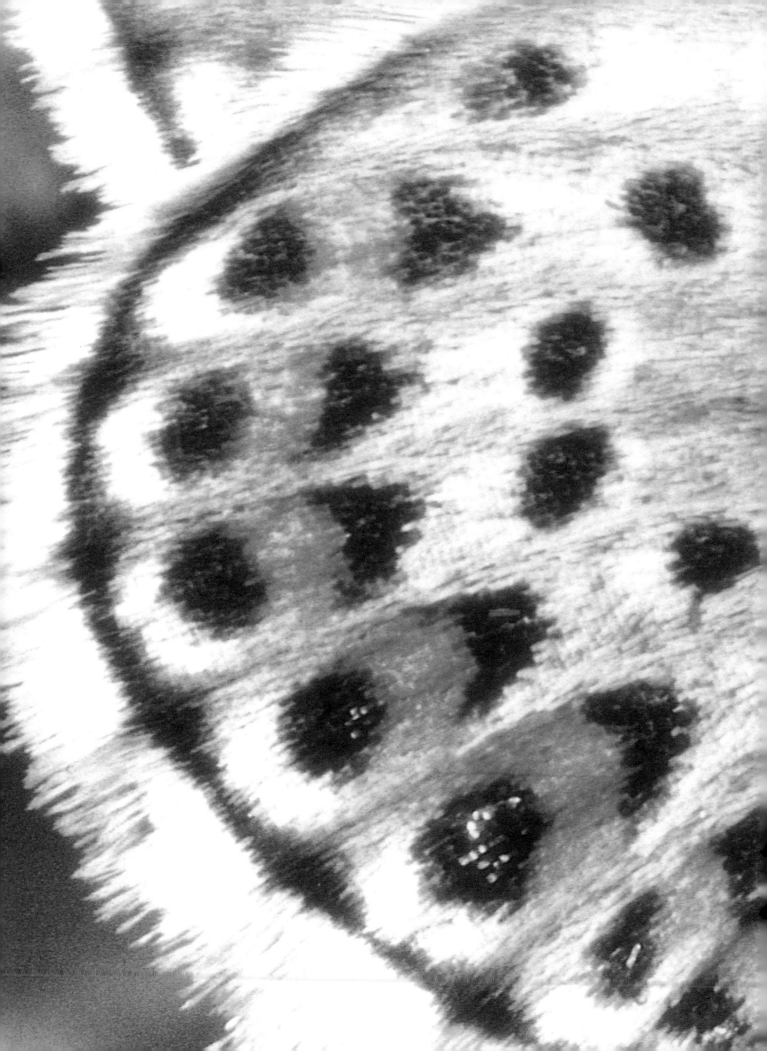

LYCAENIDAE

These include the hairstreaks, blues, and coppers, and are some of the most beautiful butterflies in the world with their rich irridescent blue, copper, and green colors. They are also among the world's smallest butterflies. The lycaenids often have tails, usually thin and tiny, often twisted, and the hindwing may also be extended. The hairstreaks are named after a thin or broken line which cuts across the underside of the hindwing. Metalmarks are closely related to the lycaenids, but they also have some nymphalid characteristics.

Lycaenids are often gregarious and breed principally on members of the *Leguminosae*, or pea family. Some are migratory, such as the Long-tailed blue, and enjoy wide distribution. Lycaenids may be found in flowery meadows, both in lowlands and mountainous areas, where they spend a lot of time imbibing nectar. (The butterfly above is *Plebjus argus.*)

GENUS
ABISARA

This is a genus of about 15 species of butterfly found in Africa and Asia, collectively called judies. They are brown butterflies, some with tails and some with a purplish tinge. They breed on *Mysinaceae*.

ABISARA SAVITRI

	ZONE 5	
2¹/₈in 54mm		

This is one of the tailed judies. The ground color is a rich fawny brown, and there is a whitish bloom across the forewings and a fainter band on the inside. The hindwing has a characteristic shape, scalloped and drawn out as a triangular tail which almost points sideways. There are two pairs of eye-spots on the hindwing, each pair a different size. The butterfly lives in the forested plains.

ABISARA FYLLA

	ZONE 5	
2in 50mm		

This is a brown butterfly with a very distinctive and contrasting orange-yellow band across the forewings in the male. The female has a white band on the forewing. Hidden in the warm brown of the hindwings is a row of black eye-spots. The butterfly occurs in the Himalayas and as far east as China.

GENUS
ABULINA

A genus of a dozen blue species from Asia and Europe.

ABULINA ORBITULUS
Alpine Argus

	ZONE 3·5	
1¹/₈in 28mm		

True to form, the male is blue and the female is brown on the uppers. The male blue is rich and dark, and there is a thin black border. The undersides are pale, and there are a few white patches on the hindwing. The butterfly lives in alpine meadows, where it breeds on *Astragalus*.

GENUS
ADELOTYPA

This is a genus of about 30 small butterflies from South America.

ADELOTYPA PENTHEA

	ZONE 2	
1³/₈in 36mm		

The butterfly has a two-tone color to the uppers. The forewings and the leading edge of the hindwing is a rich orange brown with a few black marks. The rest of the hindwing is white with three black spots on each wing.

GENUS
AGRIADES

A genus of about a dozen species found mostly in the northern hemisphere, from North America through Europe to and including Asia. The sexes are usually dimorphic, and the male is usually a colorful blue. Butterflies breed on members of the primrose and pea families, *Primulaceae* and *Leguminosae*.

AGRIADES AQUILO
Arctic Blue

⁷/₈in 22mm	ZONE 3·5

The male has silvery brown uppers; the female is brown. This butterfly is closely related to *A. glandon*, and some lepidopterists regard it as a subspecies. It is, though, much smaller and also geographically isolated as a population in arctic Scandinavia. Female butterflies lay eggs on *Astragalus alpinus*.

GENUS
AGRODIAETUS

This is a genus of about 20 species of blues from Europe to the Middle East. The sexes are generally dimorphic, and the male is brightly colored. Each species seems to have its own particular shade of blue which is useful for identification purposes. The butterflies are typical of flowery meadows and breed on members of the pea family, *Leguminosae*.

AGRODIAETUS AMANDA
Amanda's Blue

1¹/₂in 38mm	ZONE 3·5

The male is blue on the uppers with a faint black margin while the female is brown, with three orange chevrons on the trailing edge of the hindwing. Both sexes have a neat white fringe. The undersides of both male and female are pale with black and orange spots. The butterfly lives on moors and bogs and breeds on bitter vetch, *Vicia cracca*.

AGRIADES GLANDON
Glandon Blue, Primrose Blue

1¹/₈in 30mm	ZONE 1·3

The sexes are mostly different on the upper surface. The male is turquoise, especially toward the base of the wings, while the female is a uniform brown all over. The undersides are fairly similar with dark bases and black and white speckles on the outer part of the wings. Several subspecies exist. The butterfly is found in many arctic regions including around the northern coast of Greenland. It lives on flowery mountainsides and breeds on *Soldanella* in Europe and *Primula* in North America.

AGRODIAETUS DAMON
Damon's Blue

 ZONE 3 — 1¼in 32mm

The sexes are very different on the uppers. The male is mostly turquoise-blue which gives way to a darker margin around all wings. The female is a uniform brown; both sexes have a white fringe. The undersides have a tell-tale white stripe across the fawn hindwing. The butterfly lives on flowery meadows and breeds on *Onobrychis viciifolia*.

AGRODIAETUS THERSITES
Chapman's Blue

 ZONE 3·5 — 1¼in 32mm

The male is a violet-blue and is similar to *Polyommatus icarus*. However Chapman's blue differs in having a certain roughness to the upper forewing where the androconia are situated. The female is brown on the uppers. The butterfly enjoys open mountainous habitats such as found in the Vosges in France and the Atlas in Morocco. It breeds on sainfoin, *Onobrychis*.

GENUS
ALESA

A genus of four species from the rainforests of South America.

ALESA AMESIS
Green Dragon

 ZONE 2 — 2in 50mm

The male is black with three stripes of metallic green traversing the wings. The female has very subdued browns in concentric patterns radiating out from the body and four to five squarish spots on the hindwing margin.

GENUS
ALLOTINUS

A genus of at least 12 Asian and Australian species with pale speckled wings.

ALLOTINUS APRIES

 ZONE 5 — 1½in 40mm

The forewings are slightly pointed. The ground color is a speckled fawn, slightly lighter toward the base of the wings. The underside hindwing is drawn out into a series of tails. This butterfly is found in Burma, Malaya, Java, Sumatra, and Borneo.

GENUS
ALOEIDES

An African genus of at least ten species which are small and orange-brown to light brown.

ALOEIDES MOLOMO
Molomo Copper

 ZONE 4 — 1⅛in 30mm

In both sexes the uppers are orange-brown with a broad brown band along the outer margin of the forewing, and a brown mark on the leading edges of both wings. The undersides are much paler. The butterfly, which can be locally common, flies in grassy areas.

GENUS
ANCEMA

This is a genus of Asian butterflies which generally have hairy compound eyes.

ANCEMA BLANKA

 ZONE 5 — 1½in 40mm

This species is an exception as it has smooth compound eyes. The male is metallic blue with black wing tips. The gray-brown undersides have an orange blob at the base of the two small tails. The dull blue female has silvery buff undersides.

GENUS
ANCYLURIS

A South American genus of up to 20 species which have rather elongated forewings, and drawn-out hindwings which end in short or truncated tails. The hindwings are scalloped. Many of the species are black with contrasting red or white bands crossing the uppers. Little is known about the life cycles of these particular butterflies.

ANCYLURIS FORMOSISSIMA VENABALIS

	ZONE 2
1³/₄in 44mm	

The undersides are a remarkable mix of colors with bold splashes of metallic green-turquoise on the forewing, white at its base, and red and black on the hindwing. The uppers are a softer version of the undersides with less red and green, but with a row of green spots on the margin of the hindwing. This beautiful butterfly occurs in rainforest in Ecuador and Peru, up to an incredible 10,000ft (3,000m).

ANCYLURIS COLUBRA

	ZONE 2
2in 50mm	

The ground color of the male is jet black. There is a red mark which runs across both wings, with another red band almost at right angles running inside the long, drawn-out hindwing. The male has no distinct tail. The female has a tail, and a thicker red band with more orange in it. It also has a pale orange mark near the tip of the forewing.

ANCYLURIS JURGENSENII

	ZONE 2
2in 51mm	

The ground color is brown, and the amount of red is much reduced compared with other *Ancyluris* species. The red band which crosses both wings is striking. The elongated hindwing has turquoise marks on its outer edge, and a red spot on the inside edge.

GENUS
ANTHENE

This is a genus of African hairtails which have bright upperside markings in the male; females are not usually bright. Each hindwing has up to three very small tails at the ends of the veins. Butterflies breed on *Acacia* and on members of the pea family, *Leguminosae*.

ANTHENE AMARAH
Black Striped Hairtail

	ZONE 4
1¹/₈in 30mm	

The name "Black Striped" refers to the marks on the underside of the gray forewing. The uppers are gray-brown in both sexes, though the female is slightly larger and darker, and has more rounded wings. The butterfly lives in open bush country and breeds on various species of *Acacia*.

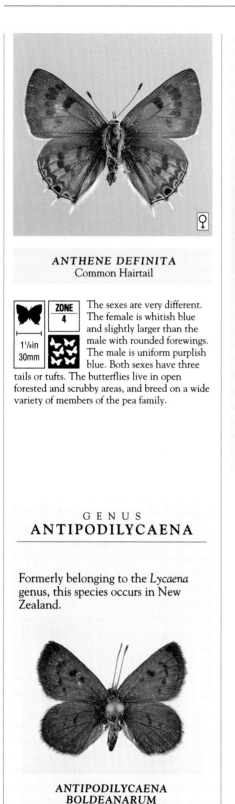

ANTHENE DEFINITA
Common Hairtail

ZONE 4
1⅛in
30mm

The sexes are very different. The female is whitish blue and slightly larger than the male with rounded forewings. The male is uniform purplish blue. Both sexes have three tails or tufts. The butterflies live in open forested and scrubby areas, and breed on a wide variety of members of the pea family.

GENUS
APHARITIS

A genus of leopard butterflies found in Saudi Arabia and Asia.

APHARITIS ACAMAS TRANSCASPICA
Arab Leopard, Leopard Butterfly

ZONE 5
1⁵⁄₁₆in
34mm

The "leopard's spots" occur only on the undersides and are more like bands of gold set against a white ground. There are also Indian and Arabian subspecies. Caterpillars live inside palms and are looked after by ants. This particular butterfly is in need of conservation.

APODEMIA MORMO
Mormon Metalmark

ZONE 1
1¼in
32mm

This pretty metalmark has white spots over a russet ground color in the typical form, though there are several subspecies. The butterfly is widespread over many chaparral, desert and dune habitats, and reaches south into Mexico. It breeds on members of the polygonum family. One subspecies which occurs in California, Lange's Metalmark (subsp. *langei*), is on the 1990 Federal List as Endangered.

GENUS
ANTIPODILYCAENA

Formerly belonging to the *Lycaena* genus, this species occurs in New Zealand.

ANTIPODILYCAENA BOLDEANARUM

ZONE 6
1⅛in
28mm

The male is shiny blue or dark blue, with one definite black spot on the forewing and more indistinct black spots and marks elsewhere. The female may be various shades of brown with more black markings than the male. Caterpillars possibly feed on *Donatia*.

GENUS
APODEMIA

This is a genus of a few species of metalmarks which occur in North and South America. They have the same spotted nature as fritillaries (which belong to the *Nymphalidae*).

APODEMIA PALMERII
Gray Metalmark, Mesquite Metalmark

ZONE 1·2
⅞in
22mm

The underside is very light, but repeats the pattern of white marks which is strong on the uppers. It is a small butterfly, with shiny gray colors. It is named after its caterpillar food plant, the mesquite, the spiny drought-tolerant trees and shrubs that cover an enormous area of desert in the Southwest and Mexico.

GENUS
ARAWACUS

This is a genus of South American hairstreaks which have brightly colored uppers and dark undersides.

ARAWACUS JADA
Jade-blue Hairstreak

1in 25mm	ZONE 2

The sexes are similar with jade blue uppers and dark brown over the outer part of the forewing. The hindwing is strongly curved and drawn out as a stubby tail. The undersides are mottled fawn and cream. The butterfly lives in Central America and is a migrant. It breeds on *Solanum*.

GENUS
ARCAS

A genus of South American butterflies with a unique wing profile. The forewings are rounded, almost elongate, and the hindwings are drawn out into two unequal tails. The undersides are often greenish. Little is known about the life cycles of these butterflies.

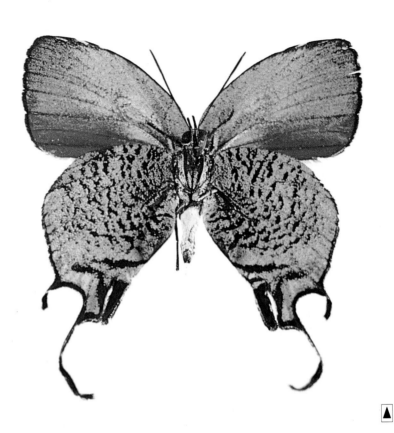

ARCAS CYPRIA

1³/₄in 45mm	ZONE 2

The extraordinary shape helps to identify this species. The hindwing has two wiggly tails, one long and one short. The forewing is very curved, almost elliptical. The overall color is bright velvety green with black tails and a black band crossing the underside of the hindwing.

ARCAS IMPERIALIS

1¹/₂in 38mm	ZONE 2

Like A. *cypria*, the hindwing has two tails of unequal length, but they are not so long. The upperside is turquoise-green with a distinct black tip and dot on the forewing. The undersides are bright green, which is much mottled in black on the hindwing.

GENUS
ARGYRASPODES

This genus of African butterflies formerly belonged to *Phasis*.

ARGYRASPODES ARGYRASPIS
Warrior Copper

| ZONE |
| 4 |

1½in
40mm

The butterfly has strong colors, bright orange-red on the uppers with a dark brown apex to the forewing continued around the hindwing margins, the underside of which is white-speckled. The hindwing margin is much scalloped. The butterfly lives in stony habitats and feeds avidly at flowers.

GENUS
ARGYROGRAMMANA

A genus of South American rain-forest butterflies.

ARGYROGRAMMANA ATTSONII

| ZONE |
| 4 |

1⅛in
30mm

A very attractive butterfly with unusual color combinations: orange at the base of the wings, turquoise blue on the forewings, and brown on the forewing tip and hindwing margin.

GENUS
ARHOPALA

This large genus of Asian and Australian butterflies are predominantly blue, especially in the male, with more subdued colors in the female. The species, which look very similar, are difficult to differentiate. The underside pattern, although very confusing and complicated, does vary slightly between individuals to give some clues to identification. This is one of the many genera of lycaenids whose larvae are cared for by ants; the larvae stop feeding on their food plants and are fed on ant grubs.

ARHOPALA AMANTES
APELLA

| ZONE |
| 5 |

2⅜in
60mm

This stunning butterfly has rich turquoise uppers in the male and metallic silver-blue in the female. Both sexes have tails, and there is a generous black border around the wings of the female. There are a number of subspecies, but the normal form comes from southern India and Sri Lanka. The butterfly frequents lowland forests.

ARHOPALA ARAXES

| ZONE |
| 6 |

2½in
64mm

Stunning in its colors, the pattern of this butterfly is very similar to A. *amantes*. The male is brighter than the female with a brilliant blue metallic sheen. The undersides are mottled brown with conspicuous spots ringed in white. The female has contrasting black borders with blue bases to the wings. The butterfly is found in Indonesia and flies in lowland forest.

ARHOPALA ARGENTEA

| ZONE |
| 6 |

2in
50mm

The silver-white color, hence *argentea*, is on the uppers of the male, which also has black tips to the forewings. The female is blackish generously suffused with blue around the bases of the wings. The butterfly lives in lowland forest on Sulawesi.

ARHOPALA AUREA

ZONE
5

The uppers of the male are green with a dark margin to the hindwing. The female uppers are blue, the shade of which may vary. The undersides are a mottled pattern made up of little circular spots evenly dispersed over the wings. The butterfly lives in lowland forests and is quite a powerful flier.

ARHOPALA CENTAURUS PHILATRON
Dull Oakblue

ZONE
6

2in
50mm

The sexes are different, but equally beautiful. The uniform bright blue of the male is distinctive, while the female has black leading edges and margins to the silver-blue wings. The brown underside is covered in white-ringed brown spots. There are a number of subspecies recorded. The butterfly haunts coastal areas and mangrove swamps.

ARHOPALA CLEANDER

ZONE
5·6

2in
50mm

The butterfly is a uniform deep purple-blue with rounded wings. A key feature is the very fine tail which sticks out sideways. The undersides are brown with numerous little brown marks each edged in pale orange. At the base of the tail, there are a few metallic turquoise marks. The butterfly lives in lowland forest.

ARHOPALA HERCULES SOPHILUS

ZONE
6

2³/₈in
60mm

Big and beautiful, this is one of the largest of the blue arhopala butterflies. The uppers are a uniform deep blue. The hindwing is particularly rounded, with a little tail. The butterfly lives in open lowland, in New Guinea.

ARHOPALA MICALE

 ZONE 6 | 2in 50mm

The male uppers are mostly metallic blue, but there is a thin strip of black around the margins of the wings which is continuous with a short curved tail. The female has larger amounts of black on the uppers. The undersides are a rich red-brown with black toward the base. The caterpillars are associated with green tree-ants, *Oecophylla*. Butterflies live in lowland forest. Although they have mouthparts, they seem not to use them for drinking nectar.

ARHOPALA WILDEYANA WILDEYANA

 ZONE 5 | 1¹⁄₈in 30mm

This is among the smallest of the *Arhopala* butterflies, less than half the size of *A. araxes*. Males have metallic blue within a thin black border which runs around all wings. Females are darker with less blue. The undersides of both sexes are brown mottled all over with tiny waves, lines and circles. Butterflies live in lowland forest. Although they have mouthparts, they seem not to use them for drinking nectar. The caterpillars are associated with green tree ants, *Oecophylla*.

GENUS
ARICIA

A genus of at least a dozen species of small butterflies which occur from Europe through to Asia. The sexes are dimorphic with blue males and brown females. They breed on members of the *Geraniaceae* and *Cistaceae*.

ARICIA AGESTIS
Brown Argus

ZONE 3·5 | 1¹⁄₈in 28mm

Separated from *A. artaxerxes*, with which it has been confused, by the absence of a white dot on the forewing. The ground color is rich brown, and the outer parts of all the wings have a rich orange band, somewhat incomplete on the forewing. The undersides are light gray, darker in the female, speckled with black spots and orange spots near the margin. At least two subspecies exist. The butterfly lives in flowery meadows and breeds on members of the *Geraniaceae*.

ARICIA ARTAXERXES ALLOUS
Mountain Argus, Scotch Argus

 ZONE 3·5 | 1¹⁄₄in 32mm

The normal form has a rich brown ground color, but the orange markings around the margin of the wing are less intense and widespread compared with *A. agestis*. The main identification feature is the presence of a small white dot on the forewing, but this is absent in the *allous* subspecies. There are at least three subspecies. The butterfly flies in flowery meadows and breeds on rock rose, *Helianthemum*.

GENUS
ASTRAEODES

A genus of small lycaenid butterflies from South America.

ASTRAEODES AREUTA

 ZONE 2 | 1½in 38mm

This is a bright yellow butterfly whose uppers are crossed by two pale yellow-brown lines. Gold metallic spots are found around the margins of the wings almost as a band. Information about the biology and ecology of this species is completely lacking.

G E N U S
ATLIDES

This is a genus of tailed hairstreaks found mainly in South America, with just one species, *A. halesus*, in North America. Butterflies have iridescent colors and are most often found in bright sunny areas.

ATLIDES POLYBE

ZONE 2

2¼in 56mm

On the uppers the butterfly has metallic green lines radiating out from the base of the wings. The extremities are black, particularly on the forewing tip. The hindwing is drawn out with one stubby tail and two other tails, one very long. The underside is brown with radiating black marks, red flashes at the base of the wings, and a yellow body. The male has a round black sex brand on the forewing.

ATLIDES HALESUS
Great Blue, Great Purple Hairstreak

ZONE 1

1½in 38mm

Iridescent blue-purple covers much of the uppers, and this is stronger in the male. There is usually a single tail on the hindwing, and sometimes a smaller subsidiary one. Parts of the underside of the body are brushed in bright red. The butterfly flies in many types of habitat, such as savanna and along streams, particularly where mistletoe, its larval food plant, occurs. Though a resident, it is a great wanderer.

**AXIOCERSES AMANGA
MENDECHE**
Bush Scarlet

ZONE 4

1⅜in 35mm

This little lycaenid is vivid scarlet in the male and orange-brown in the female. Both sexes have brown running broadly over the forewing to its tip and on the base of the thick-tailed hindwing. Butterflies live in bush and savanna, where they breed on *Ximenia*, a tropical oleacaceous plant.

G E N U S
AXIOCERSES

A genus of a few species which occur in Africa in tropical and subtropical habitats. They are brightly colored in reds, browns and oranges, and have small tails. Species breed on *Ximenia*, a member of the *Oleacaeae*, and possibly *Acacia*, a member of the pea family, *Leguminosae*.

AXIOCERSES BAMBANA
Scarlet Butterfly

ZONE 4

1⅜in 35mm

This has a rather indented and pointed forewing compared to *A. amanga*. The forewing is brown on the apex and scarlet-orange in the middle, and dark at the base. There is a tracery of black around the scalloped hindwing and more black on the forewing. The female is completely different, dull orange spotted in black. The butterfly lives in scrub and woody areas and probably breeds on *Acacia*.

GENUS
BINDAHARA

A genus of Asian and Australian butterflies in which the sexes are dimorphic.

BINDHARA PHOCIDES
Plane Butterfly

ZONE
5

1¹⁄₈in
30mm

The majestic male has velvet black uppers margined blue on the hindwing and a long pale orange tail. The female has uniform brown uppers with a bold black spot, highlighted in white, at the base of the long curving tail. This rainforest species breeds on *Salacia*, which belongs to the *Hippocrateacea* family.

GENUS
BREPHIDIUM

A genus of three species of dwarf or pygmy blues from North and South America.

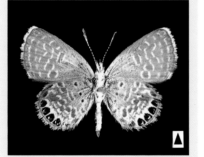

BREPHIDIUM EXILIS
Western Pygmy Blue, Pygmy Blue

ZONE
1·2

³⁄₄in
19mm

The brown outer wings are blue toward the base. The undersides are mottled reddish brown with black spots inside the hindwing margin. The undersides are unlike other blues, with a lemon apex to the forewing and a row of black dots on the hindwing margin. Subspecies of this are widespread in the southern US.

GENUS
CALEPHELIS

A genus of at least 50 species of metalmarks which occur in North and South America. Their bright shiny "metalmark" colors are often best found on the undersides.

CALEPHELIS NEMESIS
Mexican Metalmark, Fatal Metalmark

ZONE
1·2

1in
25mm

This is a small, dull-brown butterfly in which the female is the larger sex. There is a distinctive darker band crossing the uppers, and the outer margin of the forewings is slightly wavy. In the south of its range, in Central America, it is continuously brooded. It breeds on various members of the daisy and buttercup families.

CALEPHELIS VIRGINIENSIS
Little Metalmark

ZONE
1

³⁄₄in
19mm

The ground color of the uppers is rich tawny, while that of the undersides is pale tawny. The rows of black spots are heavier on the uppers than on the underside, where they appear very delicate and fine. The butterfly has three broods a year. It lives in coastal habitats of southeastern North America and breeds on thistles.

GENUS
CALETA

A genus of butterflies from the Asian and Australian regions.

CALETA MINDARUS

ZONE
6

1³⁄₈in
36mm

This small tailed lycaenid has a characteristic pattern and color. The pale lemon-white ground color is edged generously in dark brown around all the wings. This edging is continuous, with a bar across the base of the wings. The butterfly is found in New Guinea.

GENUS
CALLIPSYCHE

A genus of colorful tailed lycaenids from South America.

CALLIPSYCHE DINDYMUS

ZONE 2

1⅛in
30mm

The shape of the butterfly is important in its identification, since the forewings have a squarish look to them and the hindwings are rounded. The uppers are iridescent blue with a little black around the margins of the forewing. The underside is gray-white.

GENUS
CALLOPHRYS

A genus of small-sized hairstreaks which occur from North and South America, through Europe to Asia. There are scores of species, and they breed on a variety of plant families.

CALLOPHRYS AFFINIS
Immaculate Green Hairstreak,
Green Hairstreak

ZONE 1

1⅛in
28mm

Named after the green color of the undersides of the wings, which also have a faint yellowish suffusion. The uppersides are dark, gray-brown in the male and rust-brown in the female. The butterfly lives in mountains, canyons, and sagelands in the western part of North America. It breeds on members of the *Polygonaceae*, *Leguminosae*, and *Rhamnaceae*.

CALLOPHRYS AVIS
Chapman's Green Hairstreak

ZONE 3

1⁵⁄₁₆in
34mm

The uppersides are rich reddish brown, but otherwise this species is very similar to C. *rubi*. The male has a small bluish sex brand on its forewing. The underside is typically green with a faint white hairstreak line crossing both wings. This species is one of a few butterflies which breeds on the strawberry tree, *Arbutus unedo*. This tree is a native of the Mediterranean region and makes up some of the remaining scrubby vegetation of North Africa, parts of Spain, and southern France where the butterfly lives.

CALLOPHRYS DUMETORUM
Coastal Green Hairstreak,
Bramble Green Hairstreak

ZONE 1

⁷/₈in
22mm

The undersides of this green hairstreak lack the yellow tinges of other similar species. They are a uniform pale green punctuated by an interrupted row of small white spots. There is a very small stubby tail, too. The upper surfaces are dark brown, tinged with red-brown in the female. The butterfly lives in foothills, canyons and chaparral, where it breeds on buckwheat, *Eriogonum fasciculatum*, and deer weed, *Lotus scoparius*.

CALLOPHRYS RUBI
Green Hairstreak

ZONE 3·5

1¹/₈in
30mm

This is a delightful butterfly of springtime and early summer, which has a green underwing crossed by a faint white line sometimes reduced to spots. The uppers are a warm brown, and the hindwing is very slightly drawn out as a stubby tail. The colors are fairly constant. The female is slightly larger than the male. The butterfly lives in scrubby and woody areas, along tracks, in glades, and on mountaintops to 7,000ft (2,150m). It breeds on a variety of common leguminous plants.

CALLOPHRYS SHERIDANII
White-lined Green Hairstreak

ZONE 1

⁷/₈in
22mm

Of the North American green hairstreaks, this one has the most pronounced white "hairstreak" line across the undersides of the wings, hence its common name. The uppersides are gray. The butterfly is found in the western part of North America and lives in canyons and hillsides where it breeds on buckwheats, *Eriogonum* species.

GENUS
CALYCOPIS

A genus of small, tailed lycaenids from South America with a single species, C. *cecrops*, in North America. Members of this large genus also occur in Trinidad.

CALYCOPIS ATRIUS

	ZONE 2
⁷/₈in 24mm	

The butterfly has very dark forewings while the hindwings are a silvery blue. The undersides are a rich uniform fawn on the forewing and on most of the hindwing. By the two unequal-lengthed tails are a group of five red spots.

CALYCOPIS CECROPS
Red-band Hairstreak

	ZONE 1·2
1in 25mm	

The female is larger than the male, with dark wings and silvery blue on the hindwing. The male has brown forewings with a distinctive sex brand and a small amount of silvery blue on the hindwing. The undersides are very beautiful with an orange band crossing fawn wings and a pair of tails, at the base of which are two large black spots. Butterflies live in southeastern US in open woods and fields, where they breed on various members of the *Anacardiaceae*, *Euphorbiaceae*, and *Myricaceae*.

CALYCOPIS ISOBEON
Dusty-blue Hairstreak

	ZONE 1·2
⁷/₈in 22mm	

Similar to *C. cecrops*, but the orange lines on the undersides of the wings are less pronounced, and there are no large black spots present. The butterfly enjoys open areas in secondary forest, and breeds, somewhat curiously, on dead leaves and fruits.

A genus of small, speckled, dimorphic metalmarks from South America.

CALYDNA CALAMISA

	ZONE 2
1¹/₂in 38mm	

The male has a brown ground color, but is made very distinctive by the open bands of iridescent blue-green which radiate from the body. The female has orangey uppers and is speckled throughout with ivory and yellow marks. The butterfly is found in the Amazon basin.

A genus of African butterflies which have bright colors and breed on *Protea*.

CAPYS ALPHAEUS
Protea Scarlet

	ZONE 4
1³/₄in 45mm	

The ground color is a dark brown in both sexes with a thick red-orange band across both wings. The light gray undersides have a dark border to the slightly tailed hindwing and a light fawn patch in the forewing. The species occurs on rocky, scrubby hillsides.

A genus of metalmarks from the Amazon basin.

CARTEA VITULA
TAPAJONA

	ZONE 2
1¹/₂in 40mm	

The elongated wings and color-pattern resemble a heliconid. The dark brown wings have a bar of yellow near the forewing apex, and a red-orange band at the base of the forewing and on the hindwing. The butterfly occurs in the Amazon.

GENUS
CATOCHRYSOPS

A genus of Asian butterflies also found in Australia. They are similar to *Chilades*, but have tails.

CATOCHRYSOPS PANORMUS
Silver Forget-me-not

ZONE
5

1⁵/₁₆in
34mm

Males have delicate pale blue uppers with a single black spot near the base of the tail. The light and mottled undersides have a distinctive orange and black eye-spot by the tail. The darker females are dusted in black. Butterflies live in clearings and scrubby areas.

GENUS
CHERITRA

A genus of butterflies occurring from Sri Lanka, via India and the Philippines, to China. Members of this genus have a tuft of hairs arising from the hindwing.

CHERITRA FREJA
Common Imperial

ZONE
5

1⁷/₈in
48mm

The butterfly has two tails of unequal length; the longer is magnificent and highly characteristic. The uppers of the male are brownish purple; those of the female are dark brown. By contrast, the undersides of both sexes are white with orange-brown margins and apex to the forewing. The butterfly lives in lowland and upland rainforest. It breeds on *Xylia dolabriformis*, a leguminous plant, and the cinnamon tree, *Cinnamomum* (*Lauraceae*).

GENUS
CELASTRINA

Up to 40, mostly Asian, sexually dimorphic species of blue, of which some show seasonal variation.

CELASTRINA ARGIOLUS
Spring Azure, Holly Blue

ZONE
1·2
3·5

1⁵/₁₆in
34mm

Butterflies have pale lilac-blue uppers and paler undersides. Females have more black on the apex and margins, and in the second generation are thickly marked in black. A common, widespread species in scrub, light woodland, and gardens, the first generation larvae feed on holly, the second on ivy.

CHERITRA ORPHEUS

This magnificent butterfly has strident orange-brown on the uppers and a very long pointed tail. The spaces between the veins are suffused with dark scales which serve to emphasize the orange veins. The base of the tails are suffused in dark brown. The butterfly occurs in the Philippines.

ZONE 5
1⁵/₈in
41mm

GENUS
CHILADES

A genus of butterflies from Africa, Asia, and the Australian region, closely related to *Polyommatus*.

CHILADES CLEOTAS

A tailless lycaenid with dark purple-blue uppers and a wedge of orange on the trailing edge of the hindwing. The undersides are different, with large black spots covering the silvery white ground color and a repeat of the orange wedge.

ZONE 6
1¹/₂in
40mm

GENUS
CHLOROSTRYMON

A genus of South American butterflies, some of which occur in Central America and populate the southern parts of North America. Butterflies are dimorphic, and males are often brightly colored.

CHLOROSTRYMON MAESITES
Verde Azul, Amethyst Hairstreak, Clench's Hairstreak

ZONE 1·2
⁷/₈in
22mm

The sexes are different on the upper surfaces; the male is a spectacular and vivid metallic blue-purple, the female is dull gray-blue. The undersides of both sexes are fairly similar, being yellow-green with a broken line of black spots. This species occurs in Florida and the West Indies. Nothing is known about the life cycle of the butterfly, but it appears to like wooded areas.

CHLOROSTRYMON SIMAETHIS
Silver-banded Hairstreak,
St. Christopher's Hairstreak

ZONE 1·2 — ⁷/₈in 22mm

This is similar in size and pattern to *C. maesites*, but the uppers are not so lively in color. The male is dull iridescent purple; the female is even duller. The undersides are yellow-green with more extensive white areas towards the outer edge of the hindwing. The butterfly is found in the southern US and the West Indies. It breeds on the sapindaceous vine, *Cardiospermum halicacabum*, and the composite, *Eupatorium villosum*.

GENUS
CHORINEA

A genus of South American tailed metalmarks which have transparent wings.

CHORINEA OCTAVIUS

ZONE 2 — 1⁵/₈in 42mm

The shape and color are highly distinctive. The wings are mostly a filigree of white with black veins. The hindwing is drawn out into a very long black tail, which has a flash of red in an area of brown.

GENUS
CUPIDO

A genus of over 175 species with representatives in most continents. It includes some of the world's smallest butterflies. Sexual dimorphism is exhibited, and members often breed on plants belonging to the pea family, *Leguminosae*.

CUPIDO MINIMUS
Little Blue, Small Blue

ZONE 3·5 — ⁷/₈in 24mm

The sexes are very slightly different and are difficult to differentiate in flight. Both have brown upper surfaces, but only the male has blue scales dusted at the base of the wings. In contrast the undersides are very light gray speckled with small black dots and a dusting at the base of the wings. The butterfly can have a wingspan as small as ⁵/₈in (16mm) and is Britain's smallest species. The butterfly can be gregarious in grassy and flowery places, and breeds on kidney vetch, *Anthyllis vulneraria*.

CUPIDO OSIRIS
Osiris Blue

ZONE 3·5 — 1¹/₈in 30mm

The sexes are different, but with clear, unmarked colors on the uppers. The female is brown, the male purple-blue, and both have a white fringe. The undersides are palest gray with small black dots, and there is a delicate suffusion of sky blue at the base of the wings. The butterfly lives in flowery alpine meadows and breeds on sainfoin, *Onobrychis viciifolia*.

GENUS
CURETIS

A widespread genus of over 40 species. Males have strident red or orange uppers, females yellow or white.

CURETIS FELDERI
Sunbeam Butterfly

ZONE 5 — 1¹/₈in 28mm

One of the many sunbeam butterflies, this species is well-named for its bright color. The male has a dark border on the forewing which does not reach the base of the wing. The butterfly lives in open forested areas and engages in mud-puddling behavior.

GENUS
CYANIRIS

A genus of blues found from Europe to Asia which breed on leguminous plants.

CYANIRIS SEMIARGUS
Mazarine Blue

1⁵/₁₆in 34mm	ZONE 3·5

The male uppers are violet-blue, brown in the female. Both have a fine white fringe and light brown undersides with black dots and blue dusting at the wing bases. Butterflies live in meadows and breed on kidney vetch, *Anthyllis vulneraria*. They are somewhat migratory.

GENUS
CYANOPHRYS

A genus of green hairstreaks from North and South America which are sexually dimorphic. The butterflies are found typically in sunny places, often beside woodland. The life cycles have not been ascertained for all species.

CYANOPHRYS CRETHONA
Jamaican Green Hairstreak

1⁵/₁₆in 34mm	ZONE 2

The size of this green hairstreak marks it out from all the other species; it is the largest in the West Indies. The green undersides are unmistakable, and the hindwing has a pair of unequal length tails. The male uppers are bright blue, while the female uppers are dull blue. The butterfly frequents lowland habitats and is only found on Jamaica. Its life cycle remains unknown.

CYANOPHRYS MISERABILIS
Sad Green Hairstreak, Miserabilis Hairstreak

1in 25mm	ZONE 1

The sexes are dimorphic, the male being steely blue on the uppers, the female much duller. The undersides of both sexes are bright green. This species is distinguished from *C. goodsoni* by its slightly larger size and the presence of a single tail on the hindwing. The butterfly lives along forest margins and among scrub. It breeds on the leguminous tree, *Parkinsonia aculeata*.

GENUS
DACALANA

An Asian genus which has two groups, one with 12 forewing veins, the other with 11.

DACALANA VIDURA AZYADA
Double Tufted Royal

The male has stunning iridescent blue uppers with a thick black forewing apex. The paler blue female has a small white forewing mark. The two pairs of tails are at right angles to each other. Undersides are brownish. Butterflies live in rainforest up to 2,500ft (750m).

GENUS
DEUDORIX

Commonly called Cornelian butterflies or "playboys," these occur in the African, Asian, and Australian regions. They are brightly colored in either reds or blues. Their larvae and pupae feed inside various tropical fruits.

DEUDORIX DIOCLES
Orange-barred Playboy

The male has a bright orange bar on the forewing and over nearly all of the hindwing. The larger female has a black apex and margin, the rest of the wings being bluish-white. The butterfly is tailed, and the undersides are bluish-white with a fine tracery of thin black lines. The butterfly is found on hilltops, where it breeds on various members of the pea family such as *Acacia*, *Crotolaria*, and *Bauhinia*.

GENUS
DANIS

A genus of blues found both in the Asian and Australian regions.

DANIS DANIS
Large Green-banded Blue

The male uppers are green-blue with a large uniform white band across the hindwing. The rest of the wings are silvery blue with black margins. The butterfly occurs in northeastern Australia and many islands to the north. It lives in open flowery areas and breeds on oak, *Alphitonia excelsa*.

DEUDORIX ANTALUS
Brown Playboy

The sexes are fairly similar, though the female is the slightly larger with rounded wings. Both have blue-brown uppers, but there is a slight coppery sheen only in the male (hence the common name of Brown playboy). The undersides are similar, being white with a few delicate lines crossing the wings. There is a small tail with two dots near the base. The butterfly flies near bushy hilltops and breeds on *Crotolaria* and *Acacia* species.

DEUDORIX EPIRUS EOS
Blue Cornelian

The male is the brighter sex, with electric blue over most of the tailed hindwing and a little at the base of the black forewings. The female uppers are mostly dark with a suffusion of violet-white at the base of the markedly rounded wings. The butterflies live around open hillsides and hilltops. The butterflies breed inside tropical fruits.

DEUDORIX ERYX

ZONE 5

2¼in
56mm

The uniform dark green on the undersides of this species is both remarkable and distinctive, especially since greens in butterflies are not that common. The hindwing is drawn out as a short but stubby tail, and there is another thin tail nearby. The butterfly is found from the Himalayas to Malaya.

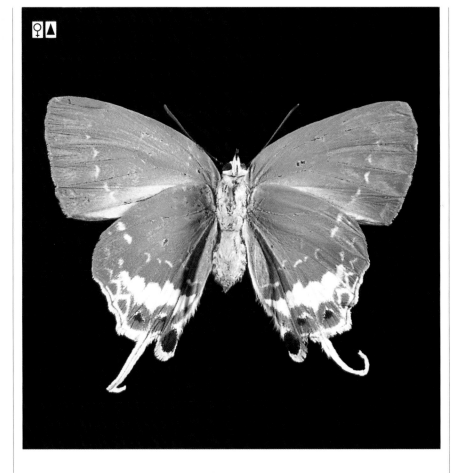

GENUS
DODONA

There are about 20 species of metalmark butterflies in this genus.

DODONA DIPOEA

ZONE 5

1¾in
45mm

The undersides are the key identification feature, since they are a rufous color crossed by three to four thin white lines. The shape of the hindwing is drawn out as a wide and stubby tail. The butterfly lives in the Himalayas.

GENUS
ELIOTA

A genus of small lycaenids from Asia which are dimorphic; males are usually bright blue.

ELIOTA JALINDRA

ZONE 5

1⅝in
42mm

Male uppers are iridescent blue; female uppers are brown with sky blue at the bases of the two long and curly tails. Undersides are light gray with brown margins. At least ten subspecies exist. Butterflies occur in open flowery areas in India, Indonesia, and the Philippines.

GENUS
ESTEMOPSIS

A genus of about 15 species of metalmark butterflies from the Amazonian region of South America.

ESTEMOPSIS INARIA THYATIRA

ZONE 2

1½in
38mm

The male is very colorful, with a wedge of brick red on the forewing and most of the brown hindwing also covered in brick red. The markings on the female uppers are yellow-brown. This particular species of butterfly occurs in the Amazon rainforest.

GENUS
EUMEDONIA

A genus with a single species of blue found in Europe and Asia.

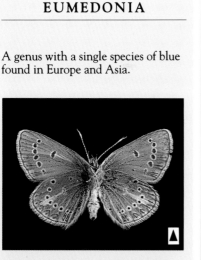

EUMEDONIA EUMEDON
Geranium Argus

ZONE 3·5

1¹/₄in
32mm

The uppers are a uniform dark brown in both sexes. The undersides have a row of orange chevrons, sharply defined in the smaller male, inside the margin of the hindwing. The butterfly lives in flowery meadows on mountains and breeds on cranesbills, *Geranium* species.

GENUS
EUPHILOTES

A genus of North American blues which are sexually dimorphic. They breed mostly on buckwheats, *Eriogonum*, and often occur in desert areas and along watercourses where their caterpillar food plants thrive.

EUPHILOTES BATTOIDES
Square-spotted Blue, Buckwheat Blue

ZONE 1

1in
25mm

Males are typically turquoise-blue on the uppers, while the female is dark brown. Both sexes have some orange markings on the trailing edge of the hindwing, and the silvery undersides are strongly spotted in black. This variable species has at least 12 subspecies. The butterfly occurs from coastal habitats to mountains at 10,000ft (3,000m). Its larval food plants are buckwheat, *Eriogonum*. Subspecies *allyni*, the El Segundo Blue, is listed as Endangered in California.

EUPHILOTES ENOPTES
Dotted Blue

ZONE 1

1in
25mm

The dots are large and well-defined, and there is a clear orange band of color around the margin of the hindwing underside. The uppers are blue in the male and brown in the female. About ten subspecies are known. The Dotted Blue ranges over the western part of the US, from the Canadian border to Mexico. Like *E. battoides*, this species also occurs in a wide range of habitats and breeds on buckwheat. Subspecies *smithi*, Smith's Blue, is listed as Endangered in California.

EUPHILOTES RITA
Rita Blue, Desert Buckwheat Blue

ZONE 1

1in
25mm

The male is dark turquoise-blue with black margins; the female is brown above with a large orange band near the margin of the hindwing. The undersides of both sexes is gray-brown with lots of small black spots mostly in ordered bands. The butterfly occurs in deserts and prairie, and breeds on a variety of buckwheats, *Eriogonum* species.

GENUS
EURYBIA

This genus of dark-colored South American metalmarks have a very conspicuous and easily identifiable eye-spot on the forewing.

EURYBIA DONNA

ZONE 2

2³/₄in
72mm

The male has brick orange on the trailing half of the hindwing, a startling contrast with the rest of the wings, which are rich brown. The female is slightly larger with rounded wings, and the orange and brown colors are less bright. The female also has a single eye-spot on each forewing. The butterfly occurs in Colombia.

EURYBIA JUTURNA HARI

ZONE 2

2¹/₂in
64mm

This is fairly similar to *E. donna* in that the color pattern is made up of orange and brown. In this species the orange is traversed by two rows of black-brown spots. Other points of difference are the eye-spot on the female forewing is surrounded by a thicker orange line, and there is a scattering of small orange spots over the brown wings. The butterfly occurs within the Amazon basin.

EURYBIA LYCISCA

ZONE 2

2¼in 58mm

The distinctive feature of *E. lycisca* is the iridescent blue hindwing edged in black. The forewings are a sooty brown, with a brown eye-spot surrounded by a thin line of orange. The butterfly occurs in Central America.

EUSELASIA EURITEUS

ZONE 2

1⁵⁄₁₆in 34mm

This bright little metalmark is dimorphic. The male, which is otherwise black, has a band of turquoise across the forewing and a splash of turquoise on the outside edge of the hindwing. The female uppers are light brown with a splash of weak orange on the trailing edge of the hindwing. The undersides of both sexes are bright mustard and brown traversed by three white lines. The butterfly occurs in Peru.

EUSELASIA THUCYDIDES

ZONE 2

1½in 40mm

The shape and color of the butterfly is distinctive. The hindwing is drawn out as a long stubby tail. Overall, the ground color is rich brown, and there are bold splashes of orange roughly in the center of each wing. The undersides are a great contrast to the uppers with almost a camouflage pattern, mottled with lines, waves, and dots over a pale gray ground color. The butterfly occurs in the south of Brazil.

GENUS
EUSELASIA

This is a large genus of over 100 species of metalmarks which occur in Central and South America. They are often sexually dimorphic and have a pattern of lines and waves on the undersides. Some species can be identified by their shape.

EUSELASIA GELIASAE

ZONE 2

1½in 38mm

The red which covers most of the uppers in the male is highly distinctive and a good guide to identification. The apex and leading edge of the forewing is a uniform dark brown. The shape of the hindwing is peculiar, being a little drawn out and geometric in shape. The female is white. The butterfly occurs in the Amazon basin.

GENUS
EVENUS

A genus of about ten South American hairstreaks which have iridescent green or blue colors.

EVENUS TERESINA

ZONE 2

⅞in 24mm

The colorful undersides are impressive and unique. The white "hairstreak" line which crosses both wings is embellished with black and chocolate, and there are two curved tails on the hindwing. The underside of the forewing has a turquoise tinge to its base.

GENUS
EVERES

A small genus of butterflies found in Europe, Asia, and Australia. They are usually sexually dimorphic and tailed, and breed on members of the pea family, *Leguminosae*.

EVERES ARGIADES COMYNTAS
Eastern Tailed Blue

	ZONE 1
1in 25mm	

This is regarded as a subspecies of *E. argiades* and is also fairly similar to *E. amytula*. The female is a uniform brown, and the male is silver-blue. On the undersides of both sexes, there is an orange spot near the base of the tiny tail on the hindwing. The butterfly occurs in the east of the US and southern Canada, in many habitats created by humans, such as roadsides and gardens. It breeds on various species of the pea family.

EVERES AMYNTULA
Western Tailed Blue

	ZONE 1
1⅛in 28mm	

The male has lavender-blue uppers while the female is a less intense blue suffused with black and brown. There is a single tail. The undersides of both sexes are very pale blue with a few tiny black spots. The butterfly occurs in a wide variety of habitats, from forest edges to meadows, and breeds on many species belonging to the pea family.

EVERES ARGIADES
Short-tailed Blue

	ZONE 3
1⅛in 30mm	

The male has violet-blue uppers. The female uppers are brown with a scattering of purple scales at the wing bases. The undersides are blue-gray in both sexes, with a row of tiny black spots. There is a single tail. This species is perhaps represented in North America as subspecies *E. argiades comyntas*. The butterfly is a migrant from mainland Europe which occasionally visits England. It flies in flowery meadows and breeds on various legumes, including medick.

GENUS
FIXENIA

A genus of browns which now has absorbed at least one species from the *Strymondia*.

FIXENIA PRUNI
Black Hairstreak

	ZONE 3·5
1¼in 32mm	

The tan undersides are characterized by black spots around the dull orange border on the trailing hindwing edge. The uppers are nut-brown with dull orange mostly on the hindwing margin. There is a single tail. Butterflies breed on blackthorn, *Prunus spinosa*, and are conserved in England.

GENUS
FLOS

This genus of Asian butterflies have bold underside markings and often frequent hilltops.

FLOS ANNIELLA

	ZONE 5
1¾in 44mm	

The exceptionally bright turquoise-blue males are slightly larger than the females, which have silver-blue in the center of each black wing. This is a tailed species. At least three subspecies are recorded. Butterflies may breed on members of the *Lyrthaceae* and *Myrtaceae*.

GENUS
GLAUCOPSYCHE

This is a genus of about eleven species of blue found in North America, Europe, Africa, and Asia. Some of the species are brightly colored, and some are highly collectable. Butterflies breed on members of the pea family, *Leguminosae*.

GLAUCOPSYCHE ALEXIS
Green-underside Blue

	ZONE 3·5
1³/₈in 36mm	

The "green underside" refers to the greenish-blue scales at the base of the wings which otherwise have a gray ground color. There are three or four prominent black spots on the forewing undersides. The sexes are different on the uppers; the male is purplish blue, the female dark brown. The butterfly lives in flowery meadows and breeds on broom, *Cytisus*.

GLAUCOPSYCHE LYGDAMUS AFRA
Silvery Blue

	ZONE 1
1¼in 32mm	

The male varies between a light silvery blue and a darker turquoise-blue. The female is often a brown-blue. The undersides and spotting vary from light to dark gray. There are ten subspecies of this variable butterfly. It lives in many different types of habitat. The Palos Verde Blue, subspecies *palosverdescensis*, was listed in 1990 as Endangered. *Xerces*, the Xerces Blue, is, sadly, now extinct.

GLAUCOPSYCHE MELANOPS
Black-eyed Blue

	ZONE 3·5
1¼in 32mm	

The key features of this butterfly are the large black dots on the underside of both the forewing and hindwing, unlike G. *alexis*. The ground color of the undersides is gray, but with no blue-green scales at the base of the wings. Above, the sexes are fairly similar, the male being pale blue and the female blue suffused strongly with black. The butterfly lives in flowery places and breeds on bird's-foot trefoil (*Lotus*), greenweed (*Genista*), and leopard's bane (*Doronicum*).

GENUS
HABRODAIS

A genus of North American hairstreaks in which the sexes are similar.

HABRODAIS GRUNUS
Live-oak Hairstreak, Golden Hairstreak

	ZONE 1
1¼in 32mm	

The uppers, in at least one of the two subspecies, are a rich straw color. The golden to yellow undersides have some bright gold flecks. There is a tiny tail. Butterflies occur on the west coast of the US, among the live oaks on which they breed.

GENUS
HADES

A genus of South American metalmarks with rounded wings; the males have a touch of blue.

HADES NOCTULA

	ZONE 2
2⅛in 54mm	

This butterfly has smoky brown uppers with no contrasting markings. The undersides have a uniform brown ground with lines radiating out between the veins on all wings. There is a whitish suffusion at the margins. At the base of the wings is a distinctive red patch. The butterfly occurs in Costa Rica.

GENUS
HAMEARIS

A genus with a single species resembling a fritillary, the only metalmark in Europe.

HAMEARIS LUCINA
Duke of Burgundy Fritillary

	ZONE 3
1⁵⁄₁₆in 34mm	

The orange spots over the dark brown ground are distinctive, more so in the female. Two bars of white spots cross the hindwings' undersides. The male has four functional legs, the female six. Butterflies live in flowery meadows and breed on cowslip and primrose.

GENUS
HARKENCLENUS

A genus of North American hairstreaks, which breeds on members of the *Rosaceae*.

HARKENCLENUS TITUS
Coral Hairstreak

	ZONE 1
1¼in 32mm	

The male is brown on the uppers and has a distinctly pointed forewing. The female uppers are orange-brown. A prominent row of orange spots runs around the gray underside of the hindwing. Butterflies live in meadows, canyons, and waysides, breeding on wild cherry, *Prunus*.

GENUS
HELICOPIS

A colorful genus of South American metalmarks which have an extraordinary set of tails.

HELICOPIS GNIDUS

ZONE
2

2in
51mm

An extraordinary-looking butterfly with unique hindwings. There are six tails, all of unequal length, one of which is strongly curved. The base of all wings is egg-yellow on the underside. The brown forewings have a large white mark in the center.

GENUS
HEMIARGUS

This is a genus of butterflies, commonly called eyed blues, which occur in North and South America. They get their name from the two or three eye-spots on the undersides of the hindwings. Butterflies breed on a wide variety of members of the pea family, *Leguminosae*.

HEMIARGUS ISOLA
Reakirt's Eyed Blue, Mexican Eyed Blue, Solitary Eyed Blue

ZONE
1·2

1⅛in
28mm

The sexes are dissimilar, which is typical of many blues. The male is a silvery blue on the uppers; the female is brown. Both sexes have a single large black spot on the margin of the tailless hindwing, which is repeated on the underside. Another key identification feature is the row of black spots on the underside of the forewing. The butterfly lives in meadows and fields.

HEMIARGUS THOMASI
Caribbean Eyed Blue, Miami Eyed Blue, Thomas's Eyed Blue

ZONE
1·2

1⅛in
28mm

The key identification feature is the pair of large black spots on the leading edge of the underside of the hindwing. The female has orange around one of two other black spots which are near the trailing edge of the hindwing. The male uppers are powdery blue. Mostly found in the Caribbean, this butterfly also occurs in southern Florida. It flies in open flowery areas.

GENUS
HEODES

A genus of brightly colored coppers, which are typically dimorphic, having copper-colored males and speckly females. Butterflies occur in Europe and Asia, and live in open flowery places, often in mountainous areas.

HEODES ALCIPHRON
Purple-shot Copper

ZONE
3·5

1⅜in
36mm

The livery of the male is spectacular, with purple-shot iridescence on the forewings and orange hindwings. The female is brown with an orange band around the margin of the hindwing. On the undersides, there is an orange-gray glow in both sexes speckled with black spots and a repeat of the orange band on the hindwing in both sexes. Two subspecies occur. This butterfly of the European wayside breeds on docks, *Rumex*.

GENUS
HORAGA

A genus from the Asian and Australian regions which live in upland and lowland secondary forest.

HORAGA ONYX FRUHSTORFERI

ZONE
5·6

1³/₈in
35mm

Males often, but not always, have more iridescent silvery or purple-blue on their wings than the females. The hindwing has three irregular tails, which are often twisted and become broken. This is a variable butterfly and one of at least nine subspecies.

GENUS
HYPAUROTIS

A genus of North American butterflies found also in Central America, members of which have a short proboscis.

HYPAUROTIS CRYSALUS
Colorado Hairstreak

ZONE
1·2

1½in
38mm

One of the most striking butterflies of North America, this species has bright purple-blue on the uppers edged in black. There are also some conspicuous orange spots on the wing margins. The butterfly lives near the native oaks on which it breeds.

HEODES TITYRUS
Sooty Copper

ZONE
3·5

1¼in
32mm

The heavy sooty colors which cover the wings in both sexes is the key to identifying this species. The very dark male has a thin marginal line of orange chevrons, mostly on the hindwing. The female has much sooty orange on the forewing and larger expanse of orange on the hindwing. The dark caramel undersides are covered in small black spots with orange marginal spots, more intense in the female. Butterflies live in flowery meadows and breed on docks, *Rumex*.

HEODES VIRGAUREAE
Scarce Copper

ZONE
3·5·6

1³/₈in
36mm

This is one of the prettiest roadside butterflies, especially the male which has a blaze of copper on the uppers. The female is of a less flamboyant nature, clad in dull orange on the forewings with black spots; hindwings are dark except for an orange marginal band. The butterfly breeds on species of dock, *Rumex*.

GENUS
HYPOCHLOROSIS

This is a genus of Australian butterflies with metallic colors.

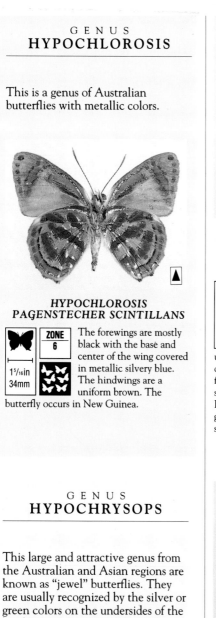

HYPOCHLOROSIS
PAGENSTECHER SCINTILLANS

ZONE 6 — 1⁵/₁₆in 34mm

The forewings are mostly black with the base and center of the wing covered in metallic silvery blue. The hindwings are a uniform brown. The butterfly occurs in New Guinea.

GENUS
HYPOCHRYSOPS

This large and attractive genus from the Australian and Asian regions are known as "jewel" butterflies. They are usually recognized by the silver or green colors on the undersides of the hindwing. Some species breed on mangroves. Like many lycaenids, the larvae of these butterflies are attended by ants.

HYPOCHRYSOPS APELLES
Copper Jewel

ZONE 5 — 1¹/₈in 28mm

The distinctive coppery color of the uppers is particularly bold in the male. The forewing tip is black in both sexes, but in the female it is also rounded. The hindwing underside is mustard crossed by four or five red-orange bands, each edged in white. The forewing underside is also mustard with a few streaks of white along the leading edge. Butterflies breed on mangroves of the *Avicennia* genus. Captain James Cook took the first specimen when he landed in Australia in 1770.

HYPOCHRYSOPS APOLLO
Apollo Jewel

ZONE 6 — 1³/₈in 36mm

This is a large orange-red species brighter in the male than the female, with a dark apex to the forewing in both sexes. It flies in coastal areas where the swamp mahogany, *Tristania*, grows. Caterpillars feed within the galleries of a large ant plant (*Myrmecodia tuberosa*), which attaches itself to the branches of the swamp mahogany.

HYPOCHRYSOPS POLYCLETUS
Rovena Jewel

ZONE 6 — 1⁵/₈in 42mm

The sexes are dimorphic. The male has metallic blue uppers and a dark margin and apex to the forewing, while the female is mostly brown with a cream center and the base to the forewing. There are two rudimentary tails. The underside is tawny with rows of black marks giving a mottled effect, especially to the hindwing. There are at least two subspecies which are dispersed around Australia and Papua New Guinea.

GENUS
HYPOLYCAENA

A genus of Australian and Asian hairstreaks, the species of which have a wide range of characteristics to aid identification. One species, *H. danis*, breeds on orchids (monocotyledonous plants), while others breed on a variety of dicotyledonous plants.

HYPOLYCAENA BUXTONI
Buxton's Hairstreak

ZONE 4

1¹/₈in
30mm

The sexes are completely different. The male has purplish uppers, the larger female is blue-white with a prominent black margin and apex to the forewing. There are two long tails, one very long. At the base of the tails on the white undersides are two eye-spots. The butterfly lives in savanna and woods, and breeds on *Clerodendron*, a member of the verbena family.

HYPOLYCAENA DANIS
Black and White Tit

ZONE 6

1¹/₈in
28mm

This black butterfly has two unequal tails, the longer one is usually twisted. There is a clearly defined bold white band across the upper surfaces of the wings, and the contrasting colors give rise to the butterfly's common name. There is at least one subspecies known. In Australia the butterfly will sometimes breed on *Vanda* orchids growing in gardens, and the caterpillars are responsible for spoiling some gardeners' prize blooms.

HYPOLYCAENA ERYLUS TEATUS
Common Tit

ZONE 6

1³/₈in
36mm

The male has a striking deep purple-blue on the uppers, the female is brown. There is a pair of tails on each hindwing which are long and twisted. The undersides are very light brown with a "hairstreak" line crossing both wings and eye-spots near the base of the wings. The butterfly is found in most habitats, including roadsides, from coastal mangrove swamps to the uplands. It breeds on *Vangueria spinosa* and *Cinnamomum zeylanicum*.

HYPOLYCAENA PHILIPPUS
Purple-brown Hairstreak

ZONE 4

1¹/₈in
30mm

The very weak purple-brown over the wings is typical of this species in which the sexes are fairly similar. The female is just a little larger, but both have two long tails of unequal length. The undersides are pale white with three yellow tracery-like lines crossing the wings. The butterfly lives in bushy habitats and breeds on *Clerodendron*, which is a member of the verbena family.

GENUS
ICARICIA

This is a small genus of butterflies found high in the mountains of North America. They are usually dimorphic, and the males are the brighter-colored sex. Various forms and abberations are recorded.

ICARICIA ACMON
Emerald-studded Blue, Silver-studded Blue

	ZONE
1in 25mm	1

The male has turquoise-blue uppers with a thin dark margin. The female is brown, sometimes with blue scales on the wing bases. An orange band on the hindwing may be present in either sex. The undersides are similar, silvery gray with black spots and an orange band on the hindwing. There is a small number of forms and subspecies. The butterfly is widespread in the western US, living in most habitats, and frequently breeds on leguminous plants.

ICARICIA ICARIOIDES
Common Blue

	ZONE
1³⁄₈in 35mm	1

This is the largest blue in the USA. In the normal form the male has violet-blue uppers, and the female is usually brown, sometimes with a flush of blue scales at the wing base. The undersides are silvery to light brown with a loose row of relatively large black spots crossing the wing. The butterfly lives in flowery meadows, usually near lupines, which are the caterpillar food plant. The Mission Blue, subspecies *missionensis*, was listed in 1990 as Endangered in California.

GENUS
INCISALIA

This is a relatively large genus of North American butterflies which live in various habitats from boggy uplands to deserts and wooded chaparral. They breed on a wide variety of plants.

INCISALIA ERYPHON
Western Pine Elfin

1¼in 32mm	ZONE 1

The key features to look out for are the apparent scalloped margins and the zigzag marks which cross the undersides of the wings. The overall color of the male is a rich brown, while that of the female is a brighter brown. The butterfly frequents forestry areas from 6,000-10,000ft (1,800-3,000m) and breeds on two species of pine, *Pinus contorta* and *P. ponderosa*.

INCISALIA MOSSII
Stonecrop Elfin, Moss Elfin

1in 25mm	ZONE 1

The uppers of the normal form are gray-brown in the male and reddish brown in the female. The undersides are a darker brown with, in some specimens, a gray band crossing the wings. This butterfly of the northwest part of the US lives in boggy land where its caterpillar food plants, the sedums, thrive, and after which it is named. The San Bruno Elfin, subspecies *bayensis*, was listed in 1990 as Endangered in California.

INCISALIA POLIOS
Hoary Elfin

1in 25mm	ZONE 1

In this species the sexes are very similar, being a dark somber speckled gray, even black. The undersides are similarly somber with just a few small lines on the wings. The hindwing is rather lobed and drawn out into an unremarkable stubby tail. The butterfly lives in various habitat types from coastal areas well into the mountains and breeds on bearberry, *Arctostaphylos uva-ursi*.

INCISALIA HENRICI
Henry's Elfin, Woodland Elfin

1⅛in 28mm	ZONE 1

The male uppers are a somber dark brown with a slight touch of orange on the trailing edge of the hindwing. The female is slightly larger and has more orange on the uppers. The undersides of both sexes are brown suffused with gray toward the base of the single stubby tail. The hindwing margin is a little indented. The butterfly lives in scrubby and boggy areas where it breeds on members of the pea and heath families.

INCISALIA NIPHON
Eastern Pine Elfin

1¼in 32mm	ZONE 1

This is generally a dark butterfly in which the male has dark brown uppers and the female has more of a tawny glow. The undersides are dark, too, with a disjointed black line crossing the wings. The margins have markings which make them appear to be scalloped. The butterfly is found in forestry areas where pines occur, since it breeds on a variety of pine species.

G E N U S
IOLANA

A genus of three species of blues which occur in Europe and Asia.

IOLANA IOLAS
Iolas Blue

1⅝in 42mm	ZONE 3·5

The male uppers are iridescent pale blue. The female has a thick dark forewing apex and a dark margin enclosing purplish blue bases. The fawn undersides have two loose rows of black spots. Butterflies live in flowery meadows and breed on bladder senna, *Colutea arborescens*.

GENUS
IOLAUS

A genus of African hairstreaks which have iridescent colors. These butterflies frequent open woody areas, along forest margins and bush country. They are associated with forest trees hosting the parasitic mistletoe, *Loranthus*, on which they breed.

IOLAUS MENAS

	ZONE 4
1½ in 40mm	

The male is blue with a bold black tip to the forewing. The larger female is white with a little blue dusting near the base of all wings. There are two unequal-length tails. The undersides of both sexes are white with two black marks by the base of the tails. The butterfly lives in bush country.

IOLAUS TIMON CONGOENSIS
Congo Long-tailed Blue

	ZONE 4
1¾ in 45mm	

As tails go, this butterfly has some of the longest, being about equal to the length of the hindwing in some specimens. There is a pair on each hindwing, and they are unequal in length. Most of the forewing is black, and this extends onto the leading edge of the hindwing. Iridescent green covers the rest of the wing, except the white tails. The undersides are in striking contrast to the uppers, being white with a few black marks near the base of the tails. It is found along forest margins.

IOLAUS BOWKERI
Bowker's Tailed Blue

	ZONE 4
1½ in 40mm	

The sexes are fairly similar, having sky blue over most of the uppers with an extensive black apex to the forewing and black on the leading edge of the hindwing. There are some white spots within the black areas, more in the female than the male. There are also two long tails of unequal length. The butterfly occurs in bushy areas and along forest margins.

IOLAUS SIDUS
Red-line Sapphire Blue

	ZONE 4
1⅜ in 35mm	

The sexes are fairly similar, though the female is the larger, with more pronounced orange spots near the base of the two tails. The male has brighter blue on the uppers; the blue of the female is less intense and suffused with white. Both have a bold black apex to the forewing. The undersides are a complete contrast, being white with two red-orange lines traversing the hindwing and a single one on the forewing – hence its common name. The butterfly is found in many types of wooded areas.

GENUS
JACOONA

A genus of about three Asian species which exhibit striking sexual dimorphism in their coloration and venation. Both sexes have eleven veins in their forewings, but males have two of them fused for a short distance. The butterflies have tails and are quite rare.

JACOONA AMRITA
Grand Imperial

2in 50mm	ZONE 5

The male is royal blue on most of the uppers. The tips of the forewings are distinctively black. There is a very long pointed tail which has a white and black eye-spot at the base. The female, which is more frequently seen than the male, is dark brown. The undersides of both sexes are orange-brown. The butterfly occurs from Burma through Malaya. It is found in open forest in lowland and upland, and is quite rare.

JACOONA ANASUJA

1½in 40mm	ZONE 5

The female has brown uppers. The male has turquoise-blue and black on the uppers; the blue occurs as an elliptical mark on the forewing tip, and at the base of the forewing and inside edge of the hindwing. Both sexes have long tails with a considerable amount of white at the base. The butterfly is a rarity and occurs in lowland rainforest, where it breeds on *Loranthus ferruginea*, a plant belonging to the *Loranthaceae* family.

▲

JACOONA SCOPULA NISIBIS

1¾in 45mm	ZONE 5

The shape of the wings is distinctive, being rounded in the forewing and the hindwing drawn out to a point, but not a tail. Most of the hindwing is sky blue, but the leading edge is black. The forewing is black with a little light dusting toward the base of the wings. The undersides are speckled.

GENUS
JALMENUS

A genus of nine species found in Australia. Caterpillars feed on *Acacia* and are attended by ants.

JALMENUS EVAGORAS
Common Imperial Blue

1⅜in 35mm	ZONE 6

The forewing tip and the wing margins are black. The pair of stubby tails has orange and blue marks at the base. There are a few subspecies which differ in the color of the uppers between blue and light green. The butterfly breeds particularly on black wattle.

245

GENUS
JAMIDES

A small genus of butterflies which occur from Sri Lanka to Australia. They are generally blue and have a short tail. They may be common along forest paths, where they fly among shrubs.

JAMIDES CUNILDA

ZONE 5

1³/₈in
36mm

The sexes are fairly similar, but there are important small differences. The male is a uniform rich metallic blue on the uppers, while the female is turquoise-blue with a black apex to the forewing. The hindwing of the female has a row of bead-like spots and white chevrons. Both sexes have tails. The undersides of both sexes are gray-brown with lots of rows of white marks resembling the speckled markings on a guinea fowl.

JAMIDES ABDUL

ZONE 5

1⁵/₈in
34mm

The male of this tailed butterfly is coppery green on the uppers with black borders; the female is brown with the black borders extending to the base of the wing. Most of the hindwing in both sexes is black. The speckled brown and white undersides have a prominent orange spot at the base of the hindwing. The butterfly flies in open forested areas.

JAMIDES CYTA AMPHISSINA
Pale Cerulean

ZONE 5

1¹/₂in
38mm

The male is pale silvery white on the uppers, which have a sheen. The female has a thick black margin around all the wings enclosing a silvery white area. The hindwing of the male has a single black spot near the small tail, but the hindwing of the female has a row of black chevrons around the margin. The butterfly is thought to breed on tropical gingers.

GENUS
LAEOSOPIS

A genus of hairstreaks found in Europe and Asia, exhibiting sexual dimorphism.

LAEOSOPIS ROBORIS
Spanish Purple Hairstreak

ZONE 3·5

1¹/₈in
30mm

Thick dark margins enclose a purplish blue area to the base of the wings. The female has less purple-blue and rounded wings. The fawn undersides have a row of orange chevrons tipped white around the hindwing margin. Butterflies live in wooded areas and breed on ash.

GENUS
LAMPIDES

A genus of one species, a tailed blue, which has colonized much of the world.

LAMPIDES BOETICUS
Long-tailed Blue

ZONE 1·3·4 5·6

1³/₈in
36mm

The tail and eye-spot on the hindwing underside mirror the head and antennae to confuse predators. Females are a darker blue, but both sexes have a rippled underside pattern. One of the most successful of butterflies, this migrant breeds on many leguminous plants, including some crops.

G E N U S
LEPTOMYRINA

A genus of African tailed or tailless butterflies with small eye-spots around the margin of the wings. They live in wooded areas, especially along forest edges where they breed on members of the *Crassulaceae*.

LEPTOMYRINA HIRUNDO
Tailed Black Eye

1⅛in 30mm	ZONE 4

This differs from *L. gorgias* in having tails, rather substantial ones which are as long as the rest of the hindwing. The black spots are present on both sets of wings, and the overall color is gray with a little blue toward the base. The sexes are similar. The butterfly lives along forest margins and in scrubby areas, and breeds on *Kalanchoe* and *Crassula* species.

LEPTOMYRINA GORGIAS
Black Eye

1³⁄₈in 35mm	ZONE 4

This tailless lycaenid is named after the black eye-spots around the margin of the hindwing and the single larger eye-spot on the trailing edge of the forewing. The sexes are similar in appearance, being pale brown with a faint blue tinge, but the female is the larger. The underside is gray with black lines. The butterfly occurs in scrub country and breeds on a variety of plants including *Kalanchoe* and *Crassula* species.

LEPTOTES MARINA
Marine Blue, Striped Blue

1in 25mm	ZONE 1·2

The male is a uniform purple-blue, while the female is dull violet with a significant brown border. The undersides of both sexes are "zebra-striped," an effect caused by lots of brown crescents covering the wings. The butterflies live along watercourses and breed on various members of the pea family. They are migratory and make northerly flights during the summer.

G E N U S
LEPTOTES

A relatively small genus of striped and generally tailed blues, small in size, which have colonized various parts of Europe, Asia, and North and South America. They are sexually dimorphic. Butterflies breed on members of the pea family, *Leguminosae*. Some species are migratory.

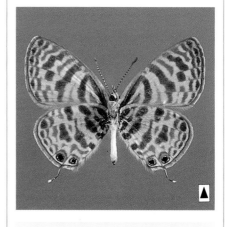

LEPTOTES PIRITHOUS
Lang's Short-tailed Blue

1in 26mm	ZONE 3·5

The male is a pale lavender-blue on the uppers, and the female is light brown with a dusting of violet in the middle of the forewing. This is a tailed species which has two small eye-spots near the base of the tail on both surfaces. The underside is mottled all over with light and dark waves and lines. The butterfly occurs in flowery places, often along coastal sites, and breeds on members of the pea family.

GENUS
LIPHYRA

A genus of two species of "moth butterflies," which are powerful fliers at dusk and dawn.

LIPHYRA BRASSOLIS
Moth Butterfly

	ZONE 5·6
3½in 92mm	

The sexes are fairly similar, though the female is slightly larger. The overall color is brown-orange with significant black borders. This rare butterfly lives in forested lowlands. It breeds on *Nauclea orientalis*, a member of the *Rubiaceae* family, and eventually pupates in ant nests.

GENUS
LYCAEIDES

A genus of European and Asian blues which are sexually dimorphic, the males often with striking blues on the uppers. They live in open flowery areas such as meadows and breed on members of the pea family, *Leguminosae*.

LYCAEIDES ARGYROGNOMON
Reverdin's Blue

	ZONE 3·5
1⁵⁄₁₆in 34mm	

The rich uniform blue-purple of the male is distinctive. The female is a uniform brown with a row of orange marks along the trailing hindwing edge. The male undersides are light gray, light brown in the female, with pronounced orange banding around the wings, especially in the female. The male has blue toward the base of the wings. Both sexes have a white fringe around all wings. The butterfly lives in flowery areas and breeds on crown vetch, *Coronilla varia*.

GENUS
LOXURA

A genus of two long-tailed species which occurs from Sri Lanka to the Philippines.

LOXURA ATYMNUS
Yamfly

	ZONE 5
1½in 40mm	

This striking golden orange butterfly has black forewing tips and yellowish buff undersides. The hindwing is drawn out as a long tail. The butterfly is found in lowland, in open areas, even around villages. Caterpillars feed on yams and are possible pests on this crop.

LYCAEIDES MELISSA
Orange-margined Blue

ZONE 1

1⅛in
30mm

The orange margins can be very pronounced in the brown female and exist as fused lunules around all wings. The male is blue. The undersides of both sexes are silvery white with a repeat of the orange band around the margins and a scattering of small black spots. There are two subspecies and forms known. The butterfly lives in meadows and prairies, and breeds on various members of the pea family.

LYCAENA CUPREUS
Lustrous Copper

ZONE 1

1¼in
32mm

Named after the bright coppery red of the male, the female is a less fiery color with darker markings. The underside of the forewing has an orange flush with the typical scattering of black spots which also appear on the gray hindwing. There are at least three subspecies known. The butterfly may be seen in alpine meadows above and below the timberline. The caterpillar food plant is thought to be dock, *Rumex paucifolius*.

LYCAENA EPIXANTHE
Cranberry-bog Copper, Bog Copper

ZONE 1

1in
25mm

The male is brown with a purple sheen, while the duller female is gray. The undersides vary from white to yellow. This is a local butterfly, sometimes of relatively small populations living in isolated boggy localities. It is a weak flier. The common name describes both the habitat and the caterpillar food plant, cranberry (*Vaccinium* species).

GENUS
LYCAENA

A genus of coppers widespread in Europe and Asia, with examples in Australia and North America. They occur mostly in temperate climates. Their colors are in the coppery and orange range, and the undersides often have dark spots. Caterpillar food plants occur particularly among the buckwheats and docks, *Polygonaceae*, as well as members of *Ericaceae*, *Rosaceae*, and possibly *Stylidiaceae*.

LYCAENA DORCAS
Dorcas, Cinquefoil Copper

ZONE 1

1¼in
32mm

The male is a dark brown with a deep purple suffusion, the female is orange-brown with muted black spots on both wings. The undersides are variable, being yellowish, pinkish or brown, with black spots on the forewing. The butterfly breeds in boggy areas on cinquefoil, *Potentilla*, from which it takes one of its common names.

LYCAENA FEREDAYI

ZONE 6

1⅛in
30mm

This butterfly resembles a dark form of the European *L. phlaeus*. The ground color is black with dark orange spots running around the inside margins of the wings, and three large dark orange spots in the center of the forewing. The female has rounded wings, and the orange spots are a little brighter than in the male. The butterfly occurs in New Zealand and frequents open flowery areas. Possibly it breeds on *Donatia*, which belongs to the *Stylidiaceae* family.

LYCAENA HELLE
Violet copper

ZONE
3·5

1⅛in
28mm

The sexes are very different. The common name comes from the male which has a strong violet suffusion over the wings, with a thin orange border round the hindwing. The female is orange with black spots on the forewing, and black with a row of blue and a row of orange spots on the hindwing. The undersides of both sexes are buff and orange with black spots and a thick orange band. This butterfly of open flowery areas breeds on knotgrass, *Polygonum*.

LYCAENA HETERONEA
Blue copper

ZONE
1

1⅜in
36mm

The sexes are dimorphic. The male has blue uppers. The female has brown uppers, sometimes with a touch of blue. The undersides are distinctive and similar in both sexes. They are white-grey with a suspicion of blue scales at the base of the wings and a few black spots are scattered over the forewing. The butterfly lives in open grassy and scrubby areas where its caterpillar food plants, various members of the knotweed family, live.

LYCAENA HYLLUS
Bronze copper

ZONE
1

1½in
40mm

The male is a uniform warm light brown on the uppers with the underside spotting showing through. The female has a bright orange forewing containing black spots and with a dark margin, while the hindwing is mostly black with an orange band around the margin. The undersides are white on the hindwing with a repeat of the orange band, and the forewing is pale orange with white towards the outer part. The butterfly lives in meadows and breeds on various species of dock and knotweed.

LYCAENA HELLOIDES
Purplish copper

ZONE
1

1¼in
32mm

The sexes are slightly different. The uppers of the male are a dark copper brown with a faint purple suffusion. The female is orangey brown on the uppers. In both sexes the undersides are ochre with black spots on the forewing. There are at least three subspecies known. The butterfly lives in many types of habitat from coastal areas well into the mountains at 10,000ft (3,000m). It breeds on various members of the buckwheat family, such as docks and knotweeds.

LYCAENA NIVALIS
Lilac-edged copper

ZONE 1

1⁵/₁₆in
34mm

The male is a uniform pale brown on the uppers with a band of orange on the hindwing. There are a few small black spots on the forewing. The female is a weak orange on the forewing which is speckled with black spots and has a dark border. The hindwing has fewer black spots. The undersides are very pale orange. There are two subspecies, one of which, *L. nivalis nivalis*, has a pink or lilac tinge towards the outside of the wings.

LYCAENA PHLAEUS
Small copper

ZONE 1·3 4·5

1¹/₈in
30mm

A small, alert and brightly coloured butterfly with a speckled copper and black pattern on the forewings which is distinctive. A row of blue spots is sometimes present around the hindwing. The undersides are light tan with a small amount of copper on the forewings which have some prominent black spots. A number of subspecies are recorded. The butterfly frequents wild habitats as well as urban sites, and breeds on docks which are very common as weeds.

LYCAENA SALUSTIUS

ZONE 6

1⁵/₁₆in
34mm

This New Zealand species looks somewhat like the European *L. phlaeus*. The uppers are dull orange with a dark border, and a single row of black spots running around the inside of the margins. There are a few other black spots on the wings. The butterfly likes warm sunny habitats.

LYCAENA ORUS
Sorrel copper

ZONE 4

1¹/₈in
30mm

This is a tailless copper with similar sexes. The uppers are coppery red and there is a small black margin round the wings. A violet sheen can be seen over the uppers in some lights. The undersides are orange-brown in the forewing and pale brown in the hindwing. This South African butterfly lives in mountain grasslands where it breeds on dock, *Rumex*.

LYCAENA RUBIDUS
Ruddy copper

ZONE 1

1³/₈in
36mm

The sexes are fairly similar, and the "ruddy" nature comes from the male uppers which are a uniform reddish orange. The female has a more subdued orange as a ground colour and more of the small diffuse black spots on the wings, mostly on the forewing. There are at least two subspecies and one form. The butterfly occurs at both low and high altitude. It breeds on members of the knotweed family, particularly docks, *Rumex* species.

LYCAENA XANTHOIDES
Gray copper

ZONE 1

1³/₄in
44mm

Rather a misnomer, the male is a uniform pale brown with a small band of orange on the trailing edge of the hindwing. The female has much more orange on the wings and this is punctuated with black spots. The undersides of both sexes are grey, almost white with a touch of blue, and with small black spots. Two subspecies are known. The butterfly lives in fields, meadows and prairies, and breeds on members of the knotweed family.

GENUS
LYROPTERYX

A genus of some 23 species of metalmarks from Central and South America, often with greenish markings. The life history of some species remains unknown.

♀

LYROPTERYX LYRA

	ZONE 2
2¹⁄₈in 54mm	

The distinctive feature of the male is that the streaky ray pattern is more elaborate on the underside. The ground color is black with radiating greenish lines on the uppers. The undersides are dark brown to black with whitish blue lines and red spots at the wing bases. The female is rich dark brown with a vermillion-red border around all the wings. One of the larger metalmarks, this butterfly occurs in Colombia and Honduras.

LYROPTERYX APOLLONIA

	ZONE 2
2in 50mm	

The sexes are dimorphic, but share the same pattern. The attractive rays on the male have a greenish hue and start from halfway in each wing. The female has much longer rays, which are white, and a distinctive orange border to the trailing edge of the hindwing. The undersides of the wings are black and have a collection of about a dozen large red spots at the base from which rays radiate out. The life history is unknown.

GENUS
LYSANDRA

This is a genus of blues found in Europe, North Africa, and Asia. They are sexually dimorphic and do not have tails. Butterflies often breed on members of the pea family, *Leguminosae*. They live in open sunny habitats and bask on flowers.

LYSANDRA BELLARGUS
Adonis Blue

ZONE
3·5

1⁵/₁₆in
34mm

The male is bright blue, its white fringe regularly punctuated with black, giving a checked appearance. The warm brown female has a sprinkling of blue toward the wing bases and a checked fringe. The undersides are light brown, darker in the female, peppered with black spots, weak orange lunules by the margin, and a small white flash on the hindwing. Butterflies live on warm sunny slopes where there are plenty of flowers, especially horseshoe vetch, *Hippocrepis comosa*, on which they breed.

LYSANDRA HISPANA
Provence Chalk-hill Blue

ZONE
3

1³/₈in
36mm

The sexes are dimorphic, and similar to *L. coridon*. The male is a pale silvery blue with a faint yellowish tinge and dark margins. The female is brown. Both have very pale undersides with orange and black spots. The butterfly frequents flowery meadows in southern France, Italy, and Spain, but its caterpillar food plant is unknown.

MACULINEA ALCON
Alcon Blue

ZONE
3·5

1¹/₂in
38mm

The male is a uniform rich violet-blue, and the female is mostly black with a suffusion of violet-blue at the base of the wings. Both sexes have a white fringe, edged in black in the male. The undersides are fawn and peppered with black spots. Two subspecies are known, each from a different altitude. Butterflies breed on *Gentiana pneumonanthe*.

LYSANDRA CORIDON
Chalk-hill Blue

ZONE
3

1³/₈in
36mm

The male is silvery blue with darker outer parts and a black and white checked fringe. The female is warm brown with a black and white checked margin, although the black is less well defined than in *L. bellargus*. The undersides are light brown, browner in the female, with a row of orange lunules around the hindwing and a scattering of black spots over the wings. The butterfly lives in flowery places and breeds on horseshoe vetch, *Hippocrepis comosa*.

GENUS
MACULINEA

A genus of "large blues" which are found in Europe and Asia. They are tailless and have darker blue colors than many other blue species. The caterpillars start by feeding on their food plant and then switch to being looked after by ants. The large blues have attracted a lot of attention from collectors, and some species are now scarce. All the large blues of the *Maculinea* genus are listed in the *Red Data Books* as Endangered in Europe.

MACULINEA ARION
Large Blue

ZONE
3·5

1¹/₂in
40mm

The bright blue male has six "teardrop" black marks on the forewing and faint gray markings near the hindwing margin. The female is heavily marked in black, with larger marks on the forewing and a thick black margin. The undersides are fairly similar in each sex, with pronounced black spots and blue scales at the wing bases, particularly the female. The butterfly became extinct in Britain in 1979. It breeds on thyme, *Thymus serphyllum*.

MACULINEA NAUSITHOUS
Dusky Large Blue

The male has a brown band around all the wing margins. The central areas are dark purple and contain four black "teardrop" marks. The female is dark brown, sometimes flushed blue near the base of the wings. The undersides of both sexes are a caramel brown with a bent row of black spots on the hindwing and a few less defined ones on the forewing. The butterfly breeds on great burnet, *Sanguisorba*, and lives in flowery meadows.

MACULINEA TELEJUS
Scarce Large Blue

The sexes are fairly similar, though the female has a wider marginal area and larger spots on the wings. The male is a dark blue with long "teardrop" marks on the forewing, this being a key characteristic. The undersides are a yellowy fawn with two rows of black spots on both wings. This rare butterfly breeds on great burnet, *Sanguisorba*.

GENUS
MAHATHALA

A genus of Asian butterflies, similar to *Arhopala*, but with slightly different tails.

MAHATHALA AMERIA HAINANI

The sexes are similar in appearance. The male is iridescent purple-blue above with a dark border. The female is the same as the male, but with a wider border. The butterfly lives in lowland rainforest.

GENUS
MANTO

A genus of Asian butterflies identified by their genitalia and by the male, which has a hindwing tuft.

MANTO HYPOLEUCA

This long-tailed lycaenid has black tips on its forewings and greenish black on the rest of the wings. The undersides are orange-brown merging to white near the elaborate black and white eye-spots at the base of the tail. It is a rare lowland butterfly.

GENUS
MANTOIDES

The species of this Asian genus are separated by differences in their genitalia and venation.

MANTOIDES GAMA

ZONE 6

1³/₄in 44mm

This butterfly is coppery brown on the uppers which have a faint dusting of blue. The hindwing is drawn out as a long tail, with eye-spots which are repeated on the much lighter undersides. The butterfly is a rarity and is found in both lowland and highland rainforest.

GENUS
MEGISBA

An Asian and Australian genus of two species which may or may not have a tail.

MEGISBA MALAYA
SIKKIMA

ZONE 5·6

⁷/₈in 24mm

This is a very small but widespread blue which has a characteristic speckled underside. The brown speckles are more pronounced on the hindwing where there are also some black spots. The butterfly lives in the plains and breeds on a sapindaceous plant.

GENUS
MESENE

A South American genus of about 20 species, which may be poisonous models of day-flying geometrid moths.

MESENE PHAREUS RUBELLA

ZONE 2

1¹/₈in 28mm

The butterfly is striking with its ruddy undersides, more strident on the hindwing. The hindwing is edged in a brown band, and the forewing is a dull orange-red, brighter on the trailing edge.

GENUS
MESOSEMIA

A genus of more than 60 species of metalmarks from South America. They are characterized by one or two very prominent eye-spots on the forewing which give them a face-like appearance. Unusually for butterflies, they tend to hop through vegetation rather than to fly.

MESOSEMIA HEWIGIS

ZONE 2

1³/₄in 46mm

The undersides have a "face," with a large pupilled eye-spot on the forewing and a thick white band crossing the dark wings. The base of the wing is light brown.

MESOSEMIA LORUHAMA

ZONE 2

1³/₄in 46mm

Both sexes of this metalmark have the characteristic face-like pattern, although the colors differ. The male has a metallic greenish hue with a black forewing tip. There is a prominent pupilled eye-spot on the forewing, emphasized on either side by a black line which runs to the hindwing. The larger female has metallic pale blue surrounded by a thick white band which runs inside the black forewing tip and across the hindwing. The butterfly is found in Peru.

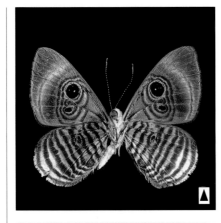

MESOSEMIA PHILOCLES

ZONE 2

1³⁄₈in
35mm

There is a single large eye-spot on the forewing which is obscured in the dark basal region. A thick white band runs outside of the eye-spot up to the black forewing tip. The hindwing is dark at the base and white on the outside, with three dark lines crossing the light area. The underside exhibits a unique streaky pattern.

GENUS

MICANDRA

A genus of metallic lycaenids with tails, found mostly in the north of South America.

♀

▲

MICANDRA PLATYPTERA

ZONE 2

1⁵⁄₁₆in
34mm

The iridescent green colors on the uppers are unmistakable and take up most of the wings. The tip of the forewing is black and continues around the wings to the black tails. By comparison the brown undersides are very dull. The butterfly is found in Central America, including Panama.

GENUS

MINISTRYMON

A genus of North and South American hairstreaks which have adaptations for living in desert conditions. They breed on mesquites, spiny trees and shrubs of the *Proposis* genus, which grow in deserts, especially by watercourses. The colors of the butterflies are blue, gray, and black.

▲

MINISTRYMON CLYTIE
Silver-blue Hairstreak

ZONE 1

⁷⁄₈in
22mm

The sexes are fairly similar. Apart from the dark tip, the male has silvery blue markings on the forewing and over most of the hindwing. The female has a similar pattern, but with a larger area of black on the forewing. The undersides of both sexes are pale gray-white with two broken orange bands and two eye-spots at the base of the tail. The butterfly lives in desert among the prickly mesquite on which it breeds.

GENUS

METHONELLA

This genus of South American metalmarks are brown and orange with scalloped hindwings.

METHONELLA CECILIA

ZONE 2

1½in
40mm

The sexes of this colorful metalmark have the same basic pattern, but different colors. The male is brighter with bright orange in the center of each dark chocolate-colored wing. The female has a big flash of pale yellow set in the brown tips of the forewing and a smaller area of orange in the center of the wings.

GENUS

MIMACRAEA

A genus of large African lycaenids which are mimics of nymphalids, particularly danaids and acraeids.

MIMACRAEA MARSHALLI DOHERTYI
Marshall's Acraea Mimic

ZONE 4

2¹⁄₈in
54mm

This species, in which the sexes are similar, looks like *Danaus chrysippus*, which it mimics. The ground color is red-brown, and there is usually a black tip to the forewing containing white spots. The butterfly flies in open woodland and breeds on lichens.

MINISTRYMON LEDA
Mesquite Hairstreak

ZONE
1·2

⁷/₈in
22mm

The sexes are similar, with sky blue colors at the base of the wings and dirty gray over the greater part of the forewing. The undersides are silvery gray with two thin lines traversing the wings and two eye-spots by the tail. This particular butterfly species breeds on the tree *Prosopis juliflora*.

GENUS
MITOURA

A genus of small-sized North American hairstreaks which are blue, brown, and greenish brown. They have formed many subspecies. Many of the butterflies are named after their caterpillar food plants, which include conifers.

▲

MITOURA GRYNEUS
Cedar Hairstreak, Olive Hairstreak

ZONE
1

1in
25mm

The suffusion of green over the undersides is usually a subtle olive, but in some cases can be rather intense. The butterfly has a typical white "hairstreak" line across the undersides and a small tail. There are about eight subspecies which have been described. The caterpillar food plants are the red cedars, *Juniperus virginiana* and *J. silicola*.

MITOURA SIVA
Juniper Hairstreak

ZONE
1

1¹/₈in
28mm

The main characteristic is the bright green on the underside. The uppers are dark brown with a little reddish brown near the base of the tail. This hairstreak is named after its caterpillar food plants: *Juniperus osteosperma*, *J. californica*, and *J. scopulorum*. It occurs in many sorts of woodland habitats where these junipers grow.

▲

MITOURA SPINETORUM
Blue Mistletoe Hairstreak

ZONE 1

1in 26mm

Sexually dimorphic, the male butterfly has steel blue uppers, while the female has subdued blue toward the base of the dark brown-black wings. The undersides have another key feature, the nutty red color which becomes lighter toward the outside. There is a typical white "hairstreak" line which crosses the wings and has a W shape on the hindwing. The butterfly lives in forestry areas where it breeds on mistletoe, which is semi-parasitic on pines.

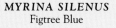

GENUS
MYRINA

A genus of African butterflies which are sexually dimorphic. The males are brightly colored, and the females are larger with duller colors. Both sexes have tails. Butterflies live in savanna and wooded country where they breed on fig, *Ficus*.

MYRINA DERMAPTERA
Lesser Figtree Blue

ZONE 4

1³/₈in 35mm

The sexes are fairly similar. The male is mostly royal blue with a black forewing apex, and some black marginal and vein marking on the hindwing. The much larger female has less blue and more black. In both sexes the undersides are a uniform gray with an orange and white eye-spot on the hindwing at the base of the large spatulate tail. The butterfly lives in savanna and scrubby country.

MYRINA SILENUS
Figtree Blue

ZONE 4

1¹/₂in 40mm

The male is the richest violet-blue with a red-brown apical patch on the forewing which is ringed in black. The female is similar though larger and with less of the flashy color and more black areas. The hindwing is drawn out to form a very long tail. The butterfly lives in wooded areas where fig trees grow.

GENUS
NECYRIA

A genus of South American metalmarks which have colorful iridescent markings. They fly along forest margins and may be involved in mimicry with other forest butterflies.

NECYRIA MANCO

ZONE 2 — 2in 50mm

This is a South American lycaenid which is essentially black. It has a turquoise-green band of chevrons on the hindwing, inside of which is a dull red band crossing both wings. This color scheme seems to be very common in the rainforests and is similar to that of *Lyropteryx*, for example. There may be some model/mimic relationships between species.

NECYRIA BELLONA

ZONE 2 — 2in 50mm

This is a metallic black metalmark which has a slight blue-green iridescence. The sexes are fairly similar. The male has uniform black and rather pointed forewings with a vermilion band which crosses just over half the black-blue hindwing. The female ground color is black with a noticeable blue dusting toward the outsides of the wings, and a thin vermilion band on both the forewing and the hindwing. The butterfly is found in Bolivia.

GENUS
NEOCHERITRA

A genus of butterflies from South America which resemble ithominids.

NEOCHERITRA FLORALA

ZONE 2 — 1½in 38mm

The elongated wings have a marginal black band. The main veins are outlined in black with white between the veins and margins. A large orange mark almost covers the forewing apex. The butterfly has been found in Colombia and lives in rainforest.

GENUS
NEOMYRINA

A genus of tailed lycaenids from Asia which look like whites, but are related to *Drina*.

NEOMYRINA NIVEA
White Imperial

ZONE 5 — 2¼in 56mm

Similar to a pierid in flight, but this species has long tails. Most of the uppers are white, the forewing tip black suffused in blue. The dark underside stripes show through to the uppers. Butterflies live in rainforest. Their life cycle is unknown.

GENUS
NEOPITHECOPS

A genus of butterflies found in Asia and Australia, but absent from Sulawesi.

NEOPITHECOPS ZALMORA

ZONE 5·6 — ⅞in 22mm

The sexes are fairly similar. The upperside is brown-black except for a white patch on the forewing which is consistently present in the female. The undersides are white with a distinctive black dot on the hindwing. The butterfly breeds on *Glycosmis pentaphylla*.

GENUS
OENOMAUS

A genus of North and South American hairstreaks which are relatively large and have iridescent colors. The butterflies live in lightly wooded areas, but their life cycles are not well known.

OENOMAUS RUSTAN

ZONE 2

1⁷⁄₈in 48mm

This hairstreak is dark brown on the uppers with a flush of light green near the base of the forewing. The hindwing is extended into one long curly tail and one very short one. The undersides are brown with two black spots at the base of the tails. It is found from Honduras to Brazil.

GENUS
OGYRIS

A genus of brightly colored lycaenids from Australia, some of which are prized by collectors.
In addition, the butterflies are vulnerable to destruction of their forest habitats, where they breed on parasitic mistletoes which often grow in eucalyptus trees. Butterflies tend to be variable in appearance, and a number of subspecies occur.

OGYRIS ABROTA
Dark Purple Azure

ZONE 6

1³⁄₄in 46mm

The sexes are very different in appearance. Like its common name suggests, the male is a very dark, almost somber purple, with a thick black margin around all the wings. The female is slightly larger, mostly brown, lighter on the heavily scalloped hindwing. The forewing has a large round yellow splash in the center of the wing. It breeds on mistletoe species.

OGYRIS AMARYLLIS HEWITSONI
Amaryllis Azure

ZONE 6

1³⁄₄in 46mm

The scalloping of the hindwing is very pronounced in the female, due to a thick wavy band of brown. On the forewing the brown band is not wavy, but wide, much wider than in the male. In other respects the sexes are similar. The ground color is a metallic rich sky blue. The undersides are a deep chocolate brown, wavy and mottled. The butterfly breeds on the mistletoe, *Amyema linophyllum*. Like many *Ogyris* species, the caterpillars are attended by ants.

OGYRIS GENOVEVA GELA
Genoveva Azure

The female has a black ground color with a pale yellow mark in the tip of the forewing and metallic silvery-green over most of the uppers. There is a modest tail from the middle of the hindwing. This very variable butterfly is one of at least six named subspecies. It is from New South Wales, Australia.

OGYRIS ZOSINE TYPHA
Purple Azure

The sexes are strongly dimorphic. The male is a bright royal blue, with rather pointed forewings and a faintly scalloped hindwing with the smallest tail. The female has pronounced scalloped hindwings and a deep purple luster over most of the hindwing and the base of the forewing. The tip of the forewing is brown with a small pale yellow mark. The butterfly breeds on mistletoes.

GENUS
PALAEOCHRYSOPHANUS

A genus of coppers with two dimorphic species found from Europe through to Asia.

PALAEOCHRYSOPHANUS HIPPOTHOE
Purple-edged Copper

The bright copper male is suffused with purple at the edges and around the inside hindwing margin. The female has less intense copper and black dots on the forewing with a dark hindwing banded orange. Butterflies live in flowery meadows and breed on dock.

GENUS
PANDEMOS

A genus of South American dimorphic metalmarks which have rather curved and pointed wings.

PANDEMOS PASIPHAE

The male has an overall silvery gray bloom with a small black mark on the leading edge of the hindwing. There are a few small white marks on the forewing. The female is a dull white. The butterfly is found in the Amazon basin.

GENUS
PARALAXITA

A genus of Asian dimorphic butterflies which have very rounded forewings.

PARALAXITA LACOON

ZONE	5
1½in	40mm

The larger male is black with a prominent dull turquoise band on the forewing. The female is brown with copper forewing tips. Eastern populations of this butterfly are also known as *P. orphana*. *P. lacoon* occurs from Burma to Malaysia.

GENUS
PARRHASIUS

A genus of blue-winged North American hairstreaks which breed on oak.

PARRHASIUS M-ALBUM
White-M Hairstreak

ZONE	1
1¼in	32mm

Both sexes have bright blue uppers with a dark margin and apex to the forewing, and are rather like *Strymon* species. There are two tails – one long, the other short. The butterfly lives near oaks. Unusually, the pupa can squeak to deter predators.

GENUS
PERIPLACIS

A genus of South American lycaenids which have strongly angled wings and brown and blue colors.

PERIPLACIS GLAUCOMA

ZONE	2
1⅝in	41mm

This species can be identified by its wing shapes. The forewings are rather rectangular, the hindwing rounded on the outer edge and drawn to a blunt point on the trailing edge. The ground color is a grey-black with a suffusion of blue on the inside, particularly on the hindwing.

GENUS
PARAPHNAEUS

This is a genus of Asian and African two-tailed blue hairstreaks.

PARAPHNAEUS HUTCHINSONI
Silver Spot, Hutchinson's Highflier

ZONE	4
1½in	40mm

The sexes are similar with large silver spots on the undersides of the wings. They have sky blue to the inside of the wings, and the black tips on the forewings contain a range of white spots. The species lives near *Acacia*, but very little is known of its life history.

GENUS
PHAEOSTRYMON

This genus of brown hairstreaks are from the south of North America.

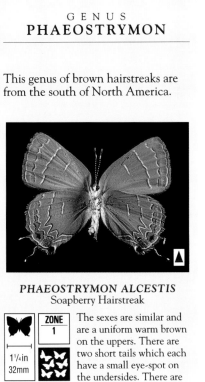

PHAEOSTRYMON ALCESTIS
Soapberry Hairstreak

ZONE 1

1¼in 32mm

The sexes are similar and are a uniform warm brown on the uppers. There are two short tails which each have a small eye-spot on the undersides. There are two white "hairstreak" lines, one prescribing a VW shape. The butterfly breeds on the native soapberry, *Sapindus*.

GENUS
PHASIS

A genus of small African coppers with tailed hindwings and varying amounts of copper and brown on the wings.

PHASIS THERO
Hooked Copper

ZONE 4

2⅛in 55mm

This rich brown butterfly has an incurved edge to the forewing. The hindwing is scalloped and tailed. There are red spots and marks on the forewing and two small red spots by the tail. Butterflies live in coastal scrub, and breed on *Rhus* and *Melianthus*.

GENUS
PHILIRIS

This is a genus of blues found from New Guinea to the Australian mainland.

PHILIRIS HELENA

ZONE 6

1⅜in 36mm

This is a relatively small butterfly. The male has electric blue on its uppers, a small black band round the wings and a white fringe. The hindwing margin of this butterfly is very slightly scalloped.

GENUS
PLEBEJUS

This is a genus of blues which occur in the temperate regions of North America and Europe. They are relatively small butterflies which exhibit sexual dimorphism. They occur in open flowery areas, enjoy basking in the sun, and breed on members of the pea family, *Leguminosae*.

PLEBEJUS ARGUS
Silver-studded Blue

ZONE 3·5

1⁵⁄₁₆in 34mm

The male has purplish blue uppers with a black margin, and pale grey undersides. The female has dark brown uppers with a set of orange lunules inside the margin; the undersides are light brown speckled with black. Both sexes have a white fringe and a distinctive band of orange lunules on the hindwing underside, but the silvery blue "studs" in each lunule are not always clear. Three subspecies are recorded. Butterflies live in grassy areas, coastal scrub, and breed on gorse, *Ulex*.

PLEBEJUS SAEPIOLUS
Greenish Blue, Greenish Clover Blue

ZONE 1

1¼in 32mm

This butterfly is true to its common name, since it often has a greenish hue to the wings. The male is silvery blue and has dark margins. The female may be either a more subdued blue than the male, or brown. The butterfly lives in meadows and waysides from the lowland to the mountains. It breeds on clovers and other members of the pea family.

GENUS
PLEBICULA

A genus of seven species of blue which occur over Europe to Russia, and in North Africa. They are generally small butterflies which exhibit sexual dimorphism. They live in open sunny areas and breed on members of the pea family, *Leguminosae*.

PLEBICULA DORYLAS
Turquoise Blue

ZONE
3·5

1⁵/₁₆in
34mm

A turquoise sheen covers the bright blue uppers of the male, which also have a thin black marginal line and a white fringe. The female is brown with a white fringe and occasional blue scaling at the base of the wings. The undersides of both sexes are gray with black spots scattered throughout and a row of orange lunules around the margins. The butterfly lives in flowery meadows and breeds on various leguminous plants, including *Trifolium* and *Anthyllis*.

PLEBICULA PYLAON
Zephyr Blue

ZONE
3·5

1⁵/₁₆in
34mm

The male has violet-blue uppers with a fine black margin and white fringe. Occasionally there are little red spots on the trailing edge of the hindwing. The female is brown with distinct red spots around the margins of both fore- and hindwings. On both sexes the red markings are pronounced on the lighter undersides, as are the black spots. The butterfly lives in warm, sunny pastures and slopes where milk vetch, *Astragalus*, occurs.

PLEBICULA ATLANTICA WEISSEI
Atlas Blue

ZONE
3·4

1⁵/₁₆in
34mm

The male is silvery blue on the uppers with a thin black band around the margins and a white fringe. The female is a warm brown with a very thick orange band around each wing, and a white fringe. The undersides of both sexes are pale gray with a white flash set in the hindwing, and orange lunules around the margins. The butterfly lives only at about 7,000-8,000ft (2,150-2,500m) in the Atlas Mountains in Morocco. Its caterpillar food plants remain unknown.

PLEBICULA NIVESCENS
Mother of Pearl Blue

ZONE
3

1³/₈in
36mm

The male has a mother of pearl sheen on its uppers with a slight graying toward the extremities. The female is brown on the uppers. Both are lighter on the undersides, the female being browner with heavier black spots on the forewing and more pronounced orange banding around the margins. The butterfly occurs only in Spain. Its caterpillar food plants are unknown.

GENUS
POECILMITIS

This is a genus of about 20 species of coppers which occur in South Africa. Butterflies are relatively small for coppers, and the sexes are usually fairly similar. They live in a variety of habitats.

POECILMITIS CHRYSAOR
Golden Copper

	ZONE 4
1¹⁄₈in 30mm	

The sexes are similar in this species, which is a brightly colored reddish copper color. There is a black band around the forewing and small black dots over the wings. The hindwing is drawn out as a partial tail. The butterfly frequents hilly and mountainous areas in South Africa, and breeds on *Rhus* and *Zygophyllum*.

POECILMITIS THYSBE
Opal Copper

	ZONE 4
1¹⁄₈in 30mm	

This is an enchanting little lycaenid whose coloration is made up of sky blue, red, and black. The sexes are fairly similar, but very variable. Females tend to have rounded wings, and the blue is restricted to the base of the wings. The orange-red may form a bold wide band, or be merely a flash by the trailing edge of the hindwing. The butterfly lives in all sorts of different habitats and breeds on *Aspalathus* and *Zygophyllum*.

GENUS
POLYOMMATUS

A genus of small blues from Europe, North Africa, Asia, and Australia which breed on legumes.

POLYOMMATUS ICARUS
Common Blue

	ZONE 3·5
1³⁄₈in 36mm	

The male has violet-blue uppers and a white fringe. The brown female uppers have a row of marginal orange lunules. Undersides are gray-brown spotted black. The orange spots on the hindwing continue onto the forewing only in the female. Butterflies enjoy open sunny areas.

GENUS
PRAETAXILA

A genus of dimorphic metalmarks found from New Guinea to the Australian mainland.

PRAETAXILA HETERISA

	ZONE 5
2⁵⁄₈in 70mm	

The forewing is mostly black with an orange band and white spots on the apex. The hindwing is mostly orange with a black base. The sexes are dimorphic.

GENUS
PSEUDALMENOS

A genus of tailed lycaenids from Australia and Tasmania which breed on members of the pea family.

PSEUDALMENOS CHLORINDUS CHLORINDUS
Tasmanian Hairstreak

	ZONE
	6
1¼in	
32mm	

The male is a smoky brown with some orange highlighting and a dark orange band around the hindwing margins. The larger, more striking female has a broad orange band crossing both wings. Of at least four subspecies recorded, *P. chlorinda* occurs on Tasmania.

GENUS
PSEUDARICIA

This genus, identified in the male by its dark borders, was formerly classified under *Aricia*.

PSEUDARICIA NICIAS
Silvery Argus

	ZONE
	3·5
1in	
26mm	

The male is silvery blue on the uppers with a distinctive pale brown marginal band and white fringes. The female is brown with brown fringes. The butterfly breeds on cranesbill, *Geranium*, and flies in alpine meadows.

GENUS
PSEUDOLYCAENA

A genus with a single species which occurs mostly in South America, but also into the southern US.

PSEUDOLYCAENA MARSYAS

	ZONE
	2
2in	
51mm	

This is a relatively large tailed blue with a curved and pointed forewing. The uppers are sky blue with black markings, and the undersides are silvery blue containing various black spots. The caterpillar food plant is unknown.

GENUS
PSEUDOPHILOTES

A genus of European and Asian blues which are small, with dainty patterns. The checkered pattern around the wings is typical. The butterflies are usually sexually dimorphic. They frequent sunny places. Probably all the species are associated with ants.

PSEUDOPHILOTES ABENCERRAGUS
False Baton Blue

	ZONE
	3
⅞in	
22mm	

The male uppers are brown suffused with blue and a checked margin. The female is black with blue at the base of the wings. The undersides of both sexes are similar in being gray with black spots. The butterfly lives in heather-dominated habitats. Its caterpillar food plants still remain unknown.

PSEUDOPHILOTES HYLACTOR
Baton Blue

	ZONE
	3·5
⅞in	
24mm	

The uppers are rich blue in the male and brown-blue in the female, both with checked margins. There is a much darker apex to the forewing in the female than in the male. The undersides are typically black spotted on a gray-blue background. This is a widespread and common butterfly of slopes, meadows, and rough ground. It breeds on thyme and is attended by ants.

GENUS
PURLISA

A genus of large and colorful Asian hairstreaks which have two prominent but unequal tails.

PURLISA GIGANTEUS

ZONE 5

2½in
64mm

This is a giant among lycaenids, and an impressive one. The male has more extensive areas of metallic greenish blue over its wings than the female. The black on the female forewing tip extends around the hindwing. This is a rare hairstreak found in mountains.

GENUS
QUERCUSIA

This is a genus with a single species, widespread in Europe, North Africa, and Asia.

QUERCUSIA QUERCUS
Purple Hairstreak

ZONE 3·5

1⅛in
28mm

The butterfly rests on leaves, showing off its deep purple uppers in the male. The female has a flash of purple only on the base of the forewings. The undersides are gray. This is an impressive woodland butterfly, which is found around the oak trees on which it breeds.

GENUS
RAPALA

A genus of about 40 species of Asian and Australian butterflies, which are mostly sexually dimorphic.

RAPALA IARBAS
Common Red Flash

ZONE 5

1⅔in
41mm

The male is reddish orange on the uppers with a dark forewing tip. The female is a coppery color. Both sexes have a single tail and a blunt protrusion on the hindwing. The butterfly lives in rainforest at all altitudes and breeds on rambutan, *Nephelium lappaceum*, a member of the *Sapindaceae* family.

GENUS
REKOA

This is a small genus of blue butterflies from South and Central America.

REKOA ZEBINA MARIUS

ZONE 2

1¼in
32mm

The male is purplish blue on the uppers, while the female is silvery gray with a suggestion of blue at the base of the wings. Both sexes have two tails, one of which is long. Butterflies live in scrubby forest and breed on legumes.

G E N U S
RHETUS

A genus of four South American species with long hindwings.

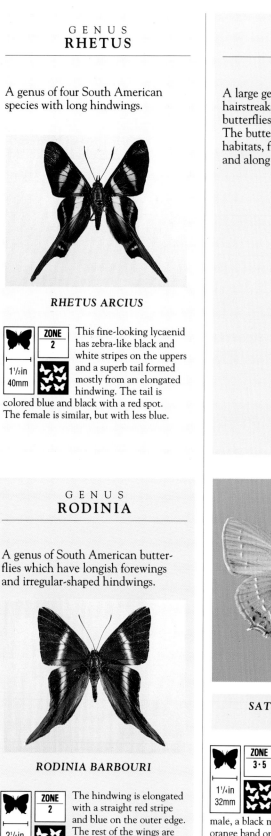

RHETUS ARCIUS

1½in 40mm	ZONE 2

This fine-looking lycaenid has zebra-like black and white stripes on the uppers and a superb tail formed mostly from an elongated hindwing. The tail is colored blue and black with a red spot. The female is similar, but with less blue.

G E N U S
RODINIA

A genus of South American butter-flies which have longish forewings and irregular-shaped hindwings.

RODINIA BARBOURI

2⅛in 54mm	ZONE 2

The hindwing is elongated with a straight red stripe and blue on the outer edge. The rest of the wings are brown with a pale band extending across all wings.

G E N U S
SATYRIUM

A large genus of European and Asian hairstreaks, which are generally small butterflies, often with somber colors. The butterflies live in a wide range of habitats, from grasslands to meadows and along woodland edges.

SATYRIUM ACACIAE
Sloe Hairstreak

1¼in 32mm	ZONE 3·5

This butterfly is a uniform dull brown on the uppers and a dull tan on the underside. There is a very small tail. In the anal region, there is a little orange mark in the male, a black mark in the female. There is an orange band on the underside of the hindwing by the tail. The butterfly lives in scrubby areas where its caterpillar food plant, sloe (*Prunus spinosa*), is found.

SATYRIUM ACADICA
Arcadian Hairstreak,
Northern Willow Hairstreak

1¼in 32mm	ZONE 1

The tailed butterfly is brown on the uppers and gray-brown below. There is a small blue dot on the hindwing and a row of orange marks. The underside of the hindwing is richly colored in red, blue, and fawn. This is a species of the northern US named after the kind of habitat in which it lives, willow woods and scrub. There are a few willow species which serve as caterpillar food plants.

SATYRIUM AURETORUM
SPADIX
Gold Hunter's Hairstreak

1¼in 32mm	ZONE 1

The uppers are light brown with a suffusion of orange. The undersides are grayish with very poorly defined markings. This butterfly lives among oaks, on which it breeds. Its name reflects the historic gold-hunting time during which it was first collected by the Frenchman, Jean de Boisduval (1799-1879).

SATYRIUM BEHRII
Behr's Hairstreak, Orange Hairstreak

ZONE 1

1¹/₈in
28mm

The orange markings on the uppers are distinctive. These are restricted on the forewing by a dark brown-black tip and margin. The presence of a male sex brand simply distinguishes the male from the female. The undersides are gray, darker in the male than the female, with poorly defined markings. The butterfly lives in mountains and canyons, and breeds on antelope bush, *Purshia tridentata*.

▲

SATYRIUM CALIFORNICA
California Hairstreak, Western Hairstreak

ZONE 1

1¹/₄in
32mm

The coppery orange uppers of the slightly larger female are a key feature. The male uppers are dark brown with just a touch of orange. Although named after California, this tailed butterfly is found in most of the western states and into Baja California. The butterfly lives in chaparral and light woodland, and breeds on a number of trees and shrubs from various plant families, including oaks, willows, and ceanothus.

SATYRIUM CALANUS
Banded Hairstreak

ZONE 1

1¹/₄in
32mm

This butterfly's common name refers to the "hairstreak" line crossing the undersides, which is made of small rectangles fused together to form a band. The butterfly is black on the uppers in both sexes, and the undersides differ in being a slightly lighter brown in the male. There are a prominent blue spot and orange marks near the base of the two unequal tails. The butterfly is found along waysides and in association with woods where it breeds on oak, walnut, and hickory.

SATYRIUM EDWARDSII
Edward's Hairstreak, Scrub Oak Hairstreak

ZONE 1

1¹/₄in
32mm

The butterfly is brown above and rich brown below, with some well-defined rectangular marks crossing the wings. Also on the hindwing are a single large blue spot and two or three orange lunules. The scrub oak name sums up the sort of habitat likely to be colonized by this hairstreak. It is not too fussy on which native species of oak, *Quercus*, it breeds; it has been found on five different species.

SATYRIUM ILICIS
Ilex Hairstreak

This is a rich dark brown butterfly which has important differences between the sexes. The male is a rich brown over its uppers. The female is the same rich brown, but has a conspicuous orange flash on the forewing. The undersides are brown-gray in the male, and light tan in the female, both with a white "hairstreak" line and set of orange marks by the sizable tail. The butterfly lives in light woodland and breeds on young shoots of oak, *Quercus*.

SATYRIUM SAEPIUM
Hedgerow Hairstreak, Buckthorn Hairstreak

The sexes are similar with uniform coppery brown uppers. There is a very small tail which is slightly longer in the female. The undersides are a dirty gray with a dull blue spot near the base of the tail and weak dark lines crossing the wings. The butterfly is found in scrubby areas as much as along hedges. It breeds on various species of ceanothus, a member of the buckthorn family.

SATYRIUM W-ALBUM
White-letter Hairstreak

The light brown undersides in both sexes are traversed by the typical white "hairstreak" line, but in this species the telltale feature is the "W" the line prescribes on the tailed hindwing close by a band of bright orange. The butterfly is dark brown on the uppers, darker in the male than the female. It frequents light woodland where its caterpillar food plant, elms (*Ulmus*), grow.

GENUS
SCOLITANTIDES

This is a genus of small-sized blues from Europe and Asia. They have checkered margins and exhibit sexual dimorphism. They occur in flowery habitats and breed on various members of the *Labiatae* and *Crassulaceae*.

SATYRIUM LIPAROPS
Striped Hairstreak

The stripes of this hairstreak are found on the brown underside which is crossed by several irregular thin lines. The uppers are different in each sex. The male is dark brown with a large area of orange and a sex brand on the forewing. The female is lighter brown with an orange glow on the forewing. The butterfly is found among waysides as well as in woods. It breeds on a wide variety of species such as oaks, willows, hawthorn, and blueberries.

SATYRIUM SPINI
Blue-spot Hairstreak

The blue spot at the base of the tail is a most distinctive identification mark, especially as the butterfly usually rests with its wings shut. The male is a dark nutty brown on the uppers, with two tiny orange spots near the tail. The slightly larger female is suffused with orange over large expanses of the wings. The butterfly lives in scrubby and lightly wooded areas, and breeds on buckthorn, *Rhamnus*, and blackthorn, *Prunus spinosa*, from which it derives its Latin name.

SCOLITANTIDES BAVIUS
Bavius Blue

ZONE 3·5

1⅛in 30mm

This is a small blue with checked margins (not unlike *S. orion*), but there are considerable sexual differences on the uppers. The male has a lot of deep blue on the forewing and black dusting near the markings. The female has more black, and the blue is restricted to the base of the wings. The gray undersides are similar in both sexes well covered in black spots, and there is a bold orange band on the tailless hindwing. The butterfly flies in flowery areas and breeds on *Salvia argentea*, a member of the *Labiatae*.

SCOLITANTIDES ORION NIGRICANS
Chequered Blue

ZONE 3·5

1¼in 32mm

The checkering around the margins, after which the butterfly is named, is pronounced on the uppers. The sexes are fairly similar, both having blue scales overlapping a greater suffusion of black. There is usually more blue on the wings in the male. The undersides are remarkably checked, with lots of bold black spots over a white-gray background and a clear orange band on the hindwing. There is no tail. The butterfly lives in flowery habitats and breeds on stonecrops, *Sedum*.

GENUS
SEMOMESIA

A genus of South American "eyed" metalmarks in which the sexes are strongly dimorphic.

SEMOMESIA CAPANEA

ZONE 2

1⅛in 28mm

The bright blue male has a pupilled black eye-spot on the forewing and three black lines or swathes occurring around the wings and including the margins. The brown female has one large white band around the forewing and several light bands on the hindwing.

GENUS
SPINDASIS

A genus of African and Asian blues called "barred blues" or "silverline" butterflies after the lines on their undersides. Characteristically, they have two pairs of tails. Their main area of distribution is in the Himalayas.

SPINDASIS NATALENSIS
Natal Barred Blue

ZONE 4

1⅛in 30mm

This is a very attractive two-tailed blue in which the sexes are similar. The uppers are suffused with rich blue broken only by dark veins, and the outer parts of the wing are gray-black. The undersides are in complete contrast, being palest yellow covered with ocher-edged white blotches of irregular size. There is an orange eye-spot near the base of the longer tail. The butterfly occurs in bush country and breeds on *Mundulea* and *Vigna*, both members of the pea family.

GENUS
STALACHTIS

A genus of under ten species of metalmarks which occur in South America. They play "dead" when disturbed, and many of the species are mimics of other rainforest butterflies.

STALACHTIS PHAEDUSA

ZONE 2

1⁷⁄₈in 48mm

The long rounded forewings are typical of this genus of rainforest metalmarks. The wings are dark blue-black with a latticed appearance of white and black marks on the forewing and an orange margin to the outer edge. The hindwing has a more complete orange band and well-defined radial blue-white marks.

STALACHTIS CALLIOPE

ZONE 2

2¹⁄₂in 64mm

This vivid metalmark resembles a heliconid. The males are very variable and, like the females, have a black forewing tip which contains some white spots. The wings are mostly orange divided by heavy black markings. The hindwing may be brown-black or banded in black and orange. Females have an area of orange-yellow inside of the black tip which emphasizes two or three black spots. The undersides mirror the uppers. The butterflies are found typically in rainforest.

STALACHTIS PHLEGIA

ZONE 2

2in 50mm

This very speckled and easily identified metalmark has some important sexual differences. The male forewings are narrow and strongly pointed; those of the female are rounded. The base of the wings, on both surfaces and in both sexes, is a rich caramel brown, but the outer part in the male is very dark brown with white spots, while the outer part of the female has a band of caramel inside the margin. The butterfly lives in the rainforest of Brazil.

GENUS
STIBOGES

A genus with a single species confined to the rainforest of Asia.

STIBOGES NYMPHIDIA

ZONE 5

1¹⁄₂in 38mm

The sexes are fairly similar in this species, which resembles a pierid. This is because most of the central area of the wings is taken up with white, while the outer parts are gray. The butterfly flies in thick forest, but its life cycle remains a mystery.

GENUS
STRYMON

A genus of North and South American hairstreaks in which the sexes are fairly similar. Butterflies exhibit seasonal variation and have a wide variety of caterpillar food plants, which include members of the spurge, elm, and mallow families, *Euphorbiaceae*, *Ulmaceae*, and *Malvaceae*. One species, *S. melinus*, is a pest on cotton.

STRYMON ACIS
Drury's Hairstreak, Acis Hairstreak,
Antillean Hairstreak

ZONE
1·2

1in
25mm

This is a two-tailed hairstreak. The sexes are fairly similar, and are brown-black above and gray-slate below. There is a thick "hairstreak" line crossing the wings and a large orange spot by the tails. The butterfly is found mostly in the Antilles, though it strays into southern Florida. It flies in gardens and beside woodland, and breeds on the attractive spurge plant, *Croton*.

STRYMON BEBRYCIA
Mexican Gray Hairstreak,
Balloon-vine Hairstreak

ZONE
1·2

1⅛in
28mm

The sexes are slightly different. The male is a dirty gray-brown above, while the female has dark patches on the forewings and some blue dusting over the hindwing. The undersides of both sexes are a slate gray with a wiggly pale orange "hairstreak" line, and an eye-spot at the base of the single tail. The butterfly lives in areas of sparse vegetation and possibly breeds on *Croton*.

STRYMON MARTIALIS
Long-tailed Hairstreak, Blue and Gray Hairstreak,
Cuban Gray Hairstreak, Martial Hairstreak

ZONE
1·2

1in
25mm

The sexes are fairly similar, though the slightly larger female is a more pronounced violet-blue. The violet-blue covers most of the hindwing and the trailing edge of the forewing. The rest of the wings are dark brown, the male having a dark sex brand on the forewing. The undersides are much lighter with blue and orange markings at the base of the two tails and a black "hairstreak" line. The butterfly lives in open lowland and breeds on *Trema micrantha*.

STRYMON ALBATA
White Hairstreak

ZONE
1·2

1⅛in
28mm

The white bloom across most of the hindwing and trailing edge of the forewing is the key to the identification of this species. The remainder of the forewing is gray to black. There is a single relatively long tail and two little black eye-spots at the tail base on both surfaces. The undersides are very light with a very slightly darker base. The butterfly is a migrant and some flights from Central America reach the southern US. It breeds on *Abutilon incanum*, a member of the *Malvaceae*.

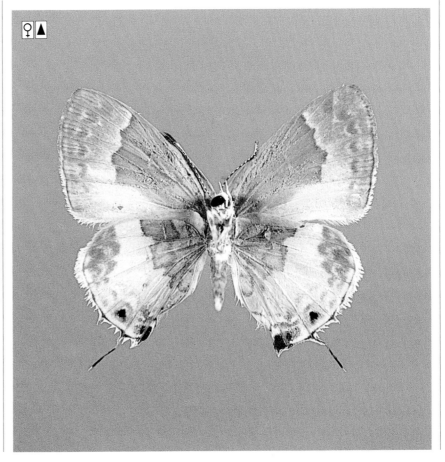

STRYMON MELINUS
Gray Hairstreak

The uppers are a uniform dark gray in the male, brownish in the female. There are two tails which are surmounted by a distinct orange mark. The undersides are distinctly gray, and there is a dark, partially disjointed "hairstreak" line and two orange marks at the base of the tail. The butterfly is widely distributed in North and Central America, and lives in many different types of open habitat. It has been recorded breeding on over 50 species of plants, including cotton, on which it can be a pest.

GENUS
SYRMATIA

This South American metalmark has an unmistakable shape with its incredibly long drawn-out hindwings.

SYRMATIA DORILAS

This is a small curious-looking butterfly with a long narrow hindwing which has the appearance of a tail. It is black, marked only by a red and white blotch on the forewing. This butterfly occurs in the Amazon rainforest.

GENUS
THECLA

This is a large genus of hairstreaks from North and South America and Europe. They are relatively small butterflies, some of which have tails and bright colors. They usually live in lightly wooded and sunny habitats.

THECLA AEGIDES

This lycaenid has wings of an unmistakable turquoise, though this merges into dark brown toward the outer parts. The forewings are strongly curved, and the hindwings have a pair of unequal tails. The undersides are rich orange crossed with thin white hairstreak lines. The butterfly occurs in Central America.

GENUS
SYNARGIS

A genus of tailless South American lycaenids with interesting black and white colors.

SYNARGIS NYCTEUS

This is a brightly colored lycaenid with snowy white uppers broken by a band across the wings, and a brown apex to the forewing. There are three black marks on the forewing and a single one on the hindwing.

GENUS
TAJURIA

A genus containing many species which occur from Sri Lanka to Sulawesi.

TAJURIA MANTRA

The sexes are dimorphic. The male is greenish blue, the female grayish blue. Both sexes have a thick black apex to the forewing. The butterfly has been seen to breed on *Dendrophthoe*, which is a member of the mistletoe family.

THECLA BETULAE
Brown Hairstreak

The warm brown male has a central black spot on the forewing, and two orange blobs by the tail and wing extension. The female has very rounded wings, a larger tail, more orange by the tail, and a large red-orange forewing band. The undersides are rich orange flushed red at the margins, especially on the hindwing, with two small white "hairstreak" lines. The butterfly lives in scrubby and light wooded areas, and breeds on sloe, *Prunus spinosa*.

THECLA DRAUDTI

This hairstreak has a magnificent set of four tails, each of a different length. The butterfly is large for a hairstreak, and the uppers are covered in a metallic green iridescence. The underside is a marvel of red, green, black, and white. The apex of the forewings verge on dark brown. The butterfly is found in Central America.

THECLA BITIAS

The male is a metallic blue, like a *Morpho*, with a distinctive sex brand on the forewing. The female has rounded forewings in contrast to the hatchet-shaped male ones, and has a duller, more subdued blue limited by black borders. There is one long tail, and a suggestion of another. The undersides are brown with fine yellow lines at the base of the tail. This metalmark species is found in Brazil, in rainforest.

THECLA ELONGATA

The shape of the wings is a useful guide to identification. The forewing is rather hatchet-shaped and the hindwing strongly curved with a suggestion of a drawn-out tail, but there is no tail. The color toward the base of the wings is a lustrous green, but to the outside this merges to brown. The undersides are a mottled brown.

THECLA GABATHA

ZONE 2

1³/₄in
44mm

The sexes are dimorphic. The male has more silvery blue on the uppers than the female, which has black forewing tips and margins. The blue areas are faintly marked by the dark veins. There are two tails, one of which is long. The butterfly lives in the rainforests of Colombia.

THECLA TELEMUS

ZONE 2

1⁵/₈in
42mm

The male is a bright blue over most of the uppers with a faint black apex to the forewing, and a round sex brand, also on the forewing. The female is slightly larger and iridescent green, with a pronounced black forewing apex and black border around the hindwing. The three unequal tails are longer in the female. The underside is a stunning green, blue, and red.

THECLA ORGIA

ZONE 2

1⁵/₁₆in
34mm

The male is deep royal blue enclosed by a regular dark margin around all wings. There is a round gray sex brand on the forewing. The female has dark sky blue to the inside of a broad dark margin, and a considerable dark apex to the forewing. The wings are less pointed than in the male. The undersides of both sexes are brown with some light tracery on the hindwing. There is one tail, on the underside of which are two eye-spots. Butterflies occur in the rainforests of Brazil.

GENUS
THECLOPSIS

A genus of South American lycaenids which have metallic blue colors and two unequal tails.

THECLOPSIS LYDUS

ZONE 2

1¹/₈in
30mm

The wings are fairly rounded with deep royal blue uppers and a black apex to the forewing. The undersides are a uniform gray-green with a dark brown base to the forewings. The butterfly lives in the Amazon rainforest.

GENUS
THERITAS

A genus of brilliantly colored tailed metalmarks from the rainforests of Mexico.

THERITAS CORONATA

ZONE 2

2½in
65mm

The male is a uniform bright metallic blue with a small marginal band. The female has more black on the forewing margin. Both sexes have two tails of unequal length, and undersides are green to the inside of a brown line, brown-green to the outside.

GENUS
THERSAMOLYCAENA

A genus of European coppers in which the sexes are different.

THERSAMOLYCAENA DISPAR
Large Copper

ZONE 3·5

1½in
40mm

The male is brilliant metallic copper with a black margin. The female is nonmetallic copper suffused with dark scales, and marked with spotted black on the forewings. Spotted undersides are gray banded orange on the hindwings, orange margined gray on the forewings. It breeds on large water dock.

GENUS
THERSAMONIA

A genus of dimorphic European and Asian coppers.

THERSAMONIA THERSAMON
Less Fiery Copper

ZONE 3·5

1¼in
32mm

The male has coppery unmarked forewings and dusky hindwings with orange margins. The female is spotted black over copper. Both sexes have slaty hindwing undersides and orange forewing undersides, both spotted black. Butterflies live in scrub and light woodland where they breed on dock and broom.

GENUS
THISBE

A genus of South American metalmarks which are brown and white, and have a drawn-out hindwing.

THISBE LYCORIAS

ZONE 2

1⅝in
41mm

The characteristic hindwing is drawn out as a stubby curved tail. The markings in this species are contrasting, with a white band across the brown wings, which are speckled with orange spots.

GENUS
TICHERRA

A genus of dimorphic Asian butterflies which have one very long tail and another very short one.

TICHERRA ACTE

The male is generally deep violet to black on the uppers with whitish tails, the female is brown. The undersides are coppery orange on the forewings, fading, on the hindwings, to a light tan with a big black-edged white mark by the tails. Butterflies occur in rainforest.

GENUS
TMOLUS

A genus of dimorphic tailed hairstreaks with dark uppers and light undersides.

TMOLUS ECHION
Large Lantana, Four Spotted Hairstreak

The black male has a royal blue flash mostly on the hindwing, the female is dark brown. The light gray undersides have two rows of orange marks and a black spot at the tail base. It was introduced to Hawaii and Mexico to control lantana, its caterpillar food plant.

GENUS
TOMARES

A genus of European hairstreaks which are relatively small in size and sexually dimorphic. They occur in open sunny areas and breed on members of the pea family, *Leguminosae*.

TOMARES BALLUS
Provence Hairstreak

The male is light brown with a touch of orange on the trailing edge of the hindwing, the female mostly rich orange with dark brown tips and a dark base to the hindwing. In both sexes, the undersides of the hindwings are green, the forewing undersides orange and speckled in black. Named after a region of France, this butterfly is found mostly around the eastern end of the Mediterranean, but also in Egypt. It lives in open flowery places and breeds on trefoils.

TOMARES MAURETANICUS
Moroccan Hairstreak

This species is very similar to *T. ballus*, but lacks the green underside of the hindwing where instead it is gray to brown. The forewing underside is only half orange with black spots. The butterfly occurs only in North Africa and breeds on leguminous plants such as *Hippocrepis* and *Heydisarum*.

GENUS
VACCINIINA

A genus of dimorphic blues found within the Arctic Circle, they breed on *Vaccinium*, its caterpillar food plants.

VACCINIINA OPTILETE
Yukon Blue, Cranberry Blue

The male uppers are violet-blue; the duller female has a less intense violet-blue within dark margins. The undersides in both sexes are dark slate speckled with black spots and have a small orange mark on the trailing hindwing edge. Butterflies live in bogs and moors.

GENUS
VAGA

A genus of Hawaiian butterflies which breed on leguminous trees such as *Acacia* and *Pipturus*.

VAGA BLACKBURNII
Green Hawaiian Blue, Blackburn's Blue

🦋	**ZONE 6**
1in 25mm	🦋🦋

The sexes are similar only on the undersides, which are a uniform green. The uppers are deep blue in the male, brown-black in the female, with a little blue dusting at the base of the wings.

GENUS
XAMIA

A genus of South American tailed butterflies which have muted orange colors and breed on succulents.

XAMIA XAMI
Xamia, Succulent Hairstreak

🦋	**ZONE 1·2**
1in 25mm	🦋🦋

In the female the orange is more intense with darker marginal areas. The light tan undersides have a white line across both wings. At the base of a tiny pair of tails are small white lines and an eyespot. Butterflies live in deserts, breeding on sedums and echeverias.

GENUS
ZIZINA

A genus of African, Asian, and Australian blues which have distinct genitalia.

ZIZINA OTIS
Common Grass Blue, Lucerne Blue, Clover Blue, Bean Blue, Lesser Grass Blue

🦋	**ZONE 5**
7/8in 24mm	🦋🦋

The sexes are fairly similar with blue uppers, but there are, generally, more darker areas on the female. The gray undersides are much speckled. There are at least two named subspecies. This butterfly of open flowery areas breeds on the sensitive plant, *Mimosa pudica*.

GENUS
ZIZULA

A genus of blues found in North America and Asia, which have distinct genitalia.

ZIZULA CYNA
Cyna Blue

🦋	**ZONE 1·2**
1in 25mm	🦋🦋

This is one of the smallest butterfly species in North America. The sexes are similar with lilac-blue uppers and an ill-defined darker apex to the forewing. Silvery gray undersides have some fine black spotting. Butterflies occur in deserts and scrubby areas, and can migrate.

Glossary

Abdomen The rear part of the body which contains most of the gut and the reproductive organs.

Aestivate The behavior of some butterflies and larvae around the world to become inactive and rest-up during periods of intense summer heat and/or dry season, a form of summer hibernation.

Aggregations A term which applies mostly to caterpillars and adults which come together to feed or sleep. Pupae rarely aggregate (as fully-grown caterpillars), but when they do, they do not feed.

Anal region The inside edge of the hindwing which is close to the tip of the abdomen. It is on the anal region of the hindwing that many key identification features are situated, such as eyespots, as well as various male characteristics.

Androconial fold A flap or fold on the inside edge of the hindwing adjacent to the abdomen, which contains the males' androconia, or androconial scales. The androconial scales contain sex scents (pheromones).

Antenna(e) The paired feelers on the head of an insect which are used for smell and touch.

Apex The tip of the forewing.

Aristocrats Members of the *Nymphalidae*, often with aristocratic names and spectacular colors; an old Victorian term.

Basking A characteristic of some butterflies of either aligning themselves side-on to the sun, or sitting with wings open and flat on the ground or on a leaf, to absorb heat energy from the sun.

Blues Members of the *Lycaenidae* to which blues, coppers and hairstreaks also belong.

Browns Formerly members of the *Satyridae*, named after the general brown colors typical of most of the family, now included in *Nymphalidae*.

Butterfly-farming Rearing butterflies under confined conditions to sell to the international trade in butterflies.

Butterfly-ranching Planting up a habitat with appropriate caterpillar and butterfly food plants in order to increase the population of a certain species to sell to the international trade in butterflies.

Camouflage The way in which butterflies and moths have colors and patterns which help them blend in with their background.

Caterpillar The stage after the egg, and before the chrysalis (pupa), the main eating stage during metamorphosis.

Cell An enclosed area of the forewing between the veins in which spots sometimes occur. Numerous identification characteristics can be seen in this region of the wing.

Chevrons A series of arrow-head marks around the edge of the wing, usually on the hindwing. This is really a description of lunules in the shape of infilled arrows.

Circumpolar Distribution of a butterfly within the arctic region around the North Pole.

CITES Convention on International Trade in Endangered Species of Wild Fauna and Flora.

Claws The end of each butterfly leg has one or two claws.

Cloud forest Tropical forest which is regularly drenched in clouds, and thus has a high humidity, with only short breaks of sunshine.

Coppers Members of the *Lycaenidae* to which blues and hairstreaks also belong.

Cryptic A color scheme which blends in with the background.

Danaids Formerly members of the *Danaidae*, also known as the monarch or milkweed family, now included in *Nymphalidae*.

Diapause A period of reduced activity, typically found in pupae, usually to overcome inclement weather such as winter.

Dimorphic Existing in two different forms; here applied to non-identical male and female butterflies of the same species.

Dorsal The topside of the body and wings.

Emigrant An insect which leaves one place for another place.

Endangered A species one step away from becoming extinct (*Red Data Book* definition).

Endemic Occurring only in a single region or locality and found nowhere else on earth.

Extinct Not found in the wild for the past 50 years (*Red Data Book* definition).

Eyespots Spots of varying sizes on the upper or lower surface of the wings, which may or may not be pupilled and surrounded in various colors. These are used to confuse predators of the whereabouts of the real head. Sometimes called false-eyes.

False-eyes *See eyespots.*

Family A major division of butterflies and moths arrived at by grouping basic characteristics such as wing shape and venation. Each family comprises a range of genera, all of which are related.

Fogging Insecticiding the rainforest canopy to knock-down insects for analysis.

Form An individual which differs from typical specimens in color, pattern, shape or size; such as seasonal variation.

Fresh The condition of a butterfly (or moth) immediately after it has emerged from the pupa. The color pattern is then diagnostic, thereafter the scales rub off.

Fringe A fine edge of scales attached to the margin of the wing; often of great diagnostic use in separating species.

Fritillaries Members of the *Nymphalidae* which are characterized by having an orange-spotted pattern (fritillary meaning spotted).

Genus (genera) The first word of the two-part Latin name given to a butterfly or moth. This name often changes, as revisions to and disagreements arise over taxonomy. The second, specific, name is a more reliable and unchanging name.

Glass wings South American rainforest butterflies which have transparent wings; otherwise called ithominids, they belong to the *Nymphalidae*.

Gregarious Living together; here applied to caterpillars or butterflies.

Ground color The main color of the butterfly which covers most of the wing and over which the pattern is displayed; also called background color.

Habitat A particular place whose characteristics are determined by the soil, vegetation and aspect.

Hair pencils A peculiar brush-like apparatus (usually paired) which is everted during courtship, and from which scents emanate.

Heliconids Members of the *Nymphalidae* which are called longwings. They are found only in the Americas.

Hibernation A means of overcoming cold conditions by going into a resting stage, sometimes called over-wintering. Butterflies can hibernate during any of their life stages.

Hill-topping A term used to describe the behavior of butterflies of either sex when they aggregate at the tops of ridges, mountains or hills, in order to find mates.

Imago (imagines) The adult butterfly.

Immigrant An insect which arrives in one place having come from another.

Iridescence The metallic appearance of some butterflies caused by light diffraction off the surface of the tiny scales which cover the wings.

Ithominids Members of the *Nymphalidae* which are called glass wings due to their transparent wings.

Lek The attraction of males and females to a communal mating area.

Lunules A series of marks, often half-moon shaped (hence the name), which often forms a crescent inside the edge of the hindwing, particularly in the *Lycaenidae*.

Margin The outer part of the wing.

Metamorphosis Literally a change in form; there are four different life forms of a butterfly: egg, larva, pupa, adult. In some butterflies it takes up to two years to progress through all four stages. Butterflies go through what is called a complete metamorphosis.

Migrant An insect which moves from one area to another and back again. Few butterflies are true migrants.

Mimic An insect which evolves color, pattern, shape of body, size, and behavior of another (the model) which it resembles.

Mimicry The copying of the behavior, color, pattern, size, and shape of one butterfly, usually poisonous, by another which is palatable in order to pass unnoticed by predators.

Model Usually a poisonous butterfly whose appearance and behavior are copied by a non-poisonous butterfly (the mimic).

Mud-puddling A term used to describe the male behavior of visiting shallow puddles, animal droppings and the moist banks of rivers and streams to imbibe nutrients.

Native species A species which has evolved in one particular place or country.

Nymphalids Members of the *Nymphalidae* which contains the aristocrats, browns, monarchs, Libytheids, Nemeobiids and glass wings.

On the wing An expression which describes the period during which the butterfly is likely to be found, between the emergence of the insect from the pupa until it dies.

Osmaterium(a) A bright orange, double filament everted from a swallowtail caterpillar when it is threatened.

Oviposition The act of laying eggs.

Palps Paired sensory devices which are present around the mouth of the caterpillar and the butterfly.

Patrolling A behavioral characteristic of some butterflies, often males, which take up position in their own territory and patrol up and down to find mates.

Perching A behavioral characteristic of some butterflies, often males, which seek to intercept and drive off other insects, including butterflies, which penetrate their territories. This behavior is used by males to find females, in which case mating may take place.

Polymorphism Existing in many forms.

Predators Any organism, such as a spider, insect, lizard, bird or mammal, which preys upon another organism.

Pupa(e) The third stage in the complete metamorphosis in a butterfly or moth, after the caterpillar; sometimes called a chrysalis.

Rainforest Tropical forest which is described as either lowland or highland, depending on altitude.

Rare Species which are one step away from becoming Vulnerable (*Red Data Book* definition).

RDB *Red Data Book.*

Resident A butterfly which stays in the same locality from where it emerged until it dies.

Satyrids Members of the *Nymphalidae* also called browns or satyrs.

Sedentary Species which do not move around much.

Setae Sensory hairs on the body of a caterpillar or butterfly.

Sex brand A darker area seen on the wings of male butterflies which produces insect scents. It is often on the forewing (in various places), but in some butterflies it is on the inside edge of the hindwing.

Snouts Members of the *Nymphalidae*, formerly classified in the *Libytheidae*; butterflies which have long palps held out underneath and in front of the head.

Species A population of individuals which have fairly similar external characteristics, and which can mate amongst themselves to produce fertile offspring.

Specific name The second, or trivial name, of the two-worded Latin name given to a butterfly or moth, which is often descriptive. It is the most cosmopolitan way of talking about any species.

Sphragis A device which closes over the female abdomen after mating to stop any further mating, present in certain genera including *Parnassius*.

Subspecies An intermediary stage between one species evolving into another species. Isolation of butterflies on islands or by mountain ranges may suggest or indicate they cannot breed with their original stock, so their characteristics evolve. Eventually a new species develops from an intermediary subspecies.

Sulfurs Members of the *Pieridae*.

Taxonomy The arrangement of species, genera, and other groups into a system that denotes their relationship.

Thorax The middle section of the body which contains the flight muscles and wings, and from which the three pairs of legs originate, one pair from each of the three thoracic segments.

Vagrant An insect which occasionally moves from one place to another, but not with any regularity; the implication is that the movement is accidental.

Variation A natural feature displayed by all organisms; all their characteristics (visible and invisible ones) are subject to small changes within all members of the same species.

Veins The supporting structure of the wing; venation is critical in butterfly identification.

Ventral The underside of the body and wings.

Vulnerable Species which are one step away from becoming Endangered (*Red Data Book* definition).

Whites Members of the *Pieridae*.

Wingspan Twice the measurement from the centre of the thorax to the tip of the forewing. Usually the forewing measurement is taken as it is normally greater than that of the hindwing.

Index to Common Names

Index to Latin Names

Bibliography

The Butterflies of the Malay Peninsula, 3rd edition revised Corbet, A. S. & Pendlebury, H. M., 1978 (Art Printing Works Sdn., Kuala Lumpur).

Butterflies of South America, D'Abrera, B., 1984 (Hill House, Victoria).

A Field Companion to the Butterflies of Australia and New Zealand, D'Abrera, B., 1984 (Five Mile Press, Victoria).

The Butterflies of Costa Rica and their natural history, Papilionidae, Pieridae, Nymphalidae, DeVries, P. J., 1987 (Princeton University Press).

Butterflies: Their World, Their Life Cycle, Their Behaviour, Emmel, T. C., 1975 (Alfred A. Knopf, New York).

The Natural History of Butterflies, Feltwell, J., 1986 (Croom Helm, London).

A Field Guide of the Butterflies of Britain and Europe, Higgins, L. G. & Riley, N. D., 1970 (Collins, London).

Butterflies of the World, Lewis, H. L., 1973 (Harrap, London).

The Common Names of North American Butterflies, Miller, J., 1992 (Smithsonian Institution Press, Washington and London).

A Field Guide to the Butterflies of the West Indies, Riley, N. D., 1975 (Collins, London).

The World of Butterflies, an Illustrated Encyclopaedia, Sbordoni, V. & Forestiero, S., 1984 (Arnoldo Mondadori Editore, S.p.a., Milano) and 1985 (Blandford Press, Poole).

The Butterflies of North America, a natural history and field guide, Scott, J. A., 1986 (Standord University Press, California).

The Encyclopaedia of the Butterfly World in Colour, Smart, P., 1976 (Hamlyn, London).

The Dictionary of Butterflies and Moths in Colour, Watson, A. & Whalley, P., 1983 (Peerage Books).

A Field Guide to the Butterflies of Africa, Williams J. G., 1969 (Collins, London).

Credits

All images in this book are the copyright of Quarto Publishing Plc except for those listed below:

pages 3, 6, 7 *Wildlife Matters*
pages 12 to 21 *Wildlife Matters*
page 22, 77 *Premaphotos Wildlife*
pages 23 to 33 *Wildlife Matters*
pages 37, 111, 211 *Wildlife Matters*

Useful Addresses

American Entomological Society, 1900 Race Street, Philadelphia, PA 19013, USA

Audubon Society, 950 Third Avenue, New York, 10022, USA

British Butterfly Conservation Society, Box 222, Dedham, Colchester, Essex, CO7 6BR, UK

Entomological Society of America, 9301 Annapolis Road, Lanham, MD 202706, USA

Royal Entomological Society of London, 41 Queen's Gate, London, SW7 5HU, UK

Societas Europeaa Lepidopterologica, c/o Zoologisches Institute der Universitat, Balzerstrasse 3, CH-3012 Berne, Switzerland

Xerces Society, 10 Southwest Ash Street, Portland, OR 97204, USA